Fleur Press
P.O. Box 6073
Gulf Breeze, Florida 32561

ISBN 0-9626593-0-4

ABOUT THE BOOK

The world of wrestling is clouded with mystery. But one thing is certain, people are not lukewarm about it: They're either very hot or very cold on the subject, and it's peppered with controversy.

"Everybody Down Here Hates Me" is a behind-the-scenes, quasi-autobiographical look at the professional wrestling business and the characters which make it up.

But this book is much more than one about life on the mats, wrestler and author Pat Barrett takes the reader on a roller coaster ride of human emotions: There's humor. There's pathos. But most of all, there are the characters who once were only subjects of stories told orally by Barrett to close friends. Now they are brought to life by Barrett's pen for the world to enjoy.

Travel to the interior of the Isle of Fiji where supper with an island chief becomes a guessing game of what's for dinner and ends with a record-setting hangover. Move on to the hills of Tennessee where messing with a hillbilly's cows brings on swiftly executed justice — southern style.

Through the pages, catch the magic of the matches, as well as life backstage with the groupies, fans, promoters, families and life on the road from the incredible world of pro wrestling.

ACKNOWLEDGEMENTS

After leaving Ireland's Emerald Isle my eyes were opened to life's good and bad, the comic and the sad, all to be found in a very concentrated form in and out of the professional wrestling arena. The scoundrels and the villains — you know who you are — are described vividly and usually appear under fictitious names for obvious reasons. The cream of humanity, whom I have fondly remembered, would probably like the same courtesy after they read this book.

Several people have been indispensable to me in making this book a reality. I'd like to thank Tim Koontz for his patience and expertise in guiding me through the maze of computer technology necessary to produce a manuscript. His wife and he graciously accepted late night phone calls from a desperate typist who had pushed the wrong buttons, watched forty pages of typed text disappear from the memory, or simply pleaded "What do I do now?" Thanks for your determined search for the computer gremlins, and the encouragement that *It* could be mastered.

Ginny MacDonald, my editor, how can I thank you? Let me count the ways. You were the first unbiased person to read my book and told me I could write. You may also be the last. Seriously though, I survived all the editing, constructive criticism, and polishing "grafs" because of your enthusiasm, your sense of humor, and your tireless expertise. I've written my first book and you've quit smoking. My friend, I think we've both done well.

Part of the reason you've picked up this book is because of the beautiful and captivating cover design by Susan M. Rand. Her artistic talent is amazing. She makes it all look easy, the true sign of a professional. I hope she will still remember me when she's the next Picasso.

Don and Carol Parker have become my mentors and my friends. They have blazed a path for me to follow and are always the voice of confidence in my ability. Even after my public speaking engagements they are not afraid to say they know me. Their wit and generous help every step of the way has shaken my faith in humanity... there really are wonderful unselfish people out there.

Thanks, Mom, for bringing me into this world, for all the love and support you've given me over the years. I always knew you were behind me 100%. Unfortunately I will have to do everything in my power to prevent you from reading this book. There are a few bad words, and a few sticky situations I've described. I wouldn't want your shining image of me, your saintly son, to tarnish.

Now to Peggy, the love of my life. Without you many things would never have been possible, including this book. Thank you for all the hard work you did and the many hours burning the midnight oil interpreting my handwriting. Mere words can never express my love and gratitude for everything.

CONTENTS

1

BAPTISM OF BLOOD

His huge left arm was wrapped around my neck, squeezing so hard my eyes were popping. He was on top of me. His massive, sweaty body lying across my chest. Breathing was almost impossible. I would have pleaded for air, begged for mercy, except this huge animal had me pinned helplessly to the mat.

My mind began playing tricks. I was back in the Roman Games. It was all a nightmare; I'd wake up any minute and be free. Unfortunately, I wasn't dreaming. The nightmare was all too real.

Of all the people in the arena, I was the only one who didn't know what was coming next. I found out soon enough as his enormous right hand bore down on my young, ripe, Irish nose. He pressed hard then began kneading it like a shapeless lump of dough, at times almost caressingly. His huge Italian lips moved close to my ear. From his bulbous rib cage came a guttural sound. It turned out to be a question to which no answer was expected.

"Do you hear them scream?" he growled. "Wait till you hear them in a minute!"

In the background I could dimly hear the screams of the crowd, a muffled roar calling for blood. Mine. What really reached me was his hot, raspy voice and the pounding of my heart. The single most important thing I wanted was for this monster to stop brutalizing my body and let me go home. What was I doing in this place, lying on my back, looking up into blinding lights with a crushing mass of muscle squeezing the life out of me? What had I done to deserve this?

I knew damned well what I was doing, and I had no one but myself to blame. I was going for the big time, trying to make a name for myself as a professional wrestler.

The call had come from Jack Dale, the promoter, earlier in the day. It was Saturday. I was off that night and glad of it. I'd made plans to have beer with a cute wrestling fan who I knew was going to be available that evening. Everything was arranged...until Jack called.

His first words rang alarm bells in my head even though I was still innocent to the machinations of the pro wrestling world. "I want you to work tonight and I promise there'll be no problems. He's changed." Jack said his piece all in one breath, which almost overwhelmed me. Almost, but not quite. I'd learned in a very short time as a pro to weigh each word spoken. After all, my body could be on the line.

I'd had a good relationship with Jack from the beginning. When I turned pro some months earlier, he'd given me his boots and dressing gown until I got some money together to buy my own. What I didn't realize was that just about everybody in the business recognized Jack's robe. Old-timers, as I called the older pros, took great delight in beating on "the boss's favorite blue-eyed boy." The old timers had a name for me too.

"Hold on, Jack, just a minute," I told him. "Who's changed? And anyway, I don't want to work tonight. I have a heavy date with a lightweight." My attempt at humor was lost on him.

"I need you, Pat," he said impatiently. "There's nobody else I can get on such short notice that will give him a good match."

The implied flattery went unnoticed, but I was growing very intrigued. Who could he want me to wrestle so badly that he was almost pleading? Jack Dale didn't plead; it wasn't part of his makeup and I knew it.

2

"Bert," he said finally, blurting it out. "I need someone to wrestle Bert." The words sent shivers down my spine, both from fear and anticipation. There was only one Bert. No need to mention his last name, Assirati. Jack didn't. Bert was enough. Without question, Bert Assirati was one of the most feared men in European professional wrestling. A stocky five-foot-seven, weighing in at 270 pounds, he was not only a powerhouse but he could move like a hard rubber ball, bouncing on his stubby muscular legs at incredible speed. In street clothes, to the unwary, he looked like a short fat man. Out of them, he was a mound of solid muscle.

Even Bert's huge Roman nose, with its giant scar running across the middle, was intimidating. The story goes that he'd smashed it while riding his bicycle, which he used in training. Speeding down a hill one day Bert's brakes failed and he rammed into the back of a double-decker bus. The bus had to be towed away but that wasn't what concerned the driver. He took one look at Bert's nose and began apologizing, believing he'd caused the accident with a sudden stop.

"Don't worry about the hooter," Bert snarled, grabbing the bus driver firmly by the lapels. "I'll get that fixed on the National Health...But who'll pay for my fucking bike?"

Bert sounded like he looked: ferocious. He talked with a deep growl but he was no dummy. In fact, he was smart enough to know that the big dome he called a head was one of his most fearsome weapons. He wasn't shy about using it in a street fight or in finishing off a match. Bert would headbutt the unfortunate victim with remarkable speed and force, right between the eyes.

The African buffalo, say hunters, is the most dangerous animal to pursue. It stalks its enemy with intelligence and cunning until the devastating charge that smashes its opponent, then tramples it to the ground, leaving a bloody mess. Bert was no different. Like an old bull, the older he got the more dangerous he became.

It wasn't just Bert's size and strength or his super agility that made him such a terror in the ring. He was a sado-masochist

3

to boot, and very unpredictable. When I first got in the business, I quickly learned to let an opponent go immediately if he gave up. That wasn't always the case with Bert. Sometimes he'd let go, other times he wouldn't, especially if he was in the middle of pounding the crap out of his hapless victim. There were times when Bert would pretend not to hear the other guy's cries. Then again, maybe he didn't want to hear. Nobody really knew what made him tick.

His favorite hold was the Boston Crab. Why it was called that I never knew, but once in it his opponents were completely at his mercy. It worked like this: first Bert would soften up his foe with short chopping elbows to the side of the head and jaw, then lunge down and grab the man's ankles, that is if his opponent was still standing. Most of the time he was on the mat, stunned.

Next, holding his opponent's ankles under his armpits, Bert would twist his body until he flipped the man over, face down. That left Bert straddling his victim, virtually sitting on the guy's head. There was no way for the man to get Bert off, not with his legs still locked under Bert's armpits, bent backward in an awkward and unnatural position. The pain could be excruciating, especially when the person on top was as short as Bert. But Assirati didn't care. He was into pain...the other person's.

Why would anyone in his right mind want to get in a ring with a man like Bert Assirati, I asked myself as Jack Dale made his pitch. Actually, there were several reasons that appealed to me. Money for one; prestige for another. Then too, I was a stubborn Irishman who not only loved to take chances but found it hard to turn down a dare. If the truth were known, I would have wrestled Bert once for nothing. I'd heard so much about this "living legend." It was hard for me to believe that he was *that tough.*

"I need you Pat," Jack repeated. "Don't let me down."

I didn't commit myself, not right off anyway. There were too many questions that needed answering. Why the last minute phone call? What had happened to Bert's original opponent for the night? Was he injured or...?

"Nothing like that," Jack answered. "the poor man's wife is very sick."

"With Assirati-itis?" I asked, my voice laden with sarcasm. "Her timing is perfect, isn't it?" I couldn't help myself.

I got no reply from Jack. He talked on as if he'd never heard my remark. Bert was making a comeback, he said, following a brief retirement. I'd heard things differently. Word had it that Assirati had run out of opponents willing to tangle with him. If I hadn't been so headstrong and greedy, I'd have been among them. I didn't ask for the moon but it wouldn't have made any difference if I had, Jack seemed so desperate to pair me with Bert. He agreed to double the normal money for our match, the main event, and the deal was made. Saturday night came all too quickly. I caught a train from Wimbledon, where I had a flat, and headed for Camberwell Green, a section in London's working class area. The people there are the salt of the earth. They work and drink hard, and have a no-nonsense approach to wrestling. They're particularly loyal to their own. I needed all the support I could get, but I knew I wouldn't get it from them. Bert would. Camberwell Green was Assirati's part of London.

It was quite early when I arrived at the hall. The line outside was long for that time of night, which meant the house was going to be very good. I made my way to the entrance under the watchful eyes of the crowd without creating even a titter of excitement. Since I wasn't yet well-known, they were no doubt trying to figure out who I was.

As I found my way inside a middle-aged lady stopped me. "Aren't you Pat Barrett?" she asked.

I replied that I was, with a certain amount of pride. I'd been recognized. Heady stuff indeed; fame and notoriety had found me at last.

"I'm Mrs. Assirati," she said just above a whisper. "I'd like to talk to you." As she spoke she grabbed my arm and pulled

5

me into a darkened alcove.

To say I was surprised is an understatement. Several thoughts raced through my head. Was she about to warn me of the dangers of being in the ring with her husband? I wondered. Did she want to find out how much money I was getting? What kind of deal I'd made? No, unfortunately. But she did want something, and her next words not only left me startled but dumbfounded.

"Please take it easy on my husband," she said in a quiet, pitiful way. "You are wrestling him tonight, aren't you?"

My jaw dropped open as I stared in disbelief. "Are you *really* Mrs. Assirati?" I asked, finally regaining my voice. "Your husband is Bert? *The* Bert?" If I sounded stupid she didn't let on. She simply looked around furtively as if she was afraid someone might overhear.

"Yes, yes," she answered impatiently. She moved closer and gripped my arm tightly. "You must take it easy on my husband. He's getting old and his hip is very bad. He's going blind in one eye and he hasn't wrestled for some time. He's very out of shape." She paused a few seconds to see what effect her words were having on me. Then she forced a worried smile and said, "You're so young and strong...please, do as I ask."

Once again I was at a loss for words. I could only nod, which seemed to satisfy her. Without taking her eyes from my face she released her grip. I didn't linger. I headed straight for the dressing room, leaving Mrs. Assirati in the shadows of the foyer.

My mind began racing. My head filled with so many thoughts, not the least of which were Mrs. Assirati's parting words: "You're so young and strong!" I kept repeating them over and over, and my chest swelled with pride. Even Mrs. Assirati feared for her husband, I told myself. I had definitely arrived. What I hadn't learned at that early stage of my career was the old Irish saying "A man is never so weak as when a woman tells him he is very strong."

My dressing room at Camberwell Green was small and musty with a mirror over a board that ran about waist-high for the length of the room. Three old chairs were lined up against the wall. A cold water sink was in the corner. Putting my bag down, I went looking for Jack Dale, peering into the different dressing rooms, saying hello to the wrestlers I knew and nodding to those I didn't. In one room I came across the man with whom I'd soon be entering the ring. He was sitting on a bench next to the door, putting on his boots. We'd never met before, but I'd seen plenty of photos of the big rugged face. It was not to be forgotten easily. He looked up when I poked my head through the door. His wife hadn't lied about his sight, one eye looked milky and in bad shape.

"He *is* going blind" I told myself. He also looked older than I'd expected. He may have been a legend in his own time, but he certainly didn't look so fearsome now. In fact, he looked a little vulnerable. I'd been brainwashed by his wife without knowing it.

Impulsively I thrust out my hand. "Pat Barrett," I blurted, "and you're Bert." It was a statement of fact, not a question. He accepted it as such.

Assirati grasped my hand in his great paw, which was so thick and hard it felt like a bicep in the shape of a hand. His grip was firm but not overly so. No big squeeze, no bone crushing power. This wasn't the dreaded beast I'd heard countless tales about. Looking down on him, he appeared to be a mild looking man, big, no doubt, with a face that showed the marks of his profession, and then some, a contradiction of his infamous reputation.

"I've heard all about you," I admitted, breaking the vacuum created by his silence. "I'm looking forward to our match."

His face split into a large friendly grin, making him look even more harmless than ever. Then a voice rumbled out from his chest. "So am I," he agreed. He made it sound as if he were looking forward to a delicious dessert after a rotten dinner.

I began to feel uncomfortable. Bert hadn't let go of my hand and he was staring at me. I got the impression he was waiting for me to say something else. "Look Bert," I started, "I've

7

heard all about you." He cocked his head to one side, as if to get a better look at the pip-squeak with his good eye.

"Yeah?"

"Well, I've heard that you sometimes don't let a wrestler give up. I mean, you keep pounding on him, or if it's a submission hold, you won't give him a chance to quit. What I'm saying is, I don't want to be mutilated or badly hurt, especially if I submit. I'd like you to respect that. And I'll do the same for you." That last part wasn't too convincing even to my ears. Yes, he looked older and not as big as I expected, but it was still hard to imagine him submitting to a greenhorn like me.

Bert opened his mouth again. He was not a man of many words but the few that rumbled out are still etched in my memory. "I've never really hurt anybody badly," he said, "except cunts. You're not a cunt, are you?" He squinted up into my face and gave my hand a little squeeze. Then he put on that big grin again, like a grandfather talking to an erring child.

I returned to my dressing room mulling over what Bert had said. One thought plagued me...I didn't think I was a cunt, but what if *he* did!

Approaching the ring in front of a packed house is almost impossible to describe. The atmosphere seizes the brain. You either love it or it strikes fear in your heart, like coming down the first big drop on a roller coaster.

My heart and stomach were heading down that first drop that Saturday night in Camberwell Green. There was a taste of excitement, a current far stronger than the electricity the senses usually perceive. Some halls or stadiums seem to accentuate the mood. No one that I've met can explain why, but it's a fact. This arena was almost perfect in that respect.

It seemed the whole town had turned out. The air was permeated with cigarette smoke and the animal smell of people packed cheek by jowl in a space too small for the size of the crowd. The hall was jammed to capacity, no fire regulations here to limit attendance.

8

The preliminaries were over. There had been an intermission during which tea, cakes, sweets and soft drinks had been sold. I suspected some of the crowd had stepped out for something stronger, judging from the raucous behavior. Now the moment had arrived that everyone had been waiting for...The Main Event.

As I strode through the fans toward the ring, I was aware of the murmuring going on around me and the curious stares I was getting, as if they were wondering who I was and how long I would last. They were looking at me like the Romans must have looked at the Christians just before they were fed to the lions. Here and there someone good naturedly shouted out, "Good luck, Paddy." But for the most part, there was little reaction to my arrival.

Without fanfare I climbed through the ropes and entered the ring, then sat in my corner. My second asked me if I wanted a massage or water between rounds. My mouth was baking hot, my tongue like sandpaper. I could only nod "Yes."

Suddenly a huge roar went up. Looking over the throng, I could see a small cavalcade approaching leisurely, coming down the aisle with Assirati in the middle. The air crackled with electricity. The fans were on their feet, straining to get a better look at the man they'd all come to see. Arms reached out to touch him in rippling waves as he passed by his adoring masses.

For the first time in my life I realized how lonely a person can feel in a room full of people. There I was surrounded by hundreds and hundreds of wildly screaming fans, feeling lonelier than I'd ever felt before, and the feeling was growing stronger every minute. Along with that came a surge of fear, a small enough sensation for the moment, but it too was on the rise. Until then I'd been an adventurer. That feeling was gone. My stomach knotted up and my knees got weak.

Into the ring bounced Bert, who seemed to have magically shed twenty years. His body, shrouded by the old robe he always wore, appeared larger than the one I had seen in his dressing room. He seemed to be tapped into the crowd, growing younger, bigger, and stronger the more they screamed and hollered, as if he was drawing some invisible life force from the adoring mob that moments before had been just a host of individuals.

The announcer stepped to the center of the ring, looking very debonair in his bow tie and well-pressed dark jacket. His English was flawless as it carried to every corner of the hall. Everyone immediately fell silent.

"Ladies and Gentlemen...On my left, from Dublin, Ireland...The up-and-coming young Irish wrestler... Pat Barrett." Polite applause but not much reaction, I noted.

"On my right...The Former British Champion...The man who has turned back all American challengers..." The voice droned on for hours, it seemed, while Assirati, who had taken off his robe, grew still larger and larger and I shrank with equal speed. "...the man who retired undefeated..." How I wished the announcer would shut his mouth. "...Ladies and Gentlemen..." Here it comes. "...I give you Berrrrrt Assiraaaaati!"

The announcer was almost drowned out by the incredible swell of voices shouting in unison, "BERT!...BERT! ...BERT!" Anyone would have thought he was going to fight to the death with a grizzly bear instead of one stupid Irishman who'd let himself get talked into such an abortion.

It was now the referee's turn. He ran his hands over our bodies (checking for oil and other foreign substances) and boots (to make sure no nasty objects were hidden and that the soles were free from resin, which could lead to glaucoma and blindness) with a professional skill born from many years of practice, then motioned us to the center of the ring. Whatever words were spoken were lost on me. I was thinking desperately how to handle the situation. But, of course, it was much too late to go over plans or strategies. The bell had rung.

I turned to face Camberwell Green's favorite son. His body was hurtling toward me from the opposite corner with amazing speed. Mercifully, my instincts took over. Moving aside, I managed to avoid being smashed into my corner. Bert turned and as he did I hit him with a chopping elbow under the ribs. To this day I'm not sure who was more surprised... Bert, myself, or the crowd.

Instantly a giant roar went up. It turned out they weren't cheering for my masterful move. They were yelling in anticipation over what was surely about to happen to me for being so brash. They also saw indications that they'd get their money's worth after all, before the inevitable kill.

Fear spurred me on. I kept taking holds wherever I could, until I heard the bell. End of round one.

It certainly didn't seem like ten minutes. It felt more like an hour. My one-minute rest, on the other hand, lasted only seconds. How could time speed by so? My second hovered over me muttering encouragement and instructions in my ear. I felt like telling him, "If you know so much, let's trade places." The bell rang and I was going full bore again.

Two rounds passed, filled with holds and counterholds, twenty minutes...a lifetime of non-stop action. Then came the beginning of the end. Assirati grabbed a headlock, and clamped on like a vice. He took me in a cross-buttock, pulling me over his hip while still holding onto my head with ferocious strength. Landing on my chest with his full weight, he completely knocked the air out of my lungs. That done, he began a slow caress of my nose, using the heel of his hand. The fans went crazy. They had come to see just this moment, and he wasn't about to disappoint them.

He smashed me again.

My mouth and nose instantly filled with blood. A film of red covered one eye. Until that moment, self-preservation had dictated my every move. No longer. Screaming like a banshee I somehow broke loose from the huge arm that held me and came to my feet in a bound. Assirati was a close second.

"You bastard!" I shouted. "You bloody bastard! I'll kill you!" My rage was so intense that I was quite capable of doing just that. Forgotten was my promise to myself to escape if I was badly hurt. Forgotten was my amateur wrestling training to be a

11

gentleman at all times. All I wanted was to smash, damage and brutalize.

Assirati's huge face was looming at me again when I hit him with my best punch, a blast powered by everything I had left in me, right where it should've polaxed him, on the chin. It landed just a little off center but it stopped him. It definitely stopped him. The crowd went silent. I smashed him again. Was I imagining it or did he stagger a little? My hand was throbbing. It felt like I'd hit a bull between the horns, and with just as much effect. Bert was still on his feet. Then that hideous hoarse guttural voice growled, "Hit me again, son. Hit me again, a little fucking harder!"

It was the sort of behavior that made Bert a legend amongst wrestlers and fans alike. He was not just a phenomenally strong man, not just an acrobat. He was a master psychologist as well. He had me psyched right there. The referee later told me I looked stunned for an instant, and that's all it took for Bert to move in fast, under my body, with a head butt. I doubled over in pain, sucking for air. He grabbed my arms by the wrists and locked them against his body. Suddenly I found myself upside-down, my legs flying overhead. A split second later he gave a mighty leap and we were airborne, locked to each other like mating flies. We floated together, with me underneath, for what seemed like an eternity. Then the roof came crashing in as blackness enveloped me. Faintly I could hear people screaming, they seemed miles away. A small voice was droning out numbers, "Three...Four..."

My own small voice tried to compete. "Get out of here before the building caves in on you!" It told me.

"Five..."

I was struggling to my feet when a hand pushed me down again. "Stay there you silly prick," someone whispered in my ear, "Or next time he'll kill you." The referee, for some reason, had taken pity on me. Not wanting to see my body take more punishment, he'd shoved me back to the canvas.

12

By the time my head cleared sufficiently to leave the ring most of the crowd had left. Only a few autograph-seekers remained, but they weren't hanging around for my signature.

I was back in the dressing room, taking off my boots, when Assirati came in. He had a big towel wrapped around his thick, muscular middle. "That was a great match, kid," he said. "You were terrific."

I stared into his broad ugly face, looking for a hint of sarcasm. I saw none, only sincerity. "Thanks," I mumbled, unsure of what else to say.

"That's okay. You've got a great future, lots of fire. I liked the match so much, I'm going to talk to the promoter. You and me can have some more great matches together." Bert shook my hand again then walked out. I didn't know what to make of his comment. Was that a threat or a promise?

On the way home that night a bus pulled up to my stop and I tried to get inside. I missed the step by about three feet. The doctor told me the next day I had a bad concussion. That wasn't all. When I went to pick up my money the promoter informed me that attendance wasn't as good as expected. "A lot of people sneaked in free," he said, "So I can't pay you as much as I'd promised."

My mother was infuriated when I told her how I'd been screwed out of the extra purse money. "Throw the check in his face." She told me. "Teach him a lesson."

I'm Irish but I wasn't *that* green. "Mum, the promoter would just keep it." I tried to act as calm as possible, but inside I was boiling. Another lesson learned, I told myself. Small consolation though it was.

Welcome to the pro wrestling business.

2

A NEW WAY OF LIFE

I have always believed in my good luck. Many times I've been told I was lucky. Things had a habit of turning out for the best, even when they looked the worst, hence my philosophy that 'tis better to be born lucky than rich.

I left Ireland by ship to arrive in Holyhead, Wales; then took a train to London, England, depending on my luck to find a place to stay, and a job of some sort to keep the wolf from my door. With almost no money and not a care in the world I spent my first night in the Salvation Army Hostel, where for a small fee, I got a meal and a bed. The meal was very plain, the bed very hard, but it was sustenance and a roof, and the price was right.

The following day I got into the underground and randomly picked a station from the hundreds that were on the board. There was no rhyme or reason to what I did, but my choice proved a lucky one, Clapham Common was a fertile ground for rental rooms, not only that, but it put me within walking distance of the only pro wrestling gym in southern England.

I ended up getting a room very cheaply from a wonderful old lady who took great care of me. Years later I tried to calculate how much it cost her to feed me. That's when I realized for her, I was a losing venture; for me, she turned out to be a great friend.

Looking back on my naivete, it's hard to believe I was really that innocent. Up until that time I'd never had sex and was very vague about the whole business. In Ireland, especially in those days, sex education was non-existent. Sports had always been my passion, long-distance cycle racing, shot putting, running, weight training and of course, wrestling, which was my main interest. Now this doesn't mean I was altogether a monk. By the time I was seventeen I could dance quite well, but dating required time which I just didn't have with all my other activities. Consequently, when I hit the Big Smoke, London, I was still a virgin.

After getting a job to pay the bills I headed for the nearest wrestling gym. In the states amateur wrestling is taught mainly in high school or college, but in Europe this is not so. Amateur wrestling gyms in Europe are as popular as amateur boxing gyms are in America, they abound in all major and minor cities. It is within those walls that a budding wrestler learns and hones his skills in the manly art, the oldest sport in the world, and the most natural form of human combat.

Sunday morning I got up bright and early, full of enthusiasm, looking forward to a good pull 'round and sweat. In wrestling lingo, a "pull 'round" is when two wrestlers get on the mat and wrestle, without one necessarily trying to beat the other. Pulling 'round to wrestlers is like sparring is to boxers. I found a gym situated in a run-down area, which was no surprise as amateur wrestling usually isn't a money-making concern. The door was locked and barred, with nothing to say when it was going to open. I banged on it two or three times but to no avail.

Watching my actions was a well-dressed individual leaning casually on what looked like a brand new Jaguar. I couldn't understand why the gym was not open. In Ireland, Sunday mornings were usually the best time to get a good workout, before a visit to either the church or the pub, or both, and not necessarily in that order.

Turning to leave, I almost bumped into the dapper man who had come up behind me. "What do you want?" He asked looking me up and down. I noticed he had this most supercilious expression across his face. It was as if he were looking at something objectionable that had crawled out of a sewer. "I want to work out. This is a wrestling gym, isn't it?" I retorted.

"Yes, it's a wrestling gym, but a *pro* one, and you're not a pro, are you?"

There was something about the man's manner that grated. I put it down to my frustration and ill humor at finding the door bolted. As time went on I got to know Les Martin better, and discovered he had that effect on everybody. At least he didn't discriminate.

"Who are you and what's your name?" Martin asked. When I answered he shook his head. "Never heard of you." He then turned abruptly and strode back to his big flashy car.

That got my Irish dander up. Most people know by now that the English and Irish have a long and bloody history of turmoil. Even today we can have our problems getting along. This man certainly wasn't doing anything to help better relations.

"Well don't feel bad," I said. "I never heard of you either." If I'd stabbed him in the back, his reaction couldn't have been more dramatic. He almost stumbled against his car, then recovering, spun around.

"You're no pro!" He spat. "You must be an amateur, that is IF you do wrestle."

It was my turn to get really hot. Irish-English glasnost was definitely headed into the polar regions.

"What do you mean IF I wrestle? I'll have you know that I'm Irish middleweight and light heavyweight champ." Modesty was never my strong point, anyway I wasn't going to take crap from this stranger, even if he was obviously wealthy and drove a big fast expensive car.

His manner changed. If I'd been more sophisticated, and less full of myself, I would have seen it coming. There was a malicious gleam in his eye, but I ignored it. After all, what could this wimp do to a fine upstanding wrestler like myself?

16

Les Martin was a business partner to three brothers who called themselves the Dales. There was Billy, who was the youngest, and John, the oldest. Jack, the remaining brother, had been a great wrestler, both amateur and pro. Never a big man, he loved the business and the sport, whatever you cared to call it. It didn't matter how well he was dressed, if he saw some young wrestler pulling around on the mat, off would come the coat and he'd be in there mixing it, forgetting about the smell, sweat, and dust. What I didn't know that early Sunday morning was that Dale Martin was the biggest promotion of pro wrestling in Great Britain. It ranked in the top three for size in the world.

Martin was hated by the Dales, but I guess he had an iron clad contract with them, for they could never get rid of him. He was a mean, petty man who loved to watch men being hurt. He would observe wrestlers pulling around with the air of a superior being watching animals mauling one another. Actually, if it hadn't been for Les's abrasive nature, I might never have become a pro.

"How would you like to try out to become a pro?" His voice was different now, softer, almost ingratiating. I had absolutely no idea what he was talking about. I'd never seen pro wrestling, with the exception of an odd magazine or two filled with pictures of such stars as Killer Kowalski and Yukon Eric, who later sadly committed suicide. At that time in my life, when confronted with a proposition such as his, I stuck to my philosophy of "when in doubt, say no thanks".

Martin had baited me, now he sprang the trap. Whether by calculation or by chance, I'll never know, but he'd found my Achilles Heel... pride. "What's wrong? Young man, you're not afraid, are you?" He didn't even look at me directly, but continued to study his car.

Afraid! It was like a slap in the face. I had not learned the meaning of the word. How innocent is youth. If I'd only known what these words were letting me in for! A time was set the next evening for my trial by fire.

EVERYBODY DOWN HERE HATES ME

When I arrived there were a couple of men working out on the weights. The ring was empty and surrounded with rope, which I was not expecting. I was just used to normal amateur mats, with no ropes or corner posts. Looking around I started to feel a bit uneasy. This was not going to be what I had anticipated. Standing still, drinking in the atmosphere, I became aware that Les Martin had entered the gym through another door. He spotted me right away and beckoned me over to where he was talking to another well-dressed man. This I learned was Jack Dale, the driving force behind the huge promotional empire.

Right away I felt more at ease. Even though he had two huge cauliflower ears, he wore an air of affable business that I liked. His ears just confirmed that he was my kind of man.

Turning around to the two men exercising, he asked who was available to try me out. Before he was answered, Martin jumped in.

"I've already got it all arranged," he said. "Les Kellet will be here shortly to take care of him."

The way he looked in my direction told me somehow I'd made an enemy. What I wasn't aware of was he'd put off an evening at the theatre just to watch me being hurt. Jack Dale's head snapped around. The air was electric. "We don't have to wait for Kellet," he said. "Arthur here will try him out."

I thought Les Martin would have a heart attack on the spot. His face suffused with blood and I could see his body trembling. His voice had gone up three octaves. I thought he was going to stamp his feet he was so enraged. "I want to see him with Kellet! Let's wait. He'll be here any moment!"

In the meantime I was stripped and into my wrestling gear, but taking everything in. This Kellet must be something else, but what? When I met him, much later, I realized what a narrow escape I'd had.

Les Kellet's appearance was deceptive in many ways. He was tough, hard-bitten at times, very sadistic and slightly crazy. He was a contradiction to anyone who thinks that huge biceps and

18

a flat stomach are what makes a man dangerous in the wrestling business. He was fairly short, but not on guts; slightly rotund; with pale eyes, pale hair, pale skin, and some varicose veins on his legs. His round cherubic face was the picture of innocence. His hands were huge. They looked almost out of place dangling on the end of his wrists. His fingers were like big English sausages. With his long arms, he looked almost like a white orangutan — the same innocence with the same brute power. It wasn't only his strength that frightened other wrestlers, it was his indomitable will. Once he set his course on destroying someone, that's precisely what he did, not caring how, using whatever means he could, with a single-mindedness that scared those who knew him half to death.

In years to come I witnessed him in action. He was famous for his unorthodox holds, such as grabbing a handful of cheek, twisting and tearing, at the same time hooking his fingers into the side of the mouth and ripping away at the flesh.

This was the man Martin had wanted to brutalize me. My guardian angel was in my corner that day! For some reason, Kellet didn't show up until it was too late.

"Don't be bloody stupid, Martin." Jack snapped, his voice taking on an edge that wasn't there before. "Beaumont, here, will do fine." Then turning his back on his fellow promoter, Jack signaled us to get into the ring. "I'll give you five minutes in there," he said, looking at his watch, "to see what you can do." Turning to face the man who was to try me out, I got my first real look at one of the finest submission wrestlers at his weight in the world.

Arthur Beaumont was about five-feet, eleven-inches tall and weighed about one-hundred and ninety-five pounds. Strangely enough, he looked Celtic to me. He had sandy hair and white skin, that alabaster color that the Celtic race seem to possess. His cheekbones were high, with deep sunken eyes that were neither friendly nor unfriendly. Without a moments hesitation he moved in, smooth as silk, fast, but unhurried. The knots in my stomach disappeared. This was my language, my forte. I suddenly felt at home. This was no different than the hundreds of mats and opponents I'd met before.

Suddenly I found myself on the mat, with him behind me, a very dangerous situation to be in. Instantly I sat through a move that would take my body out of trouble, and put me in a position where I would be facing my opponent, and hopefully be on my feet. Everything worked out fine until I spun to a standing position, then my plan went awry. As I surged to my feet, he slapped a front face lock on me, at the same time hooking my leg with his, tripping me expertly. I'd been in similar positions before, but never quite like this. I was blacking out. My neck muscles screamed with pain. I couldn't understand what was happening. The more I struggled, the more pain in my neck and blackness in my head. Trying to fight seemed to be speeding me to oblivion. Suddenly I was released.

Sitting there, trying to marshal my senses, I looked up into a pair of amused eyes. Beaumont was looking over me, extending his hand. I came to my feet and gasped "What was that you had on me? That's never happened before."

Dale's voice cut in. It was all business...wrestle on.

Again we moved around the ring, each searching for an opening to take a hold. I could tell this man was in great shape. I was in the best condition of my young life, but he wasn't even breathing hard.

What happened next was like a bad dream. This man from the north of England ended up with my body in a position where I couldn't move. Not only that, the pain was excruciating. This was not wrestling as I knew it, the holds he used were basically the same, it was his application of them that differed. Again, just as suddenly, I was released. Getting gingerly to my feet, I turned to face my opponent.

"Give me two minutes of pulling around." Jack's voice cut into my thoughts. "No submissions." No submissions? What did he mean? Then my mind went back to the business at hand.

Still not understanding what was going on, I wrestled my best. This time it was in the amateur style I was used to. No more of those weird holds. My confidence started to return. This was what wrestling was all about. What I didn't know then, but have since learned, is that to men like Beaumont, wrestling was not a game, but a war, to be won at all costs. Dale's voice pierced through the grunting and heavy breathing. "Time." Then it was all over.

Laying down on the mat, sucking in air, I realized that was the hardest five minutes I'd ever wrestled. The reason was of course, amateurs cannot use bone-breaking holds to win. This is to protect the participants. In the pro sport, just about anything goes; submissions, including the use of arm bars to exact greater leverage. To the pro wrestler, pinning is not that important. To submit your opponent is all important. They have a saying "I'm pinned, but I'm not beat." Sometimes if a lot of money or pride is at stake, a man will not give up. At times like that bones are broken, or men are rendered unconscious.

Arthur Beaumont and I became good friends later on. He had a streak of kindness in his nature not found in many men. That was why he didn't take advantage of my ignorance. He's dead now. He died at an early age, like so many other wrestlers who die from an accumulation of internal injuries. But to this day, I thank him for not abusing his position of power. Many times since, I've seen people just like me ground into the mat, punched or kicked into unconsciousness, just on the whim of a wrestler or promoter. All they wanted was a pull 'round, and instead got totally brutalized. In one wrestling office, the promoter had would-be pro wrestlers sign papers absolving the promotion of all liability for the horrendous injuries they were about to receive. I've always hated it, and I still do.

Jack Dale obviously liked my style, for whatever reason. We went back to his office upstairs while Les Martin left in ill humor.

The offer he made me was one I couldn't refuse. A business in which I could do all the things I enjoyed, wrestle, travel, and make money. Who could ask for more?

So now I was a pro, or at least a semi-pro, working at a job during the day, working out at night. Fortunately for me training was not a chore, in fact to this day very few things in life do I enjoy more than sweating it out in a gym. A great many people in sports hate the grind of training, and I believe this ends successful careers. At times I've heard sportscasters talk about boxers, aged thirty and upwards, as being finished because their legs were going. If this is true, how is it that most marathon runners don't hit their peak until age forty? My belief is that some athletes lose their desire for the grind of gym work, especially if they are successful and have made a lot of money. So consequently, they lose the edge that put them on top.

After I finished at the gym I'd head back to my room for a late dinner and sleep. Not being able to afford a car, there was no public transportation at that hour, I'd walk a distance of perhaps four miles. The shortest route was across Clapham Common.

A common in England is a piece of unenclosed land, set aside by various kings and queens for the use of the common people in a district. Originally, in every manor there was a tract of uncultivated land, over which the local inhabitants had rights of common, principally the rights to pasture animals, to fish, and to cut wood. These privileges are defended righteously even today. Any talk by government or big developers to annex even a tiny portion of the land is met with howling protests. They range in size from a few acres to thousands. For example, Wimbledon Common is one of the most famous in the country. It has a windmill in which families of the park attendants live, a golf course, lakes and deer. It's like a wilderness area, right in the heart of one of the largest cities in the world.

Clapham Common was nowhere near the size of Wimbledon, but it had a couple of ponds and many large trees and shrubs. These shrubs were the nocturnal hiding places of the ladies of the night and their followers.

My return home would take me across this common where, to my surprise, every night one or two young and not-so-young females would accost me, linking my arm affectionately and whispering in my ear something about "a short time, very cheap." I had no conception of what they were talking about. One particular woman was very persistent. Most of the others recognized me after a while, and would remain in the shadows, figuring rightly that I was a waste of time. I could see their dim forms lounging against the trees. They were surrounded in the background by other dark images, whom I found out later were watchers — people who spent their evenings waiting for the prostitutes to pick someone up, then watch while they performed the act under the stars.

It was almost like a jungle scene. The marks or Johns were like the zebra or wildebeest. The prostitutes were like the big cats waiting to pounce. The watchers behaved like the hyenas and jackals, hanging around waiting for whatever opportunity might present itself.

The one persistent woman must've had a room or flat nearby because her pitch was always the same. First she would step from the darker shadows into the half light thrown by the street lights. She was, I judged, about thirty, but with my limited experience with women at the time, she could've been sixty under all the makeup.

"Good evening, sir." She would say. My reply, because I was a well-mannered young man, was always good evening, in return. My heart would race a little. My stomach got that butterfly feeling. For though I wasn't sure what was going on, my primitive side was responding to the situation. She would then hook my arm and whisper her words of intrigue.

"Short time dearie...and I makes a nice cuppa tea." This was how I knew she lived close by.

Shaking my head, I would mumble a fast "No thank you, ma'am," and turn bright red. I could feel the blood in my hot cheeks. I'm sure she had a good laugh at my reaction. If she'd

23

been in her business any length of time at all, she knew the effect she was having on me.

Finally, after this went on for months, I decided to find out exactly what she meant. But I was too embarrassed to ask her, and I didn't want to look a complete fool. I turned to the only person I felt I could trust in London, my landlady.

She was an old, very fat, very jolly cockney with a heart of gold.

A few weeks before I'd come back from the matches with one eye closed, and a gash over my eyebrow. She'd been upset telling me that pro wrestling was no fit business for a well brought up young gentleman. I liked her loyalty, even though it must've blinded her to what I was really like.

As I came in the front door, her head popped out of the door at the end of the hall.

"How are you luv?" she said. "Everything all right?" The concern on her big, old, lined face was beautiful to see. It gave me a warm feeling to know that someone in England was worried if anything happened to me. My mother and sister lived in Ireland, so other than letters home, I had no personal contact with anyone.

"I'm fine." I answered. "No problems at all." I guess she knew me better than I thought, or perhaps I was still transparent. She came out of her room and turned on the hall light. She looked up into my face searchingly and questioned me.

"What is it? Is something bothering you?"

"Yes!" I blurted out. "Yes, something is bothering me." I told her the story about the ladies who were approaching me on the common. She was incredulous.

"You mean you honestly don't know what's going on? I figured you for an innocent, but this is hard to believe. You'd better to come into my flat. There are a few things you need to know."

That's where I got my first real lecture on life. I was astounded at how I could have been so blind, so dumb. Looking back, it wasn't a bad way to be. Knowledge doesn't necessarily bring happiness. Still we had a good laugh about my ignorance, then I asked her the last question on my mind.

"Why the cup of tea?" She really laughed hard, but the question was genuine. It had bothered me why the drink was thrown in.

"To help you get your strength back, silly!"

Shortly after all this, the streets and commons of England were cleaned up by the police. What brought this about, I was told, was an American serviceman's mother was accosted by a man who mistook her for a lady of the night. She was so incensed that she complained to her congressman. Other mothers and wives joined in. Pressure was brought to bear on the powers that be. The majority of the common prostitutes, as we knew them, were doomed.

3

REVENGE IS SWEET

It was hate at first sight between him and I, no ifs, ands, or buts about that. People talk about how they felt the first time they met their loved ones, how there was a chemical reaction, a sunburst of emotion for the other person, an immediate attraction that they were both aware of. Many years later they can still conjure up that moment. That's how it was with me. Between Sonny Keene and I there was the opposite reaction, just as strong, just as violent.

It was near the beginning of my career. I was still very much a babe in the woods in the business, but learning fast. The first time I met Sonny it was at one of the halls he was promoting. I was working for the Dale-Martin consortium, which comprised many under-promoters, people who ran one or more towns while paying Dale and Martin a booking fee. These local men earned a precarious livelihood, and still do to this day. If they aroused the ire of the central office, which sent them the wrestlers, made up the cards, in other words did the matchmaking, they could, and often were punished. Sometimes they were squeezed out altogether. This could easily be accomplished by sending second class men who were dull to watch, or not known by the fans. After a couple of bad shows, people would just stay away from the matches, and the under-promoter would go broke. On the other hand, if an under-promoter had a good grip on his town, or towns, and was rich enough, plus had local political clout, he could hold off a move on his interests.

A case in point was Fred Ward, an under-promoter in Georgia. He ran towns like Macon and Columbus. The central office was controlled by Tim Bernard, who later became one of the powers in the WWF, and is now affiliated with Ted Turner. Bernard had a disagreement with Fred and tried repeatedly to get rid of him, with no success. The reason they couldn't squeeze him out was he had power in local politics. Born and raised in the area, he was a member of different organizations such as the Elks, and the Moose lodges. One night I had to wait twenty minutes before I could wrestle because Ward was giving out tailored blazers to the head men in one such organization. The fact that President Carter's mother Lillian was a big wrestling fan, seen often at ringside at one of his towns, didn't hurt him, I'm sure. Mr. Wrestling II, a masked wrestler, has a photo of President Carter with a headlock on him. Also in Ward's favor was the fact that his Georgia towns were all money-spinners. Fred Ward is still there, while Bernard has moved on to greener pastures.

Sonny was one of those local sub-promoters who had a lot of influence with the central office, because most of the towns he promoted were popular wrestling towns. With a minimum of publicity, fans would turn out in droves, thus making the promoters a lot of money. This put Sonny in a very influential position, as in this business money talks, and talks big. The fact that he didn't like me could make my life very difficult. It meant that I was butting heads with a very influential person, who could, with enough bad reports to Dale and Martin, get me fired. A top class wrestler could be put in a bad position. For a rookie like me it was just about death. I already knew that instant dismissals were the norm, and still are. Wrestlers have absolutely no redress if they are dismissed; on top today, ostracized tomorrow.

He was a repulsive man to look at. He was extremely obese

27

and dirty looking, always wearing food stains on his shirt, or suit, or both. He had one short arm which was a deformity from birth. His hair was parted in the middle and matted, always slicked down with lots of oil like something out of a nightmare. Then there was one of his eyes, which never looked at you, but seemed to have a will of its own.

"Hope you can wrestle better than you look!" Were the first words of greeting from the man I'd never met, but had heard so much about. His voice had a whining quality that grated on my nerves. "They've been sending me a lot of drach recently."

Instantly I got hot, my Irishness showing through. I didn't know what drach meant, but it didn't sound good, the way it was delivered spoke multitudes.

"If you don't want me to stay, I'll leave right now." Saying this, I picked up my bag.

"Don't be a silly fella... Can't you take a joke?" His bad eye had difficulty focusing and he couldn't seem to stop fiddling with his dirty tie.

"Sometimes." I said. "It depends on who's making it." Turning his back he waddled away, leaving me holding my bag.

It turned out he was the announcer and the time-keeper, as well as the promoter. That was so he didn't have to pay anybody else. His wife, who was a rather large blonde woman, ran the concessions. Between the two of them, they cleaned up cash-wise every wrestling night, and controlled everyone and everything. Most of the wrestlers hated him for reasons I was yet to discover. During the matches, if he didn't like a particular bout with any of the wrestlers in it, he would fall asleep, or pretend to, and let the time run over between rounds. Another favorite trick he had was to pretend to forget the name of a wrestler he didn't like when announcing the contestants before a match. Then he'd start rummaging through his pockets, trying to find the scrap of paper the name was supposedly written on. If he really wanted to get to the wrestler, he would eventually find the paper. Holding it in his long arm, he would throw it to the short one, which invariably missed the catch. He would then spend about five minutes trying to pick it up. This would bring howls of laughter from the audience and kill the prestige of whoever he was putting down, to say nothing of what it would do to the match. He did this to me a couple of times on different occasions, getting me so steamed up I wanted to kill him, but with great difficulty, I contained myself. This must have given him a false sense of security, as both he and I were aware of his power. But alas, he wasn't satisfied with doing his normal tricks to me. One night he decided to carry it a step further. My match was in full swing. He had already done the whole gambit, announcing from the outside of the ring instead of the middle, then pretending to lose the paper with my name on it; when found, it was tossed and missed with the short arm, and he'd gotten his laugh. Sitting at ringside beside the bell, he read a newspaper out loud, like he was in his living room. It was hard for me to believe that a grown man, a businessman supposedly, would do things like this, but he was extremely vindictive, and in my mind, childish.

During my match, which had been going very well for me, I was suddenly surprised by a sound I'd never heard before in the ring. I'd heard boo's, hisses, raspberries, slow hand claps, stomping, bad language, and all kinds of other noises. But what creature was at ringside that could sound like a pig rooting for its supper? Jumping away from my opponent, looking wildly around, I beheld a sight never to be forgotten. Half-lying, half-sitting in his chair, his tie loosened, shirt opened showing a lard-like fat white chest, was Sonny. His florid face was thrown back towards the ceiling. His drooling cavernous mouth was wide open from whence came the most horrible sounds imaginable. It was obvious by the crowd's reaction that it could be heard all over the hall. People were standing up, not in excitement or anger at the match or the wrestlers, but were craning their necks to catch a glimpse of this fat hog doing his thing.

Obviously, he wasn't asleep. In a fit of snorting his head rolled to one side, then I saw one eyelid slowly lift, and a small bloodshot eye look straight at me for just a split second before it slammed shut again. This was the final straw. Laughter rose, then swelled all through the hall. My blood boiled. If I'd been a member of the audience I would've seen the funny side of things too. But I wasn't, and I didn't.

He'd gone too far. If it was open war, so be it. Waiting until the other wrestler had broken out of my hold, I started to run, with my opponent in hot pursuit. Charging at full speed, I launched my two-hundred and thirty pounds over the ropes without touching them. Turning my body in mid-air, I smashed the big ugly face with both feet. Instantly there was blood everywhere. His face was a mess, lips split, nose flattened. The snorts and grunts turned to howls of pain. So great was my impact that I kicked his three-hundred-plus-pound body several feet up the aisle. With my momentum going strong, I let my body continue its forward direction, landing on top of him again. His eye, that is the good one, was staring up in sheer terror. The other one was like a fruit in a slot machine, dancing around at a terrific speed. Still supposedly unaware of what I was doing, (two could play his game) I ripped the shirt from around his neck, tore his bow tie right off, flung it to the audience, never to be seen again, and lastly, elbowed him on the side of the jaw, which actually straightened out both eyes for a couple of seconds. Scrambling to my feet, I stepped on his face which had opened up like an overripe tomato, then pushed away from the bloated body, which was no longer snoring, but emitting long high-pitched hysterical screams, like a pig sounds while being slaughtered.

Without a backward glance I re-entered the ring. Nobody had to tell me how much damage I'd done. It took six people to carry the body, which by now was quivering and crying. The match fell to pieces. My opponent seemed to lose his stomach for wrestling, and kept back-peddling away from me. When I got back to the dressing rooms it was like I had the plague. No one talked to me, I was left strictly alone. Sonny had already been whisked away to the hospital. I knew my goose was cooked, but I had no remorse, in fact I slept very soundly that night.

I got a call the next day from Jack Dale to come and see him. He berated me, said I would be fired and never work for a promoter again. I never doubted that they had the power to do that. But I detected, as he harangued me, a glint of amusement in those eyes. I thought I must be mistaken, but there it was again. I had to be wrong, after all from my experience promoters stick together. Then it hit me. Jack hated Sonny as much as I did, maybe more.

Jack Dale had been a pretty tough wrestler before becoming a promoter. He still had his big cauliflower ears, which he wore with pride to testify to his years in the ring. Even though he was now a millionaire and could afford to have them surgically corrected, they were untouched. He loathed Sonny's methods of harassment. It wasn't manly, and to Jack being manly was very important. Wrestlers without balls were not for him. I believe he secretly wanted Sonny's towns, if he could have gotten them. Jack, no saint, was a bit greedy. Why settle for a little when you can have the lot? I was starting to understand politics. We came to an agreement. I would go overseas to Germany for awhile, until Jack took care of the damage I'd done at home. When I returned six months later, all was smoothed out. Keene didn't speak to me for years. Though he announced my matches from the middle of the ring, he never sat ringside again. Also, to my surprise, he never messed up my introductions anymore.

Years later, when I returned from the USA to England on a trip, I'd heard that he'd had all kinds of health troubles. I can't say I felt bad about his misfortunes. For this I was not unhappy. Then his wife of many years had left him for his chauffeur. The story goes that she ran away to Brighton, a small English town on the south coast, taking the deeds to three or four properties, plus a great deal of money, and was living with her lover. Sonny wanted the deeds back, not the wife just the property, so he hired two thugs from the east end of London, which is the real rugged part of the city. The idea was for the men to grab his wife from the house, throw her in the car, then leave in a hurry. After that they were to somehow get the deeds from her.

Everything went according to plan. They found the house, rang the doorbell, and a large blond woman answered. She was promptly snatched like a sack of garbage, thrown in the back seat right on top of Sonny, and the car sped off.

Sonny's voice couldn't be heard above the screams of the victim who pummeled and abused him relentlessly. It turned out not to be his errant wife. They had gone to the wrong house and grabbed someone else's wife. By the time all this was sorted out, they had driven several miles back to London. There was an argument about what to do with the lady in question. The unwilling baggage was left by the side of the road to make her own way back to Brighton. Word quickly spread through the neighborhood. Sonny's wife was alerted to the danger of being kidnapped, so she immediately moved.

Sonny went rapidly down hill following that. The last time I saw him, he was a pathetic figure. For some reason he went out of his way to talk to me. Strangely, he asked if I knew anybody who would take care of him, sort of a house matron, for a small weekly wage. He died shortly after, I heard. I can't honestly say I was sorry.

when his name was announced, there would be a pregnant silence, or at best a splutter of applause. This did very little for the ego of the man in question. Especially if his name was announced right after a popular pro, who would get a thunderous ovation. It didn't matter if the fickle fans loved or hated you. What was of paramount importance to the wrestler and promoter was their reaction, and there had better be lots of it. The reason for this was simple. One of the ways a promoter gauges a wrestler's worth is by crowd reaction. TV shows are judged by the Nielsen ratings, wrestlers by cheers, boos, catcalls and hisses. The greater the volume; the greater the worth. So consequently silence in the wrestling business is not golden!

I remember the shame I felt for the first few nights when my name was announced. I stepped forward resolutely, waving all around, only to be deafened by the silence. I knew instinctively that I was not long for that tournament if the reaction from the onlookers didn't pick up. Also I noticed that the men who chanced to stand next to me got resounding applause. This made it seem all the worse. Thinking about this phenomenon I started to realize that it was no accident where they stood. Any reaction sounded deafening compared to the silence I was greeted with, therefore prolonging their stay. The promoter had a built-in sound meter which, I believe, could gauge the hand-clapping, foot-stomping, and whistling to the nearest decibel. In some ways it was like an Agatha Christie mystery. Who would be the next to disappear? Sometimes it was only one body that was gone, other times it was none. But then three or four would vanish without so much as a "good-bye." There was a certain stigma to being dismissed from the matches. In fact there was even a stigma attached to being friendly with someone that was about to do the vanishing act. The trick I was told was to be able to figure out on whom the axe would fall next, and disassociate oneself from them as rapidly as possible, just in case their downfall was contagious. In this climate it was very difficult to develop a secure outlook. Of course there was always the ever-present threat of injury looming over the participant which would terminate his contract. The contracts weren't worth the paper they were written on, I found out. Men still got the sudden call to the promoter's office for dismissal. The strange thing was there were always other bodies to take the places of the missing. It was as if there was a huge warehouse somewhere where pro wrestlers were kept on ice for just such an occasion.

I had a nightmare where I could see the promoter calling this cold storage place, saying that he needed three bodies tomorrow... Send him a medium one that could move fast, a large one that's good looking, and give him a super big one, not to worry about looks as long as he could get the fans boiling. He was returning three. The one with the red hair was the shits, needs a tune-up or something... The frightening part was the red-haired one looked a lot like me!

The men were of all nationalities, mostly German or Hungarian. There were also Greek, English, Polish, and sometimes American, especially a Negro. Negroes were always in demand. Outside the ring there was a certain amount of camaraderie, despite the language barrier. Inside the ring, everything was different. It was a real dog-eat-dog world. Everyone would try to out-do everyone else, by whatever means at their disposal.

It was during my third match when a strange thing happened that I couldn't quite understand, but it gave me a big lift. I was in the ring against a giant Hungarian, who was doing a good job of manhandling my body and my pro career, it only being three months old. I was green as grass, which must have been obvious to everyone but me. Suddenly, during my match, the promoter's voice boomed out over the public address system, which caused quite a stir with the fans. The bored crowd came alive with excitement. I could even see people sitting up high and taking notice of the contest, but I couldn't understand why.

Then it was all over with, the massive Hungarian picked me up in the air like a sack of garbage, and dropped me on the back

35

of my head and neck. While I was lying on the canvas stunned, he casually dropped his bulk across my body for the pinfall. The crowd went wild. Something must be wrong. The other nights when I was beaten nothing happened. The fans just kept on talking to each other like there was no match at all. They acted like they were resting their emotions, taking time out to replenish their beer or go to the toilet. Some of the more voluptuous girls seemed to have two main problems. One was finding the bathrooms, which was never in the direction they were headed. The girls paraded right past the ring in full view of all, accompanied by whistles and cheers. The second was how frequently they felt the need to go. Up until tonight the attitude of the fans seemed to have been let's save our energies for the real knock-down, drag-out matches yet to come, between two real men. Let's not waste it on this pale, freckled boy who calls himself a wrestler. This time, as I left the ring, several people shook my hand vigorously!

The promoter was standing his full six-foot, two-inch height, smiling in my direction, the microphone still in his hand. He was an ex-wrestler from the school of hard knocks, steeped in the Prussian tradition of absolutely no surrender. Smiling was not a specialty of his, so I felt honored. As I passed him by, still stunned by the fall and the crowd's enthusiasm, I heard him say in a gentle German accent what sounded like, ''goot, goot.'' At that kind of praise from him, I would've single handedly attacked a brigade of tanks, so profound was the awe and esteem I held him in. Looking back now it would seem foolish to have felt like this, but it did me no harm. Perhaps it gave me a sense of pride in myself that up until that night had been draining away.

My first night in the dressing room Kaiser, the promoter, caught me with my pants down, so to speak. I checked into my hotel that morning, then being a fitness maniac and an ambitious young wrestler, went straight to the gym and worked out strenuously for three hours. I mainly wanted to get the kinks out after the long train journey, but there was also the sheer joy of working out.

On my way back to the hotel I passed a Hungarian restaurant where I was surprised to see several large men with big necks and cauliflowered ears sitting at various tables that were arranged on the pavement outside. They were eating meals of strange origins and drinking turbid black Turkish coffee in small china cups. They all looked very relaxed to me, like big, well-fed lions the morning after a successful hunt, wearing equally as benign expressions on their faces as they puffed on their cigars or chatted with the locals who clustered around periodically looking for autographs. Like the resting lions, they looked almost like big cuddly toys, no hint of the menace or violence that they were capable of was allowed to show. It was virtually like an afternoon tea party.

Finding myself a seat in a corner, I watched the scenario with fascination while eating fantastic Hungarian goulash. It was the first time I'd eaten this wonderful dish.

The food was excellent and priced right, but then I already knew it would be. I was green, but a survivor never the less. I'd picked up early in my career that if wrestlers frequented a hotel or restaurant then it would rate high in three major categories. First, it had to be priced reasonably. Secondly, the food had to be good. It surprised me to find how many pros were gourmets in their own right. Thirdly, and very importantly, there had to be plenty of it. None of your little helpings for these men. They were mostly very large, with corresponding appetites. God help the waiter or waitress that brought a small platter of food! Staying in the background, I absorbed the scene before me. Each man held court with his fans, basking in the attention they got from their minions. In return for the adulation, a fan would get an autograph or a handshake from a thick paw. If they were very lucky, the fan may even get a conversation, but that was never for too long. I noticed how the wrestler would limit the time given to each person, unless of course, they were pretty females.

Right away I could see who was the most successful, by the

quantity and quality of the attention he got. Unconsciously I was learning my trade, not just the ring part, but important just the same, how to handle fans and what image to present. At that moment I was not aware of this, but in retrospect I can see how much of an impression that scene, and many other similar ones that followed in Germany, left on me.

Suddenly I was spotted in the corner by a girl of about eighteen. She came toward me with her autograph book outstretched. Speaking in German she stood before me waiting, not so much shy, for fans are almost never shy, but unsure. Since she had never seen me before she was only guessing, by whatever instinct fans have, that I was indeed a wrestler. My heart swelled with pride. My first day in Germany and already I was being recognized. I had only been around a few months in the business and still had some doubts in my ability to survive in the hectic world I found myself in, let alone make a good living from it. Reaching out, I took the book from her. The instant my hand touched the cover of the book it was like an alarm went out to all the world, especially to all the cauliflowered ears in the vicinity. Every wrestler in the place turned to stare at me, and I mean turned! Because of the size of their necks, or maybe it was their injuries, I still don't know why, but wrestlers very seldom turn their heads. If they want to see something behind them, the whole body turns. This is how it looked. All the heavy bodies shifted so their owners could get a better look at this interloper. The stares were not unfriendly, neither were they friendly, just calculating for the most part, with a frown thrown in here or there as they searched their memories for a recollection of who I was. Now I've never been a shrinking violet, but all this was unwelcomed attention from men who were, in my eyes, and most likely theirs, much more than my peers. To make matters worse, most of the fans left their gods to rush to my table. I was a novelty, someone they'd never seen before. I might be a world champion or some other famous luminary that they had overlooked. Until they had found out exactly what they had here I would be treated with fawning respect. If it became known that I was just another pro I'd be dropped like a hot potato.

Jumping to my feet to get some room, the fans behind were pushing the ones in front so hard they were literally falling in my lap, I turned over my coffee. Going red with embarrassment, I looked in the direction of the other wrestlers to see what effect my clumsiness was having. All I got were cold hard stares. These men, if they were asked, would tell you what a terrible nuisance fans were, and how they didn't want them around. On the other hand, they obviously didn't like the idea of their retinue suddenly deserting them for a whipper-snapper, for that is all I was to them. No matter that once I was discovered for what I was, a green un-tried pro, there would be a stampede in the other direction even faster than they arrived. Right now I was getting the attention they deserved. The tension was a living thing. I could feel it hitting me in waves. Instinctively I knew I didn't need to make such formidable enemies.

Ignoring the people around me I gave what I hoped was a friendly smile, and with my palms turned out, an apologetic shrug. Suddenly one of the biggest men, a Hungarian, with his history stamped and beaten onto his face, broke into a huge infectious belly laugh. It was wonderful music to my ears. It was a friendly laugh and made me feel like I'd come home from some test that I almost failed. Then his voice boomed across the open space between us. His accent was atrocious, his English, horrible. But the words were marvelous.

"Welcome to Germany, my friend... whoever you are. Welcome!"

The tension dropped instantly. The large bodies turned away. There were no smiles from them, but at least I wasn't getting those frigid stares.

It's amazing how quickly fans can find out your status, even when they don't speak your language. With a speed that would make my head spin, they stripped away my veneer, laying my soul bare to the world, then left me with my bruised ego, sitting

alone again, just like before, only now I had coffee all over me
and the table. Welcome to Germany, my ass!

That evening the dressing rooms were full. This was a large
tournament with about twenty-two wrestlers, all shapes and sizes,
most weighing two-hundred-eighty-pounds and up. Germany,
like the USA, likes its men big, the bigger the better. In England
and in some other countries, size isn't important, many top men
weigh only one-hundred-sixty-pounds. It's amazing how much
room twenty or so bodies take up, especially when they are
sprawled out on benches or chairs. There were four big dressing
rooms, all interconnected, but with no doors. They had been
taken off long before by the looks of the paint on the hinges.

I was lying down on the wooden floor feeling quite relaxed.
It had been a long heavy day so far, what with the train trip,
plus the workout, and the episode in the restaurant. I wanted
as much rest as I could get before the match. I've never been
one of those unfortunate men that get the gitters before the bouts.
Some even get sick, or their blood pressure goes so high that
they have trouble convincing the athletic doctor to let them
wrestle. My attitude had always been to get myself ready the
best way I knew how, then let the chips fall where they may.
No point in worrying about what may or may not happen. My
mind was drifting pleasantly to that in-between world, neither
sleep nor conscious. I had not a care in the world. Nothing to
do now until the match, which was about an hour away.

Somewhere in the back of my subconscious I could hear what
sounded like a platoon of Romans marching to battle. It was like
a dream. Maybe I was dreaming, but right then I didn't want
to find out. I was too content just the way things were. I must
have dozed off, but I could hear the Roman general bellowing
in my ear. He seemed to be getting closer and sounded mad as
all hell. Trying to shut him out was impossible. He was getting
louder. How could this be? It was certainly a very realistic dream!
Suddenly I was brought awake very rudely by a massive hand
shaking my shoulder violently. Leaping to my feet, I was instantly

awake. This must be an emergency! Perhaps the stadium was on fire! Most of the ones I'd seen were death traps anyway.

"What's wrong? What's happening?" I said glancing around wildly. I knew from past experiences that dressing rooms were not the place to grab a sleeping body. You were more than likely to have a fight on your hands. So on that basis I presumed it had to be a disaster or I would not have been so violently awakened.

My wandering gaze stopped. In front of me was standing a very well-dressed man. His suit, even to my untutored eye, looked expensive. That diamond ring on his pinky finger, nobody had to tell me it was real. He just didn't look like the kind of man that would dream of wearing anything fake, let alone a diamond. There was an air of authority about this man that said he would brook no nonsense. He was obviously used to command. What really shocked the hell out of me were the other wrestlers, who I'd seen in various states of undress and somnolence. I couldn't believe my eyes! They were madly exercising. Some were doing push-ups like their life depended on it, some, sit-ups. Two were in the corner pulling necks, while another pair had a towel twisted like a rope and were mightily trying to pull it away from each other. All of this was accompanied with the appropriate grunts and pants. Right away I knew I'd done something wrong. I also knew these big bastards weren't doing all of this for the good of their health, least-wise not the good health I knew about. "Barrett! Herr Barrett!" The voice brought me back to earth. It was a full-bodied voice, the accent heavily German, but the English was good.

"Yes." I mumbled. Something was wrong with my mouth. It tasted like the inside of a Turkish wrestler's jock strap. Right then my tongue was stuck to the roof of my mouth.

"I am Gustav Kaiser." The voice boomed. "Your promoter." At the mention of the name, maybe it was the way he said "Your promoter", I felt I should jump to attention, that it was expected of me, and that I should stick my hand out at the same time and shout, "Ya, Mein Promoter!"

Still not taking any chances, I did straighten up and stared him in the eye, trying to look alert and ready for action, but not insolent. Instinctively I knew this was required, anything less would bring me lots of grief. In this I was very right.

"What were you doing there?" He asked, pointing to the space on the floor I had just vacated. It was a stupid question, but from him I also knew he wanted an answer, and it had better be prompt and truthful. He must have seen me asleep, after all someone woke me up. It must have been him. Had I known him as well as I was to later on, I would have realized he let other people do things like that for him. It was beneath his dignity to stoop down and shake a sleeping wrestler.

"Sleeping." I said. "Didn't you wake me up?" This was like a slap in the face. Here was this snotty-nosed wrestler talking back. He stiffened visibly his already ramrod-straight body. His face flushed.

"I did not. But why were you sleeping?"

It was then that I saw the large Hungarian standing behind and to one side of Kaiser, his face in an easy grin. Seeing me looking at him, he gave a conspiratory wink of his eye, which helped me to relax. I was fast approaching my instinctive fight-or-flight decision. Even though in awe of this promoter, if he had pushed some more verbally, without my relaxing, I would've ended up telling him to stick the tournament up his German ass. Then I knew who woke me up. His grin and wink made me feel that at least I had one other friend in this place. It made the tirade that followed easier to take. To this day I can't abide someone shouting orders or reprimanding me, but somehow Gideon, the Hungarian, made it a little more palatable. I had no illusions about myself, even at that early age. Desperately though I wanted to stay, both for the wrestling experience and to see the country. I could've thrown it all away in a fit of uncontrollable Irish rage, or willfulness. Call it what you like.

"Why were you sleeping?" I was asked. But no answer was

expected. "You are a young man. You should not need to sleep before a match! You should be like my champions!" This was said with a grand wave of his hand, encompassing all the dressing rooms. Following the sweep of his arm I saw that the workouts were continuing unabated, sweat pouring off bodies that five minutes ago were in repose. At that moment I hated them all. Why hadn't they told me what to expect from this maniac who was berating me?

Then his manner changed. His voice softened, his demeanor relaxed somewhat.

"Yes, you have come here to learn your profession." He said, never stopping it seemed to catch his breath. "I, Gustav Kaiser, will teach it to you! I will make you a champion! You will sweat and train until you hate me!" I could've told him that I didn't have far to go for that. "But when you leave here you will be one of the best! You will have discipline! You will hold your head up with pride!" Now nobody ever accused me of being overly modest, even then, but I thought I knew what he meant. "My men here," again the god-like sweep of his hand, "Will help you anyway they can to become like them." Turning to a dark-haired pro who was doing Hindu squats, "You will help this young man if he asks you, Herman." He said in English.

"Ya!" Came the quick response between gasps.

"See," said the promoter turning his back to me. "They are all ready to help a young professional become a great champion." But he didn't see what I saw, the look of pure dislike that was shot in my direction. I knew there would be no help from that quarter.

My instincts were right. In all the time I was there, Herman Ifland never spoke a word of English to me. If I passed the time of day with him he would not answer or look at me. Why he took such a dislike to me I'll never know. Other German wrestlers tried at least to be pleasant, but he never changed. As suddenly at it began, the lecture stopped. I was dismissed. Kaiser turned his attention to his other men.

43

Kaiser rattled something in German which stopped all activity. Gideon shouted to the other dressing rooms which brought men spilling through the doors, all of them sweating and panting. They formed a semi-circle around their promoter and stood listening in rapt attention for the next ten minutes. They were treated to a barrage of propaganda about the joys of clean living, working out, training, and no over-indulgence in strong liquor, over-eating, and definitely no fraternizing with the nasty women that hang around the ring, dressing rooms, hotels, restaurants, or even gyms just waiting for the chance to sap your manly strength.

The reason I know all this is I found out later that the lecture was almost word for word the same, every night. Kaiser believed in what he said. Unlike most people who tell others how to live, he practiced what he preached, moderation. The only thing was, it was wasted on these men. They lived hard, loved hard, ate and drank as much as they could, and screwed anything that came their way. The Hungarians especially had a zest for life, staying up all night consuming vast quantities of food and booze, singing and dancing, then staggering to bed with at least one girl on their arm. The Germans, I found out, were not far behind.

My time in that town was a happy one. I learned a lot, as Kaiser said I would, but it wasn't all business. What I did learn was to listen for that footfall down the passageway to the dressing rooms, for Gustav's approach was always well-advertised. Once I knew what to listen for, I would be the first to start exercising.

Another trick I learned was to splash water on myself to achieve the instant sweat. He would march in, in all his majesty, with his entourage and stooges trailing in behind, then stand looking around with a proprietary air, nodding his head slowly with approval. I knew I had my technique mastered when he strode over to where I was doing upside-down push-ups against the wall between chairs. This was a very impressive exercise that took a great amount of upper-body strength. Using two chairs placed shoulder width apart, I'd go into a hand-stand position, my feet against the wall. My hands on the chairs, I'd dip between them fifteen or twenty times before dropping to the floor, almost kicking him in the head as I dropped to the ground by his side. His face wore his strong paternal look as I came to my feet.

"My boy, you are doing very well with all this exercise. Already I can see a change in you." Putting his hand on my still heaving shoulders, I was trying desperately hard not to have a heart attack, while controlling my breath, not to show him how winded I really was. Turning to face the crowded dressing room, his voice boomed out for all to hear.

"Look at this young wrestler!" He spoke in his heavily German-accented English. "He is going to be a champion if he continues to listen to me and follow my instruction. When he came here he was very lazy, laying around all day doing nothing. He had many bad habits, but I will change all that. Wait and see."

Inside I didn't know whether to laugh or get mad. Since I'd arrived there I'd had to cut down on my workouts drastically. My energy did have its limits. It was not to be wasted on such a mundane thing as sweating my ass off in a gym, when it could be consumed by much more interesting pastimes, like partying to all hours of the night with gorgeous fräuleins of various ages, of which there was an unending supply.

I must admit I did owe his champions something for their example of how best to live. They believed in doing it to the hilt morning, noon, and night, and not necessarily in that order.

By now he had the attention of all the wrestlers. When he spoke, everyone listened, or suffered the consequences, which I'd heard could be quite drastic, like doing the disappearing act. Trying to look suitably humble, I still allowed a small smirk to suffuse my face as I saw the hatred his attention to me was getting from some quarters.

Back in the ring I was getting the treatment from a German who had all the qualities of a modern-day Marquis de Sade, putting his large boots to parts of my body I never knew I had. The promoter's voice was bellowing across the stadium again. He did this every night now in my match, doing a German monologue that I couldn't understand. As I lay pinned beneath the German's bulk, I decided to ask some of the wrestlers again what he was saying. I'd already asked a few before, but got no response, just evasive answers.

Back in the dressing room, tired and sore, I cornered the only person who was friendly with me, the big Hungarian I'd met the first day at the restaurant.

"You've got to tell me. Nobody else will. What is Kaiser saying during my bout?"

Pulling me into an empty room, he made me promise I wouldn't tell anyone in the tournament what he was about to divulge. What could he be saying that would make all these people so closed-mouthed? I was going mad with curiosity. It must be one hell of a build-up to get that reaction from the crowd. Perhaps what he said was true, maybe I was his next champion. After all, he didn't do it with anyone else. Then I heard the truth. Whoever said ignorance was bliss knew what he was talking about. All my dreams of grandeur were shattered. Another person with a lesser ego might have quit right then and there. Although I was damaged, it wasn't fatal. I'd live to fight another day.

He'd been telling the audience that I was a lazy shiftless young wrestler whom he was trying to change, an almost hopeless task, but he would persevere against the odds. Every night he would tell them that I hadn't won a match, but despite all this, he would keep trying.

I was so hot I was speechless. I wanted to confront him and shout obscenities in his face, I already knew a few in German. But my friend, reading my face, laid a restraining hand on my shoulder and reminded me of my promise.

"All right, all right!" I yelled. "But something I don't understand... Why do the fans get so excited? If I'm such a loser, why do they bother cheering me when he tells them all this?" My friends craggy face broke into a smile.

"You must not be mad. It's for your good! Remember now, everybody knows you!"

"Yes... A loser!" I interjected.

"Maybe," He said. "But that does not matter. What is important is that they know your name and face!"

"You still haven't told me why they get so excited. What else does he say?"

"Okay, Pat. If you insist I will tell you, but you must relax a little. During your match he tells them the time it took for you to lose your other bouts. Then he asks them to time you that night to see if you can beat your record, and if so, by how much."

"You mean he whips them up by saying that I'm getting close to my loss time... If I can pass it he tells them the time... To be sure to record how much past I get before I lose again?!"

It was so blatant that I couldn't get mad anymore. Here I'd been thinking all kinds of nice things were being said about me, when in fact, the opposite was happening! Life was never the same for me again. I'd lost some of my innocence.

Despite this set-back to my ego and morale, I managed to hang in and finish the tournament. Then I signed on for a three-week stay in Reglinhausen, a town which never had professional wrestling before. From what I was told, it was a mining town with a reputation for being quite tough.

Arriving at the train station, I wasn't surprised by my first glimpse of what looked like a north of England mining town, dirty and smoky. The hotel we were to stay in was equally as depressing, being very plain and workman-like clean, but without the little frills that German hotels tend to have.

That night was a disaster from the point of view of a crowd. It was like we didn't exist, only a couple of hundred people showed up for the matches. I didn't need to be a mathematician to understand that it would take a couple of nights like this and we would have to close down, which meant a real dead-end for me. It translated into no work for three weeks, until the end of the tournament, which meant no money in a strange country, that is *if* I was invited to join the next tournament. At this point it looked quite doubtful, even though I felt I was improving by leaps and bounds.

The matches were poor. There was no incentive for anyone to hustle. It's amazing what a bad audience will do to wrestling matches, but no audience had even been worse.

Kaiser's face was like a thundercloud at his pre-match lecture. Although I couldn't understand most of what he was saying, I could understand empty seats and what they meant. There was an air of gloom in the dressing rooms that night. We all expected the wrestling to close down if the audience didn't pick up.

After the matches the wrestlers all went to their respective hotels. It so happened that I was booked into one of the larger ones where several other wrestlers were staying. As I didn't speak much German, except a few swear words, my bookings had been done for me by the office.

The drinking hall downstairs was reasonably full of salty-looking miners. From the looks of all the photos of soccer teams playing or sitting together posing, it was not only their drinking place, but their social hall as well. The walls were lined with glass cases full of silver cups and medals, which showed I supposed they were a fairly athletic bunch.

The air was filled with smoke and pungent with sweat and food odors, mixed with the strong beer smell. It was assuredly not the place to take your best girl, or any girl for that matter.

Most German hotel lounges are usually family-type places where all members can eat, drink, and make merry. It wasn't unusual for a complete stranger to burst into song, only to be joined by most of the people there, even though they had no idea who or why the person was singing. Also the Germans at play are a very hospitable people, loving nothing better than raising a glass or mug in a toast with a total stranger. In my brief stay in that country I had found this to be so, making many fine acquaintances of all ages and both sexes.

This place was different. I could tell the moment I walked through the door into the lounge that this was no family place. All heads turned in my direction. Was it my imagination or was there hostility in the onlooking eyes? Hesitating, not quite sure where to sit, but determined not to be put off by the stares I was getting, and driven by a dying thirst, with a mouth as dry as a mummy's tomb, not to mention a ravenous hunger that insisted on being satisfied, I continued on into the room. I must confess that my stubborn Irish nature would not allow me to leave now, no matter how hostile the looks or how thick the antagonism in the air.

Then I saw some of the other wrestlers who were staying at the hotel clustered together at a table. They were the only people who hadn't looked in my direction as I entered. But I also knew they were aware of my arrival. The heightening in the tension wouldn't have gone unnoticed by old battle-hardened men like them. The fact that they were all together at one table told me that they didn't feel too comfortable or at home. Normally they were like bull elephants, keeping distance between each other, or at most, two or three, on special occasions would spend some time in each other's company. Competition has a way of keeping friendships in a state of flux. When drinking heavy they'd been known to do goofy things, tempers would get frayed, then fights would break out.

Here they were. I counted seven of them, all nationalities and temperaments, sitting together at one table. Striding down the long walk between tables to the other end of the hotel social hall, I reached the place where they were drinking. Without a word, a space was made for me to get a chair in between two huge bodies of entirely different structure.

Kovacs, the Hungarian to my left, was about five-feet, ten-inches tall and weighed two-hundred, eighty-five pounds of solid bone and muscle. His legs were like tree trunks with huge thick ankles, his upper body didn't look anything near its actual size, so large was his lower body. All of this was topped by a massive shaved head on a neck that seemed as large as a waist. To simply look at him was to know here was a man not to be trifled with. Both ears were thickened with congealed blood under the skin,

49

for that is what a cauliflowered ear is really made up of. Indeed his reputation had preceded him in England, a silver medalist in the Greco-Roman amateur wrestling at the Olympic games, a barroom brawler first class, and a man about whom it was said was a good companion in a drinking spree, and whose depths in that direction had never been plumbed.

Ski Hi Lee was so totally different that it was hard to believe they were of the same species. Ski's six-foot, ten-inch frame was on my right, with the lion-like face that so many giants have. He was near the end of his career by this time, but even though he was stooped by life's turbulence, he was still a man that people stared at in awe. His shoulders were unbelievably wide. His hands were twice the size of the average wrestler. The legs were slightly bowed, but it was the rib cage that was incredible. It was so wide at the bottom that it appeared to be in the shape of a funnel, with the broader end poised above his waist. He was, I believe, from Texas. His way of dressing bore this out. His cowboy boots only added to his height. The wide-brimmed cowboy hat put the finishing touches on a man that once seen was never forgotten. His body carried no extra flesh. The frame, though massive, was not deep in comparison to its width. His muscles were flat, as opposed to the heavy bulging muscle people imagine wrestlers to have. His drinking was also monumental, but of the worst kind, at least a fifth of bourbon a day. The fact that he was an alcoholic wasn't obvious unless you spent a whole day in his company, or carefully studied his form, seeing that it bordered on emaciation for such a giant. The reason for his heavy drinking I was told, was when he was a big star in Canada, a cook in a roadside cafe recognized him from TV and ordered him out. Ski, at that time, was one of the most hated men in wrestling, on a par with Roddy Piper today. He made the mistake of not leaving as he was asked, but insisted on being served. In the end the cook made a meal for him, but laced it with rat poison. Why he didn't die at that time was a miracle, but he never totally recovered. Whether that was the reason for his heavy drinking is conjecture, but I'm sure it hastened his early death a few years later in London. Ski had his books piled on the table. He was an avid reader and I noticed his late evening bottle of bourbon was already half empty.

The other wrestlers were all big men. The German, Ifland, was there. A Polish wrestler, whom I was only on a nodding acquaintance with, was another. There was also a Hungarian named Nadar, a Dutchman who was new to me that day; and the last — but by no means the least — was the German champion, Fritz Meuller.

Meuller was a good all-round athlete, seven times the national amateur champion. Or was it ten? No matter, a man built like the proverbial German oak, with the heart of a lion. I'd worked out with him a few times and we became friends, even in the short time I was there. I had the utmost respect for Fritz as an athlete and as a human being.

Into this august company I squeezed my body, saying hello to nobody in particular and everybody in general. Five of them were playing poker, only the Dutchman and Ifland were not. They were just observing, and conversation was at a minimum, mainly, I suspected because of the language barrier.

The fräulein who was serving got me a large tankard of the house's draught beer. She took orders from everyone for food, which consisted of sausages and sauerkraut. I began to relax after killing my main thirst with a few swigs of excellent beer that Germany seems to abound with. There I was, basking in the company of these giants of the mat world, men who, from my position at the bottom of the totem pole, a mere beginner, were almost god-like. My instincts for self-preservation, though juvenile compared to today, were growing fast, and right then alarm bells started ringing in my brain.

Trouble in the shape of several large, apparently half-drunk miners were heading toward our table, their voices loud and boisterous, their laughter just a little forced, or at least to my ears it sounded that way. They had linked their arms like good comrades might, but what I didn't like was the direction they were moving — directly toward us. The position we were sitting in the room left no doubt in my mind of their destination. There was no exit from that end of the room, nothing that I could see that would attract such a large group of half-drunk patrons. Being right didn't make me feel any better. My stomach started to knot as it always did before I'd get into a fight.

Sure enough, they were coming for us. They crowded around our table, directly behind my chair, overlapping Ski and Kovacs. I'd heard about the hair on the back of people's necks standing up in moments of stress, but this was the first time it ever happened to me. The aura of the miners enveloped like a blanket. I looked at the others to see if they felt it, but they were acting like they were alone in the room. The card playing continued unabated.

Then the first move in the escalation was made by a big burly miner with a cigar in his mouth. I saw the movement out of the corner of my eye and swiveled my head like a frightened deer so I could see what was happening. The miner in question had maneuvered himself between Ski and the Dutchman, and was apparently watching the game. He made some comment in German, out of the side of his mouth, in a very loud voice which brought peals of laughter from his friends. I didn't understand what was said, and though others at the table must have, they still never batted an eye. I stole a quick look to see.

Then the second step came. Our burly friend did what was a deliberate act of provocation. I'd seen enough western movies to understand what he was doing. He was trying to pick a fight obviously, but to do it this way was ludicrous. Taking a deep drag of the half-smoked soggy cigar, he then removed it from his mouth in his big dirty fist, then blew a noxious cloud of smoke right in the face of Ski Hi Lee. It was a ridiculously stupid act of aggression, one that was so patently obvious that a child of three would have known what was happening. If I hadn't seen it myself I wouldn't have believed that in the twentieth century this sort of ploy was used to provoke a fight.

Ski's expression looked pained, but he didn't look up from his cards. It was as though his tormentors didn't exist. Then the thick dirty paw came up to the mouth again and took another deep drag. I watched in disbelief. He was going to do it again!

Sure enough, another big cloud of cigar smoke enveloped Ski's head, this time making him cough.

What would this giant of the ring do? I knew he had a punch like the kick of a mule. Even though physically wasted from booze and injuries received in and out of the ring, this three-hundred-fifty pounder still had tremendous strength. I had seen him in action. I knew what he was capable of.

The cloud hung around his head like an evil halo. Surely this would prompt swift retaliatory action. Abruptly Ski stood up. The miners backed away a couple of paces, looking in awe at this gentle giant that one of their number had tried to provoke. The whole place was silent. The drama that was unfolding at our end of the hall had everyone's attention. The unexpected surge to his feet of this colossus had drawn every eye in our direction.

"I'm getting out of here." Said Ski in a deep growl, so low it sounded like it came from somewhere in his boots. "The air is foul since these cocksuckers came around." Nodding his head at the silent crowd, he did, what to me was a surprising thing at that time of my life. He walked away from a fight. Throwing his hand in, he picked up his books, his bottle of booze, then slowly wended his way through the tables to the stairs leading to his room.

The wide boney shoulders were slightly stooped, but it was his massiveness that really accentuated his humiliation. If he'd been my size, a mere two-hundred-twenty-pounder, the effect on that half-drunken crowd wouldn't have been so dramatic. We were pro wrestlers. That was common knowledge. I'm sure there wasn't a soul in the place who didn't know that by now. Being realistic, we didn't look like your normal happy hour crowd, even in a town that was used to hard-bitten men.

The place once more came alive. The tension eased. Everyone started to talk and laugh again. Everyone, except the six remaining wrestlers. Watching him go, I felt sorry for Ski. He didn't pick up his provocateur and smash him across a table. Anything would've been better than what he did, I felt. What I didn't understand then was, it took more guts to do what he did, deliberately walk away from a loud-mouthed bully. It was only after seeing him rush to the rescue of another wrestler who was surrounded by a howling mob, later that year, that I realized he was no coward. He'd just gotten to the stage of avoiding any trouble whenever possible, no matter how chicken it made him look.

In the meantime, trouble was definitely brewing in the wings. Our miner friends were emboldened by the sudden, and I'm sure, unexpected exit of one of the seven, especially one so large and awe-inspiring. The laughter behind me became deafening. I didn't dare look around for fear of saying something to the lout whose laugh I now recognized above the others. I knew I was next, I was the obvious choice being younger and smaller than my companions, also my face didn't reflect the brutalizing effects of my profession, like the broken noses and bulbous ears that surrounded me.

I sensed movement behind. Something loud was spoken in German. I waited for the next act in this macabre play that was unfolding. What would I do if he blew smoke in my face? Thoughts raced through my electrified brain. My position would be precarious. If I attacked him, would his comrades go to his aid? More to the point, would my companions go to mine? If I'd known them better, I would've been able to base a decision on my knowledge of their reactions to my perceived plight. But I was basically a stranger to them all, a Johnny-come-lately to boot.

The card players in the meantime had dealt another hand, as if nothing had happened. They were masters of the poker face.

I kept wondering what thoughts were going on behind these craggy exteriors. Did fear of the unknown grip their bellies like it did mine? Did they wonder would I back them up, like I worried about them? I moved my chair a little away from Kovacs, I could do that now that Ski had left such a big space. The reason for the move was like the gunfighters in the bar rooms of the old west, I wanted more room to maneuver, even though at that point in time I wasn't aware of my motive. I felt rather than saw the burly body squeeze between the Hungarian and myself. I could smell the reeking body odor. Maybe my senses were more acute because of the situation I was in, but the stench of old sweat, stale tobacco, booze, and what I know now was fear assailed my nostrils. Slowly I looked up into the beefy face. The small piggy eyes were looking down at me in derision. Then, as if in slow motion, the dirty paw reached once more for the infamous cigar. The face was so magnified in my vision that the enlarged pores seemed like small craters, the blackheads, like chunks of coal embedded in his leathery hide. My body tensed. I still didn't know what I was going to do. My heart was pounding like a hammer on an anvil. The only thing I did know was no stinking drunken miner was going to shit on me!

He took a slow deep drag on his cigar, savoring the moment, still looking down, his eyes locked on mine. He sucked the smoke deep into his lungs, or that's how it looked to me. Then almost nonchalantly he withdrew the soggy mass from his hideous mouth, gave me a last contemptuous look, then turning his head, blew a mammoth cloud of the vile blue smoke right into Kovacs' face.

Things happened so fast, had I not been watching so intently for any movement, I might have missed the beginning of the final act. As the cloud hit the bald head, an enormous muscular arm came at incredible speed from the table, still clutching the cards which were crumpled so tightly I could see white patches under the skin. The knuckles smashed into the red meaty cheek like an old war mace wielded by a savage warrior. Under the crashing impact, the miner's face opened like a squashed tomato, spewing blood and flesh all over the table and me.

Leaping from my chair to avoid both the red deluge and being trapped in a sitting position, the mayhem erupted all around me. The huge Hungarian was living up to his ring name, The Butcher of Budapest, one he had earned for his cruel tactics in and out of the ring. He was already on his feet and moving forward, smashing the crowd aside with his body, reducing the miner's face to a bloody pulp with short chopping blows that were having a devastating effect.

All hell broke loose. The miner's friends were taken by surprise by the speed of the events. They were behind Kovacs who had, by now, lifted the hapless unconscious man shoulder high, then run him head-first into a nearby wall. This was too much for most of the miners. They let out howls of rage and attacked. Pandemonium reigned.

Gone was the knot of fear in my belly. No time for fear now, if I was to survive. Offense was the best defense. I knew if I went under here, not to expect any mercy. The Butcher of Budapest had set the rules, if there had been any in the first place.

Instinctively the remaining wrestlers formed a tight group to meet the onslaught that was quickly coming. I found myself ducking a chair swung by a brute that would've brained me if he could. Coming up under the swinging chair, I punched him a terrific blow in the gut, which though large, was surprisingly hard. I could hear the air leaving his body in a rush, in spite of the battles going on all around me.

Then a thought hit me. Why not use the Les Kellet hold to finish this man off? He was the rotund wrestler with the disproportionate hands, who was supposed to try me out when I was breaking into the business. He didn't show up, thank god.

I'd met him a short time later. I was fascinated by his unconventional holds, especially one I'd heard he used with incredible success, his favorite.

What he'd do is thrust his first and second fingers in behind the bottom teeth of his victim's mouth. The thumb would press up under the chin, then he'd squeeze and twist, causing excruciating pain and dislocate the jaw. It was diabolical in its simplicity, so I thought that this was the perfect opportunity to try it out and finish this slob off at the same time.

Right then I learned the truth of the saying, the best laid plans of mice and men often go astray. Mine certainly did. His mouth was wide open, the chair dropped on the floor out of harm's way. He was gasping for breath. Now was my chance. Keeping a wary eye at the same time on the shenanigans going on around me, I didn't want to be Pearl Harbored, I inserted my fingers almost clinically. There would be no need to hurry. His demand for oxygen was so great it would keep the mouth open long enough for me to finish him. Getting the grip was child's play, then I started to exert pressure. That's when things went wrong. Jesus Christ! This son of a bitch wasn't feeling anything, at least not the pressure I was applying! His jaws closed like a vice on my defenseless fingers. His teeth had a fine cutting edge to them. I could feel he was starting to bite into the bones! I was in agony. Tears of pain were filling in my eyes. What the hell was I going to do? I cursed myself for sticking my hand into the oaf's mouth, especially as I could see now he had jaws like a bulldog. It was then that I realized enormous hand and finger strength was necessary to apply Kellet's hold effectively. I remembered his orangutan hands. Understanding came quickly. I simply didn't have enough power. My position was hairy to say the least, absurd if the truth were known. Here was the pride of old Erin with his right hand stuck in the jaws of a human alligator. To make matters worse, I'd put them there myself. How could I ever tell my grandchildren what I'd done? That is, assuming that I lived through this, and ever had grandchildren. Suddenly the solution hit me with the clarity born of desperation. If the famous Les Kellet hold wouldn't work... use the Pat Barrett infamous one! It had a tried and true formula for getting out of trouble. It was absolutely perfect for opening reluctant jaws.

EVERYBODY DOWN HERE HATES ME

Reaching down with my left hand, almost seductively, I felt for his testicles, which was no easy matter. I was dancing about in pain like a child wanting to go to the bathroom. Groping around, I was beginning to panic. Where the hell are they? In the cold light of day all this sounds comical, but time was running out for my fingers. I thought God Damn! He hasn't got any! Then I found them, hanging like two ripe figs waiting to be plucked, and that's exactly what I'd intended doing. Who knows in this crazy world, he might have had them cut off for some reason. How was I to know? At that point in time I wasn't really thinking straight.

There wasn't much time. The pain in my fingers passed all belief. He was gathering strength. His nostrils were flared by the huge vacuum sucking in air, replenishing his engine. Carefully I surrounded the little round devils with the fingers of my left hand. I knew I'd only get one chance to break loose, better make it a good one! When my hand was in the perfect position I squeezed, this time I was sure of the result. No matter how drunk a man was, or how caught up in the throws of a fight, I've yet to see one continue whatever he was doing when his balls are being squeezed by an expert. I considered myself one. Squeezing with all the power in my hand, I twisted at the same time. The scream that came from his lips was almost like a woman's. His eyes were wide and staring, but most of all, his mouth shot open, releasing my right hand which was on fire. The blood from my fingers ran down his face, making him look like a beefy Count Dracula. Seizing the initiative, I grabbed his throat with my mutilated right hand, still squeezing his balls with my left. I mustered all of my strength and hurled him backwards into a glass trophy case. When his body crashed into it, the case disintegrated into a shower of glass, splinters of wood, and assorted trophies, tearing the back of his neck and slicing one of his hands with a shard of razor sharp glass. Even then the bastard wasn't finished. He was certainly one tough cookie!

By now my Irish was up. To hell with being a gentleman! This was a fight to the finish! Reaching down, I picked up the heavy base of one of the trophies that now were strewn all over the floor. My miner was pulling himself out of the case when I smashed him on the side of the head with the improvised club. He dropped like a stone. There'd be no more problems from him. He looked in such bad shape, I hoped I hadn't killed him.

Turning to survey the battle, I could see that the wrestlers were cleaning house, at least the part of the house that had given us the trouble. Fortunately, other than the original group that had come to our table, nobody else had joined against us. They were a salty bunch, and if we'd had to fight the rest as well, we'd have been in desperate trouble.

The police arrived, but by then the action was all over. They thought the whole thing was a huge joke. No one was arrested. The miners carried their wounded to cars and took them to god knows where. After pouring whiskey over my fingers, I went to bed, sleeping like a baby.

The next night in the dressing room I looked around. We had definitely not come away unscathed. Everyone from the hotel had injuries from chairs and bottles, except for Ski and Kovacs. Kovacs, who had been in the thick of the battle, from what I could gather, personally took out three opponents, and didn't have a scratch — not even skinned knuckles.

While I was looking over the damage, down the passageway came the footfalls I knew so well. Kaiser strode in, again his face black as a thundercloud. Oh shit! I thought. Here it comes, we're going to be fired. He's not going to want men who cause trouble outside the ring, particularly ones that smash up the hotel he booked us into.

No one was working out as usual this time. We were all on our feet, waiting for the tirade that we knew was coming. Walking slowly past his men, like a general on inspection of his troops, he examined the wounds of his champions. Stopping in front of me, he looked at my hand, which was taped up. Then a big smile broke over his normally stern visage. Looking around

59

the room, where by now everybody had gathered, he broke into a fifteen-minute exhortation in German, praising his troops for a job well done. Even though I couldn't understand what he was saying, the pride in his voice was unmistakable.

I couldn't understand why we were getting praised when a good bawling out was more in order. Slowly it dawned on me, what kind of a man Kaiser was. Failure was something he would not tolerate. If we'd taken a beating, no matter what the odds, the axe would've fallen swiftly, without hesitation.

He took care of the damage in the hotel. When we returned that night I entered with trepidation, half expecting to be attacked. Instead I was met with big smiles and raised beer mugs, as were the other wrestlers. To cap it all off, business boomed. The matches were packed every night with exuberant fans. As for the men we had mutilated, there were suspicious bandages amongst the miners in the beer hall, but their owners were just as friendly as everyone else.

I had great difficulty paying for a beer in the hotel, as had the other wrestlers involved in the brawl. When I would produce my money it would be waved away with a friendly smile from the landlord. He would point to a miner across the room to let me know who my benefactor was. These men were a hard living bunch who admired toughness. I guessed we passed the test.

5

RUN SILENT, RUN FAST

England has been the cradle of many great wrestlers. One of the finest was Harry Kendall. What set Harry apart from other wrestlers was that he was a deaf-mute. He had represented England many times as an amateur and was a talented technical wrestler. Couple this with a killer instinct and Kendall was the almost perfect wrestling machine. In a quiet and insidious way, he enjoyed beating and hurting other wrestlers, but it wasn't apparent to the average onlooker. Because of his affliction, the crowd was always on his side. They felt sorry for him, thinking that his deafness was a drawback to his craft. Actually, I always felt it was an asset. As a deaf wrestler, you can't hear the moans and groans coming from someone you've just hurt. Wrestling him, for me, was always a pain in the ass, mainly because the fans made very little noise during the bout, no cheers just polite applause, mainly for him. Many times when wrestling him I would make a clever move that should have gotten crowd reaction. Instead there would be silence. When Harry did something similar, the crowd would react enthusiastically. This never sat too well with the other wrestlers. It's a very competitive business and crowd reaction was sought after avidly.

Harry couldn't speak a word when he turned pro, but that didn't mean he was an introvert. Far from it! He was a great mimic and enjoyed picking out the flaws of other people. With mimicry, he could make them look foolish, much to their discomfort. The business soon changed him from a non-speaker to one that could utter intelligible words. The first one was "cunt", which he would illustrate while shouting at the unfortunate person he was venting his spleen upon. The next word was "queer", which he used mainly on promoter Johnny Dale, for some obscure reason. He would spot Johnny walking down the street with his clothes immaculate, not a hair out of place, puffing on his pipe. Johnny was the dandy of the three brothers in the Dale family. Although the eldest, he had the least power in the promotion. Kendall would mince along behind Johnny, one hand on his hip, the other primping and brushing his hair back, or sucking on an imaginary pipe, and shout in that peculiar high-pitched voice that he was developing.

"Queer Puff" he would shout, knowing he was understood by the different reactions he got. In all fairness, I don't think he realized how loud he spoke. If he did, he didn't show it. Johnny was furious, but that never deterred Kendall. He tried to have Harry fired. Jack, who was the boss, refused. He admired Kendall's wrestling ability, plus I believe he got a certain sadistic pleasure out of watching his brother pilloried.

Harry's wife eventually went into the office one day to complain about his language. She told Jack Dale that she was happy to see her husband learning to talk, but unfortunately the only words he was speaking were the wrong ones. She wanted Jack to stop the wrestlers from teaching her husband rude, vulgar words. Harry may have been coached, but he took to bad language like a duck takes to water.

The thought of going deaf was always a fear of mine, since I had lost the hearing in one ear myself. I conjured up what a terrible place the world would be if I couldn't hear the voice of a loved one. To me, not being able to hear beautiful music among other things would be devastating. The simple truth is we who have our hearing have no conception of how situations that we could cope with under normal circumstances, can become a nightmare to the deaf. This was brought home to me when I heard what happened to Harry the night he was dropped off by the wrestling bus in Brixton.

Dale and Martin supplied transportation in the shape of a bus. This was not for benign reasons alone, but so they wouldn't have to pay traveling expenses of every wrestler. These buses saw life in the raw. The stories they could tell if they could only talk...fights up the aisle; sex on the seats and floor as the boys took the flower of some far-off town or city to bed — except in this case the bed was the inside of our transportation. Many times I have gone to have a little romance with some not-so-shy beauty, only to find the seats overflowing with ample thighs and buttocks, naked as the day they were born, pounding or being pounded in the age-old ritual of sex. Often times the outside of the bus was crowded with people peering in through the soiled windows, trying to get a glimpse of the orgy that was going on inside. Their titterings and gigglings were matched only by the grunting and labored breathing within.

The bus went from the office in Brixton, London to whatever show was on that day. You had to find your own way to the meeting point. There is the story of the wrestler who was retired and asked Jack Dale if he could he borrow the bus for a weekend. The reason was his sex life was non-existent at home. He couldn't make it in a bed anymore, he'd done it so many times in the coach. Although it's a joke, so many hours were spent on the road by wrestlers that the transportation became their second home. They ate, slept, got drunk, fornicated, and some even died within its walls.

It was January, not the most pleasant month in London. The coach had dropped Harry off at the office. He had walked from there to the center of Brixton, about half a mile. It was 1:30 a.m. and he was hoping to catch a London transport bus to his home. At that time of night, buses ran every hour and a half or so. If you missed one, it was a long wait for the next, especially on a cold, wet winter's night.

Harry's wife told the story...He'd been walking along at a brisk pace, swinging his wrestling bag containing the usual boots, towel, dressing gown, trunks, two or three pairs of socks, and various other things, depending on the keeper. Most tried to keep the extras to a bare minimum because they could get heavy. Over a period of years, some bags almost developed the same personality as their owner, especially in physical looks and smell. Some, when opened, would bring demands from people in the dressing room to "Shut that thing before we all die!" You could tell a lot about a guy by his bag, if he was single or married to a loving wife. Or on the other hand, if he was married to a wife who didn't care. Even the cleanest bag was not a place to thrust either your face or your hand, particularly after a match.

As Kendall walked along, he suddenly observed his bus warming up in the distance, by the steam coming from the exhaust pipes. He knew by the Brixton town hall clock that it was time for its departure. His pace quickened, the wrestling bag swinging by his side. Out of the night, behind him, rolled a roving police car with two constables in front, and a rather large German Shepherd dog in the back.

Their experienced eyes saw a fairly large man, muffled to the ears, striding briskly away from them, carrying a bag. At 1:30 a.m. anyone walking was viewed with suspicion, a man with a bag - doubly so. At that point Kendall was hurrying across a pedestrian mall where the police car couldn't follow without mounting the pavement, which in this case was too steep.

The policeman on the driver's side lowered his window and shouted at him, "You! You with the bag! Stop right there!" At that moment, the bus was starting to move into position to leave on its nightly expedition through London. Harry started to jog, not wanting to spend half the night waiting for the next bus.

By now the police were both shouting for him to stop, but of course, being deaf, out intrepid wrestler was oblivious to all. He was just intent on getting home. Why should he look around?

There is a myth about the English police: that they are wonderfully nice people who pat criminals and the public on the head, tell them the error of their ways, then send them home with a courteous caution. The English didn't conquer the world by being entirely nice. What they have done is learned to hide their ruthlessness beneath a polite veneer. The police have this down to a fine art. Remember that underneath that crisp uniform lies a force that's as effective as any army in the world. There exists a no-nonsense attitude to the criminal, or perceived one, especially at 1:30 a.m.

To their trained eyes this was a very suspicious situation. Why would this man be carrying a large bag at this hour of the morning? Why, when ordered by Her Majesty's Police Force to halt, did he start to run? It was time for unusual force - the dog.

Now British police dogs are, I'm sure, very well-trained. I believe the theory is, if you don't resist they will only hold you. The theory is excellent, except if you happen to be on the receiving end of the holding. It can be very frightening, primarily as you don't know just how well-trained and polite this canine is

The first thing Kendall knew, a large police dog landed on his shoulders from out of nowhere, tearing at his coat and head, trying to get the so-called holding grip. By the time the police arrived Harry had had the shit scared out of him. To make matters worse, when they tried to question him, he'd lost his new-found vocabulary. To be exact, he couldn't talk at all. Maybe this was just as well, after all his vocabulary wasn't the best, and it might have antagonized the police even more. All that would come from his lips were high-pitched screams of fear and anger. It was only when his bag was opened and the contents disgorged on the pavement, that the police started to realize that maybe they'd made a mistake. That also was when Kendall found his voice and newly learned words. Brixton's air almost went blue with the bad language. Even at that hour a small crowd had gathered who were being entertained by the red-faced policemen berated by the deaf-mute. All credit to them when they understood they

65

had an innocent man on their hands. They did not compound the damage by trying to cover up.

They took him to the station and gave him some hot tea, and tried to calm him down, which was no easy feat. I was told for a long time afterwards Harry could be seen periodically looking over his shoulder with a wild-eyed stare. I suppose under the circumstances he can't be blamed.

6

THE GREEK
MEETS HIS MATCH

I was wrestling in Tennessee which, at the time was definitely the pits. It was known as the asshole of the pro wrestling business. The promoter was a Greek who had come up the hard way. Before he reached his pinnacle of success, he used to get the boys cups of coffee, sold programs to the fans, cleaned the toilets, and do any of the dirty work around the halls. The story goes that he was made to ride at times on the floor of the car on the way to matches while the wrestlers put their feet on him. There were stories of other indignations he'd suffered at their hands which were a lot worse, such as making him lick their bare feet. I'm inclined to believe them knowing how sadistic some of the men in the business are. I was told this was the reason he was such a shit head, but then again, maybe he was just naturally that way. When I arrived in Tennessee I found out that the Greek was not the main promoter, but only a junior partner. This came as a surprise as I had heard a lot about Gulus the Greek, but nothing about Walsh, the real boss. The top man and I came to an understanding early on in our relationship. I'd been in the area two days before I met the Greek, though I'd been forewarned of how he liked to treat wrestlers like dirt. One particular man was always sent to towns a long distance from his home, which happened to be Nashville. The Greek would tell him not to hurry back, and schedule him to wrestle last. The reason for this was he was screwing the man's wife. The wrestler knew it, but wanted to work so badly he did nothing about the situation.

The first time we met I guess I was ready. Being in the USA only about three months, I was wet behind the ears in many ways, but confrontations I never shirked. Into the dressing room strode the Greek. Looking around he spotted me sitting, reading a book. Striding over to where I was he said, "Hey you! Get your boots on!"

"My name is Pat." I told him.

He studied me carefully then said with contempt in his voice, "To me you're just 'Hey You.' "

Rage boiled up inside me. I couldn't believe my ears. He certainly didn't mess around. Well, two can play that game.

"You can stick 'Hey You' up your Greek ass..." I snarled. "Along with Tennessee." I didn't care, or wait to see his reaction, just threw on my coat, my bag was still packed, and I left. In some businesses this might be called overreaction, but I've found out quite a long time ago there could be no half measures, at least not for me.

The next morning, about 7 a.m., I got a call from Roy Walsh's secretary. Walsh, the man in control, wanted to see me. I was still angry and not interested in seeing anyone, least of all him. I had the urge to see other pastures that I'd hoped would be greener. His secretary, who happened also to be his lover I'm told, convinced me to come in and talk.

When I arrived at the office I expected to find Gulus there. I was loaded for bear but Nick the Greek was nowhere to be found. I was ushered into the inner-office and treated like royalty. Would I like a coffee, soft drink, or whatever? I wasn't sure this wasn't a dream. This office, which had the worst reputation in the business, was giving me the V.I.P. treatment.

"What seems to be the problem?" Asked the kindly man across the desk. "I've heard that Nick has been giving you a bad time. Tell me all about it."

I explained how I felt. I wasn't going to be treated like shit. The words poured out. It was like confessing to a kindly priest, whose only role in life was to take care of my well being.

"What? That no-good son of a bitch!" The outburst was a shock. I thought it was against me. "Nick Gulus, I've told him so many times don't treat my boys like shit, I won't have it!" This went on for a full three or four minutes while he paced up and down. His performance could only be described as awe-inspiring. He reached the apex of his tirade with the words, "I'm going to fire him. He's done this once too often!" For a moment I was shocked at his rage. Then it all started to click into place. Looking up at him I started to get a glimmer of what was happening. I'd been snowed before, but not like this, never by such an expert.

"Let me ask you something Mr. Walsh . . . " I took the opportunity to interject while he was catching his breath.

"Yes son," He turned his kindly face in my direction. "By the way, just call me Roy. Now, how can I help you?"

"How long have you been in this business together?" I asked quietly, beginning to relish the game being played. He looked a little puzzled by my question.

"Why... twenty-five, twenty-six years, it must be."

I kept my face as innocent as possible. The hook was baited. I had the old bastard. My theory was bearing fruit.

"Why has it taken you so long to fire him?" I asked again. At these words his face went completely blank. There was a complete and utter silence while we looked each other in the eye. Then he laughed, a big belly laugh, his whole face lighting up.

"Son," He said, "It is taking me a long while, but don't you worry. He won't give you any trouble in the future. Any problems . . . anything at all . . . come direct to me."

It was then that I understood who the real villain was. The old man liked to make the bullets and enjoyed watching the Greek firing them. From that point on my stay in Tennessee was fairly

7

THE WOLFMAN
AND THE BEAR

The Wolfman came to wrestle in the northwestern United States and British Columbia, Canada, for promoter Rod Fenton. He would enter the ring chewing the thigh bone of a horse or steer. His wild look definitely made one believe all the stories that were told about him. He was supposed to have been found in the wastes of Russia, as a teenager — running wild with the wolves. The fur trappers who caught him smuggled him into Canada, where he ended up in a circus. How he found his way into wrestling was shrouded in mystery. He couldn't speak, only grunt and growl. He was driven to the halls by a manager who took care of the business arrangements for this wild creature.

Rod Fenton, the promoter, and I were friends of a sort. For some unknown reason he took a liking to me. This was the second time a promoter had done this. The first one had been my mentor, Jack Dale. While flying on some of our longer trips, Fenton and I would play cards. It was on these trips that I learned how to play a mean game of Rummy. On the longer ones we would play for hours. Rod, who was a great player, forced me to improve my game. He was a real betting man, and would bet on almost anything. He loved to gamble. Though he loved cards, horse racing was his real passion. When I got my purse money after a match, which was supposedly based on the number of people in attendance, I could always tell if he'd had a losing streak at the track by how much my pay amounted to. When you've been in the business for awhile, as I had by then, you could look around the hall and tell, within a couple of hundred dollars, how much the take was. So when my money was smaller than the take I counted, I'd say to Rod, "Bad time at the races, eh?"

This was always met with self-righteous indignation. "Why do you always complain?" He would grumble. "I gave you your first real break... all you ever do is bitch about not making enough money." This was not a question, but a statement of fact. No answer was expected.

I'd never get the money he'd taken, but he would be more careful for a few weeks. Then the cycle would start again. Sometimes I wondered what would happen if I didn't complain. Would my money go right down? As I am tight with my purse strings, I never stopped complaining, so I never found out.

The Wolfman had been going strong around the Northwest, which was basically Rod's territory. Let me explain a little about territories. Promoters had an area, which could be as small as a few towns or cities, or it could be the size of the New York office, which stretched from Canada in the North, to the Carolinas in the South, and out as far West as Chicago. Today they operate worldwide.

Wars between promoters did not break out too often. But when they did, they were very messy. They were nasty affairs and could go on for long periods of time with the wrestlers, or "boys" as is the common term used in the business, capitalizing on the situation. A "boy" could be any age, from sixteen to sixty, as long as he wore wrestling trunks. Usually arguments were settled between the territories by the National Wrestling Alliance. This was a confederation of promoters, created for just such problems, and to keep the boys in line. It also had the added bonus of controlling the money paid out to the wrestlers. As you can imagine, when promoters quarreled, the boys seized the opportunity to hold them up for a bigger share of the purse. Stars made out like bandits in such troubled times. On the other hand, when peace reigned the payoffs were reduced. There was and is no wrestlers union, so there remains no place to mediate disputes between parties. Currently there's a giant struggle going on between the promotion that controls the New York office, namely Vince McMahon Jr., and the promoters in the rest of the country. They have been, and are, moving in using TV as a battering ram to eliminate the competition. In this national struggle New York has become very innovative, using the rock music scene and rock stars, like Cyndi Lauper, to enhance their TV shows. Mr. T has been roped into the scene, which I'm sure is giving several other promoters heartburn, knowing his popularity and drawing power. New York also has involved the WWF men in movies such as Hulk Hogan's recently released film "No Holds Barred."

New York has become a supernova. The promotion has broken with the "hands off" tradition and is now expanding all over the world. Money generated by this giant on a world scale is staggering. It's definitely caused consternation among the wrestling promotion fraternity, even put many out of business. Vince McMahon Sr. was of the old school, ruthless in business, but with a soft spot for hard-luck cases. He was also a great believer in respecting borders. His son is of a very different cloth and very ambitious. It appears Vince Jr. wants to control world wrestling. Who knows how successful he'll become?

Now, back in the Northwest Territory, where Rod Fenton had the Wolfman, I found myself based in Vancouver. The area ranged almost to Alaska in the North, over to Calgary in the East, and South to Seattle. Into this area came the Bear, all five or six hundred pounds of him!

This was a real bear, a wrestling bear, of which there are only a few in the country. Bears are natural wrestlers, loving to rough and tumble, having great balance, intimidating size and enormous strength. But they also have a few unsavory habits.

One of the first things a trainer does is declaw a bear if he intends to put it in the wrestling ring. The reason for this is simple. Bears, like the big cats — lions, tigers and leopards, etc. use their claws to hold their prey. When they lose them, it's one less weapon in their formidable arsenal. Even though their claws are gone, they still have their teeth. Wearing a muzzle has not prevented them from sucking fingers or ears, anything sticking out, into their mouth. They do this by pressing their muzzle tight up against the unfortunate wrestler and biting off anything they can get. Now this won't occur every time. Usually they are big semi-friendly brutes, but the first time I saw a live bear in the dressing room I had my reservations about wrestling one! I made a point of talking to the Bear's owner about training techniques. For some time I'd fancied myself somewhat of a dog trainer, having trained quite a few Dobermans, Rottweilers, and German Shepherds. The first thing I noticed was there was something not quite right about the man's hands. A few joints were missing from his fingers. What had distracted me from seeing this earlier on was that he was an Eastern European and waved his arms and hands all of the time while he was talking. It turned out he'd lost them by cavorting around with this big hairy beast. When I asked how this could happen if the bear was wearing a muzzle, he explained that it was his own fault. He accidently let his fingers stray into the animal's mouth while wrestling around, and the animal chomped down by mistake. I didn't believe that story for one minute. What really happened I didn't know, and wasn't about to find out. I decided then and there that Bear wrestling was not for me. Bears have also been known to cuff a man or two. For instance, there was a heavyweight boxer, who had once fought Joe Louis, who had a wrestling match with a bear. All the animal would do was sit on his ass and look playful. The boxer got so mad because he felt the animal was making him look stupid that he punched the bear on the nose for not living up to his contract and wrestling. The animal went berserk and cuffed him on the side of the head, knocking him clear out of the ring. Not content with that, it chased him up the aisle toward the dressing rooms, dragging its trainer plus five ushers behind. The boxer ended up taking sanctuary in his dressing room, while the bear tried to beat its way through the door. Anyone who knows anything about bears understands how unpredictable and temperamental they can be. Add to this a high degree of intelligence and they make a formidable opponent.

Rod got the idea to match this bear against the Wolfman, but wasn't sure how it would draw. Sometimes he would use me as a sounding board, not always taking my advice, but using what he wanted of my ideas and discarding others. I never took offense at this. I just watched his operation and learned a lot about human nature. Rod could control audiences with his matchmaking.

"What do you think about wrestling the Bear?" He asked.

"Not much!" I quickly replied, wanting to squash any idea he might have of matching me with the beast.

"Would you like to work with him?"

Again, a fast reply. "Definitely not, Rod!"

He started to shake with silent laughter. I knew he was playing with my head.

"Come on..." I snarled, not enjoying the game and wishing to put an end to it quickly. "You know me well enough. I enjoy taking chances, but that's ridiculous. What have you got in mind?"

"The Wolfman against the Bear," he answered. "How do you think it would draw?" At first I thought he was joking, matchmaking to him was a science. Putting two or four men in the ring together, especially in the main event, was calculated on drawing power, the amount of money the match would draw at the gate. As little as possible was left to chance. Even with all the careful preparation, some matches bombed out. The fans just didn't buy what you were selling. Promoting could be a very precarious way to earn a living as it all depended on the whims of the fans, "mobs", I believed they were called in ancient

Roman days.

Here Rod was really going out on a limb and he was asking my opinion. Did he just want to bounce an idea off me or was he asking me to stick my neck out? If this match came unstuck, who would be left holding the bag? Right then it looked like I would.

Knowing an answer was expected, I racked my brains. What advice could be given? Then I hit on the solution, I hoped. "Why not try the match out in a small town, somewhere not too important. If it stinks, it won't hurt your business too much, or your reputation."

Fenton gave my idea some thought, then his face broke into a grin. "Okay, I'll go along with that, but where?"

I'd already given that some thought. "Chilliwack! That's the place!" This town was about sixty miles from Vancouver, B.C., and ten miles from the U.S. border. In my mind this would be an ideal town to try this wild experiment. The people there were a no-nonsense bunch who liked their wrestling tough and rough.

Sucking on his cigar for a few minutes Rod seemed to hesitate. Then as though a bit reluctant he grunted an affirmative. So Chilliwack it was. By taking my advice Rod had subtly shifted the blame for any failure on to my shoulders. We both knew that.

My reason for picking that particular town was based on my knowledge of the territory. What was needed was a town with responsive fans that liked the unusual. For me, this one filled the bill.

On the night of the match the hall was packed, not a seat was vacant. I guess the advertising had caught the imagination of the crowd. "Beast Against Beast" the billboards had proclaimed. "Can the Bear tame the Wolfman?" the TV announcer had asked. It's hard for non-wrestling fans to believe, but the Bear had the crowd's support. Everyone I could see in the hall was rooting for it. To think that a six-hundred-pound animal, as tough as a bear, was the underdog to a two-hundred, forty-five-pound man shows you the impact the Wolfman had on the populace.

After studying the bear in the dressing room I believed it had the black heart of a scoundrel, if that's possible in an animal.

The other matches were finished. Now for the main event. The crowd was agog, expectation on every face. People talked to each other in rushed sentences, as if the match would start unexpectedly and they might miss some crucial moment. They rushed even faster than normal to get their drinks and popcorn. Suddenly, there it was. Down the aisle came the shambling bear, on a thick chain, led by its trainer and owner. This bear was an old campaigner. He knew what was expected of him. He climbed between the ropes, then stood up on his hind legs and turned around, with his paws held up over his head, just like the old pro he was, he then dropped down on all fours, and headed for his corner.

Suddenly the crowd came alive, screaming abuse, hissing and booing. Little children were shouting adjectives unpunished that would make a longshoreman blush. The Wolfman was on his way. He snarled and growled his way down the aisle, making lunges at the crowd. Climbing onto the ring apron, giving a last glare at the audience, he leaped into the squared circle with his big bone clutched in his hairy hand, and headed for the Bear, snarling and panting. The referee jumped in between the opponents while the onlookers screamed for action and blood. This mob hadn't spent their good money that night to watch scientific wrestling. Violence was what they wanted, violence they would have, or someone would have to answer to them. This was the crowd that had broken a two-hundred, eighty-pound wrestler's arm with a board torn from the seating, when he made the mistake of pursuing one of their numbers among the bleachers.

The introductions over, the bone was hurled to the ground outside the ring, but not before Wolfman had tried to attack the Bear with it. The match was on!

The Wolfman went straight at his huge opponent, charging it like a mad thing. The hulking black bear had raised up onto its hind legs, its big front paws extended before it. To say I know what the Wolfman tried to do would be lying. I was just as fascinated as everyone else in the hall. If I were in the Wolfman's place, what would I do? This thought ran through my head as I watched like a fan for the outcome. What tactics would the Wolfman use? How would he handle the nearly four-hundred-pound disparity between their weights? Suddenly he grabbed the Bear around the neck and flung himself backwards. I guess he was hoping to throw the animal across the ring. Unfortunately for the Wolfman, the Bear was not thrown. This behemoth of the woods was not to be downed so easily. Instead the big hairy brute landed squarely on top of him. All that remained free were the Wolfman's arms and legs. These started to swing and thrash about wildly. There was an air of desperation about the movements. The referee, after counting three started pulling on the Bear's collar. Nothing happened. The trainer, who was ringside, produced the bottle of Coke, which was the Bear's reward for its performance and normally got the animal moving, but this bear appeared to be in a perverse mood. It was not budging one inch. It lay in magnificent splendor, full length, and quite content, like it was resting on a prime feather bed, seemingly oblivious to the writhing body underneath. The hands were pulling out tufts of hair frantically, the kicking was now frenzied, but still no movement from the contented Bear. By now five or six wrestlers were in the ring, having been ordered there by Fenton. With a concentrated effort wrestlers, referee, and trainer finally got the mammoth furry mass to stand up.

The Wolfman moved from underneath like lightning, surging to his feet. From the back of the hall where I stood watching all of this, I could see his face was almost purple, he was taking large gulps of air, while leaping around the ring. Then he started screaming abuse, at the top of his lungs, in perfect plain English. Now I won't say his diction was flawless, nor his grammar the choicest, but his delivery was rated a very high ten. His vocabulary was descriptive, not what you'd want your children to hear, but concise.

This man, raised by wolves, who couldn't do anything but grunt five minutes before, now suddenly exploded into voice. "Fuck you!" He shouted at the Bear. "Fuck you! You rotten fat son of a bitch!" He swallowed and gasped for air. The trainer, who was trying to get his ward out of the ring, came under fire next. "Fuck you too, Rubie!" He screamed, directing his spleen at the unfortunate man. It was amazing how articulate he became in a matter of moments. The trainer reeled back as if struck across the face. This whole episode was fast becoming a nightmare for him. He could see his and the Bear's bookings being canceled when word of this debacle got out.

Fenton had moved to ring-side, you could tell he was agitated. His cigar was not clenched in his mouth, but in his hand. "Wrestle on!" He shouted. "This is a three fall match!"

The Bear, in the meantime, unconcerned by the furor he had caused, was looking for his Coke. As far as the animal was concerned, the match was finished, a job well-done; the trainer, like everyone else, was mesmerized by the savage torrent of abuse that came from the Wolfman's lips. His sudden education took them by surprise. The Wolfman fixed his bloodshot eyes in the promoter's direction, then leaped forward and thrusting his head through the ropes, so his face was only inches from his boss, shouted, "Fuck you... FUCK YOU FENTON! You want three falls?... You wrestle the mother-fucking bear!!"

So forceful was the torrent that Fenton moved back a couple of feet. The crowd until this time was speechless. Other than the shouting in the ring from the Wolfman, the rest of the hall was completely silent. Everyone was stunned. My mind was moving fast. This was worse than anything I could have imagined. Should I leave town before Fenton came to vent his spleen on me? He would conveniently forget that the match was his idea in the first place. I would be carrying the can. Suddenly the entire hall erupted into laughter. People were rolling in the aisles, holding their sides, slapping each other on the back. I'd never seen a whole mob laughing so hysterically before, not insanely like this! It was so infectious I joined in, leaning against the wall, helplessly caught up in the merriment. Gone were my fears of a few moments ago. The Wolfman stormed out of the ring, up the aisle to the dressing rooms, still shouting obscenities at the audience, punctuated with gestures. He left no doubt what he meant, or what the people could do to themselves.

As I look back at the whole affair, I realize how ugly it could have turned out. Audiences at wrestling matches can become very irate if they feel cheated. They have been known to set fire to halls. Chilliwack had a reputation for being very explosive. As for the Wolfman, he disappeared into the wilds. Every time I'd broach the subject with Rod he'd just start laughing, shake his head and walk away. I knew by then to leave well enough alone.

8

SLEEPING BEAUTY

The Vancouver area was especially good for me. I was making money, not a fantastic amount, but it was comfortable. It wasn't a rich territory, it didn't have enough big cities for that. Even though I was predominantly in the main events, I wasn't getting wealthy, but I was happy. I was honing my professional wrestling skills. I really liked the people of the Northwest. They were open and friendly, and win or lose, they didn't change. Around that area, I was recognized in the business as a good draw card. There were large numbers of people of Scottish and Irish descent which certainly didn't hurt my appeal.

The country is magnificent. I would drive up to Prince George to appear in a match, a trip of about four-hundred, eighty miles. I never got over the size and beauty of the countryside. The mountains and valleys were stupendous in winter and summer. All shapes and sizes of animal life roamed in profusion. The city of Vancouver is one of the most beautiful in the world. Among all this I was very happy.

Rod Fenton talked to me one day about becoming one half of a tag team. This surprised me, believing I was doing great on my own. Why would I need a partner? He explained that it would extend my wrestling life, as I would have someone else to fall back on when hurt or burnt out. Professional burn-out is a prime time to get injuries, one of the main pitfalls in our business.

Tag team wrestling is entirely different to individual matches in many ways. To begin with, there are four men involved in a match, two to each side. Supposedly there are only two men in the ring at one time, but of course that usually goes out the window very early in the bout. This all adds to the excitement from the fans' point of view. From the wrestlers view point, more personalities are involved, which can and does cause more than double the problems. Having a partner can be great when there is complete trust and harmony. If a bond is lacking, or if a conflict of interests exists between partners, then all hell can break loose. Many a fight has started in the dressing rooms, not necessarily between opposing men, but between two on the same side! In such a highly volatile business, friction has often erupted between strong men with even stronger personalities. I've seen trouble brew between partners because one man was injured too often and perceived by the other as not carrying his end of the load. Or one man felt his partner was stealing too much of the limelight. All of these things would have to be considered if I was going to take the step Fenton suggested.

Faith won me over. I believed in Rod. Perhaps I was naive, but I did believe he had my best interests at heart. In the pro wrestling business, belief like mine could end up being disastrous. An unscrupulous promoter could take all kinds of advantages of the unwary. Many wrestlers have been broken in body, mind, and bank balance by being too trusting. Knowing all this I still took the chance.

"Okay Rod. What do you suggest?" I asked.

He looked at me for a long time as if he was thinking hard, trying to decide who to pick. I knew him too well. He'd already decided on someone. Whether I wanted the wrestler or not would be my decision. This is not always the case with most promoters. If you didn't agree to what they wanted... Bingo! Your number was up, very quickly too. I mean out the door. Out of the territory. I've known wrestlers who'd moved their families thousands of miles, leased a home with everything that goes with it. They paid for phone, water, garbage, gas and electric, and sent their children to school, only to be fired or forced out in one night. No one was immune. Even stars or draw cards could say or do the wrong thing with dire results. Promoters' powers could be awesome.

As it turned out Rod and I had no conflict. He'd decided upon Timmy O'Mally, another Irish wrestler, whom I'd never met but known by reputation. Pound for pound he was very strong, especially in the hands and fingers. He could bend and tear coins with relative ease. At two-hundred-thirty pounds not many could match his unusual muscular prowess. Here was another deceptive man. With his slightly flat-footed walk and open face, he didn't look as dangerous as he proved he could be.

When I first met Timmy I liked his sincerity. Very intelligent and knowledgeable in many areas, he was an expert in yoga, nutrition, and hypnotism. Despite all this expertise he was extremely naive. Though older than I and seasoned in the wrestling business, he had not changed his outlook. For me, he was far too trusting, reminding me of how I saw things when I first became a pro. He and I got along like a house on fire. If I was to have a partner, it must be someone I could trust and depend on, in or out of the ring. O'Mally fitted the bill perfectly. I could always count on him to back me up.

Rod, on the other hand, regretted his choice. He wasn't happy with Timmy's wrestling style, saying to me that he was slow and outdated. This was somewhat true, but his mastery of the Sleeper Hold was so phenomenal that it made up for any perceived inadequacy.

The sleeper hold was something he'd perfected. Many were those who said it was fake to his face, but became fast believers after he'd put them to the test. It was fun for me to watch a skeptic being put into a state of somnolence with his consummate ease. All the while Timmy would be murmuring words of comfort, like a mother over her baby.

In his Irish accent, still very pronounced, he'd say, "There now, t'will be allright... It will," as he applied the pressure. Why he even said these words I'll never know, because these people usually went out so fast I doubt they ever heard them. It was amazing to watch. He showed me how to do it several times. Though he said it was easy, I never really mastered the art quite like him. Not only could he apply the hold, but he knew its history. The Tibetan monks used it for thousands of years to perform simple surgeries or for pulling teeth. In the ring he would invite members of the audience to come up. It's surprising how many I would have to stop because the ring would be already full of sleeping bodies. It never ceased to amaze me how many people would voluntarily give themselves into somebody's hands to be put into a hold that literally rendered them unconscious. Especially as they could see the end results lying around the ring... a whole row of unconscious people. The only thing that frightened me was sometimes the fans were a little difficult to revive. Watching them laying there with their slack jaws always made me feel uneasy.

Once on TV a fan did not recover like he was supposed to. Seemingly the blood supply to the brain is diminished and if it's not restored fully within minutes, brain damage could ensue. There are a lot of people in this world I'd have been happy to see this happen to, but that fan wasn't one of them. Fenton was watching us on a monitor in the dressing room and almost crapped when the commercial time was finished. Timmy was still hard at it, massaging the forehead and neck trying to restore consciousness to one of his victims. I could tell by O'Mally's face, which had gone completely white, that things were not as they should be. All I could see was a brain-damaged person and a gigantic lawsuit coming! I started asking myself if wrestling in India was as popular as ever... Would I like the climate? Suddenly the guy came to life. Everybody cheered, loudest of all me.

The one time I derived real satisfaction from his hold was in a weight-lifting gym in Vancouver where I trained. It was one of my favorite gyms, clean, lots of up-to-date equipment, and a nice atmosphere. The owner, Jock, was a full-blooded Scot from the old country. He ran a tight ship making sure wrestlers using the facility were not bothered by the public. He prided himself on keeping harmony among the various people training there, that's why what happened almost caused him to have a heart attack.

A man whom I'd seen training there many times was introduced to me by Jock.

"Pat," He said. "Meet Bill. Pat's a professional wrestler you know." Jock said this with pride. He seemed to enjoy the idea that wrestlers who were on TV worked out in his gym. It was obvious Bill didn't know, or if he did, he didn't care. There was a strained silence while Bill and I took the measure of each other. Jock rambled on about how I was one of the top stars of wrestling in the USA and Canada. He gave me such a build-up it was starting to become embarrassing, especially as Bill didn't want to hear any of it. I was beginning to get that gut feeling that trouble was ahead. I was right. Without letting the owner finish, Bill jumped in with a loaded question.

"Is it the fake kind of wrestling you do?" He asked, looking me right in the eye. I glanced from him to Jock. Although I got along quite well with Jock, he was a typical Scot, loving a little conflict or dissention... but not in his gym, surely. His face was a picture, torn between stopping any trouble and curious to see what would happen.

"What do you do for a crust?" Was my reply, trying to deflect the question. The morning had started well. I didn't want to see it deteriorate.

"I'm a policeman... so what?" He certainly wouldn't get full marks at a charm school.

"Well, that's a tough job!" I said. "I can understand why you want to stay in such good shape." My ploy didn't work at all.

It rolled off him like water off a duck's back. In every business there are assholes. I knew I'd just found one in the Canadian police.

"Yeah, it's a lot tougher than that fake garbage you do for a living. It is the fake stuff you do..." He left the question hanging in the air. My insides began to boil. I agree that everyone is entitled to their opinion on things. That's okay by me. But if I don't ask for it, then I don't want to hear it. I've met many jockeys and I've never asked them if they pulled the horses, or if a tennis player threw a match, or for that matter if a boxer took a dive. In my travels I've met, wrestled, and associated with football players. Never have I asked them if the receiver fumbled on purpose, or did the quarterback throw wide for whatever reason. As for cops, I've trained, got drunk with, and been arrested by police all over the world. Never have I asked one if he took bribes. Now this asshole was beginning to badger me with his bullshit.

I was just about to give him a classic Irish reply like "Fuck you me boy!" when, on the horizon, came the answer to my problem.

Summing up the situation rapidly, I could only see two solutions. One, I could just turn and walk away, but probably face this confrontation some other day with the same prick. Or else I could see how far his macho image would carry him, which I believe would be physical violence, right there in the gym. I knew I was not prepared to simply leave. My machismo was on the line. In any gym, respect is very important for a pro wrestler. If I had walked away, my pride would've gone out the window. I believed that that kind of trouble never went away completely. It always comes back to haunt. The solution was in the shape of Timmy, who'd just come through the door and was heading our way. His big benign smile was spread across his face. Instantly I changed my tack. An idea hit me that excited the Machiavellian side of my nature.

"What do you mean the sleeper hold doesn't work! Of course

it does!'' I raised my voice somewhat so it would carry to O'Mally, who'd stopped to talk to another member momentarily. Bill looked bemused. His mouth opened to say something but I didn't give him a chance.

"What do you mean it wouldn't work on you!? The Sleeper works on everybody!" Now O'Mally was right behind him, his head cocked to one side, obviously interested in our conversation, especially at the mention of his beloved Sleeper. Bill, seizing a momentary break in my tirade, jumped in with both feet and said the wrong thing. His face was suffused with blood. He wasn't used to being treated the way I was treating him.

"Sleeper Hold? I don't believe that bullshit either! Nobody can put me to sleep with a hold!" With those words his doom was sealed. Though he didn't know it, he'd played right into my hands. Now I'm not going to argue the ethics of what I did. All's fair in love and war. I was not the same Irishman that left God's Emerald Isle several years before.

"Timmy me boy..." I said. "Show him the Sleeper. He doesn't believe it works." Before Bill could do anything he was caught from behind in the steel-like arms of my partner. Timmy locked on him like a Pitbull locks onto a rat. The hold he had on Bill was vice-like and unshakable. He went out like a light to Timmy's soft murmurings.

"There now... T'will be allright..."

The Scottish gym owner was holding on to an iron upright. He was speechless, white and shaking. You would think the hold had been put on him by the way he looked. Things had taken a very unpleasant turn. The gym was his living, the last thing he needed were his customers being put to sleep, especially if they were policemen. He now had a frothing body lying in the middle of his weight room.

"My God!" He exclaimed. "What have you done?!" He looked wildly from one to the other of us. I was laughing. The Scot's face was so comical. He'd gotten more than he bargained for. Timmy added insult to injury by his innocence.

"He'll be allright." Tim reassured Jock. "I'll bring him 'round. He'll be right as rain!"

All of this was said very matter-of-factly. As far as I was concerned, it was just another wrestling fan, one of thousands, that he'd put to sleep in his career.

"Do something! Wake him up! Bring him around!" Jock could only bleat. "He might die!"

Tim went about his wake-up work efficiently. Within seconds Bill was standing up staring around the room.

"Well..." I said somewhat sarcastically. "Did you enjoy your little snooze?"

"Snooze!" He bellowed. "What snooze?" He denied while shaking cobwebs out of his still befuddled head.

"You were unconscious." I confirmed, while my partner looked at him like an indulgent father looks at a slightly wayward child.

"Shit! I was never asleep!"

The strange thing is many people have this reaction when they come to. Never having had it done to me, I've no idea why they can't remember going under. But under they do go!

"Right!" Said Timmy. "I'll show you again." This spoken in a voice as soft as an Irish spring. He made a gliding move toward the luckless policeman. He had a very deceptive way of homing in on his victim. My Irish partner could move like lightning when he wanted to. His eyes were fixed hypnotically on Bill, like a boa constrictor fixes on a rabbit. The intrepid gym owner had found both voice and locomotion. Jock jumped between the Irishman and his erstwhile victim. Facing Bill, Jock clenched his teeth.

"You dumb silly bastard!" Strange how strong his accent sounded right then under stress. I'd never noticed it before. I also detected a note of hysteria in his Scottish burr.

"You were out to the world! He's liable to put you out for keeps next time!"

Bill's whole bearing dropped. Fear flicked in his eyes. He

could tell that Jock was serious. Facing a situation that was out of his control was something that he didn't understand. Abruptly he turned on his heel and left muttering under his breath. I almost felt sorry for him... almost, but not quite.

9

ASSIRATI STRIKES AGAIN

He was at it again. I could hear the blood curdling screams coming through the thick walls of my dressing room. I'd been on earlier in the night in one of the preliminary matches and was now relaxing. Luckily for me I'd been on before the main event, not after it. If the noise coming from outside the dressing room was any indication of what was going on inside the ring, it would be almost impossible to follow. It would be like following the lions eating the Christians with poetry reading! By that I mean after the action, blood and gore of Assirati's match, who would stay to watch good clean scientific hold-for-hold wrestling?

Anxious to see exactly what mayhem was going on, I hurried up my shower and rushed into my clothes. My match had been twenty minutes of fine upstanding wrestling, lots of good clean holds, everything that the public likes to see, if I was to believe what they always say.

My match, which ended in a draw, was politely applauded. On the way from the ring, voices shouted, "Good show!" or "Fine wrestling!" "Marvelous!" But somehow I detected a note of insincerity in the praise. Perhaps I was a bit more sensitive knowing that the packed hall, crammed to capacity, all the way to the rafters, a promoter's dream, was not here to see me or my opponent, but to watch the match that was following the intermission... The Main Event.

Normally, when I could, I watched the top of the bill at work. After all, they are at the top of the heap, the cream, the epitome of my profession. Right where I and every other wrestler worth his salt wanted to be. But tonight it was even more imperative that I watch, for a past opponent was doing battle with an unknown import from Holland.

The Dutchman was a big handsome brute, standing about six feet, four inches and weighing in at two-hundred, sixty pounds of bronzed bone and muscle. This was his first time in England, but he had quite a reputation on the continent as a great draw card and a tough cookie.

In England, foreign wrestlers are limited to twenty matches a year. English promoters, when bringing in an outside man, try to get them booked as many times as they can in as short a time as possible. This helps to cut down on the expenses which the promoters have to pay.

The hall was in the midlands, not one of the largest, but of a goodly size, and that particular night it was overflowing. I was told that a large crowd had to be turned away because it was full to capacity. The promoter would make a killing.

I finished dressing, and hurried outside into the maelstrom of red-faced screaming fans, and was instantly swept up into the animal excitement of the mob. I hadn't taken the time to cool down. Even though my bout hadn't been particularly stressful, it still took time for my body's cooling system to shut off. Tonight I hadn't waited. I was too anxious to see the action.

After I pushed my way down the aisle, I slipped into a seat beside the timekeeper who was so immersed in the action that he never noticed my arrival. All eyes were riveted on the ring. My presence was ignored completely, which didn't do my ego any good. Normally a wrestler not involved in a match will keep as far from the ring as possible, so as not to incur the wrath of the participants performing. It's not considered good form to take attention away from the match in progress by parading close to the ring. In this case my appearance so close caused not a ripple amongst the fans, nor the combatants.

The tall muscular Dutchman was in a lot of trouble. His shorter opponent had just head-butted him in the face, leaving it a bloody mask. By the looks of things, I was going to be in on the kill. The excitement in the hall was electric. Fans were standing, their bodies taut, their mouths agape, and all eyes were straining to see the action.

The taller man was looking around with a dazed and frightened expression on his face, too stunned or too proud to make an escape through the ropes. The referee was searching his face with concern from a distance, but made no move to halt the proceedings. Bert Assirati moved in for the kill with the assurance of the invincible.

Balling his fist up, he slammed the luckless Dutchman across the stomach with the inside of his forearm, doubling him over completely winded. Then with a short violent tackle, knocked him flat on his back. Everyone went berserk. Men, women, and children were jumping up and down shouting encouragement to their favorite to finish off this once-handsome foreigner. Assirati needed no encouragement. He was going to give them their money's worth, but he was going to do it in his own time, and in his own way. This was what made him the enormous draw all over Europe, and the bane of other wrestlers' lives.

Straddling the bronzed body that was now covered in blood, he started to pound the ill-fated face, slowly and methodically, with his closed fist, palm down. The man from Holland made a feeble attempt at defending himself, but the beating he had just received and the weight of the squat massive body were too much. So engrossed had I become, I never saw the arrival of the promoter at ringside amongst the fans who were crowding around chanting "Assirati! Assirati! Assirati!" Bert was pounding away on the face underneath, only a couple of feet away from me, when the promoter reached through the ropes and grabbed the thick muscular arm.

"Bert! BERT!" He shouted above the din. The authoritative voice attracted my attention. Assirati's arm halted its downward swing in mid-air. The large sweating face turned to see who had the audacity to grab his arm. The promoter's feet were off the floor, his body was halfway into the ring. Clutched in the other hand was a black bag. I recognized it as the money bag that this particular businessman always filled with the take from the night. He would sit at one of the windows, count the money and then stuff it straight into the old black bag. It was then carried around for the rest of the night, white-knuckled tight, almost in a death grip.

Only once have I seen it put down after it was filled. A few months before, in another hall, an exciting match was in progress. One of the wrestlers was breaking so many rules that the fans were starting to climb into the ring. Jack Dale, who still loved to participate in the matches, couldn't help himself. He was also afraid a riot might start and the building, which he was responsible for, might be wrecked. As he shouted at the wrestler in question to desist from his incitement of the fans, he was driven to a fit of temper. The wrestler he was admonishing grabbed his hat, revealing his balding head.

This was insult enough, but when the man jumped on the hat, it was too much. Incensed, he threw the bag on the ground, mad as hell, then leaped in to do battle. Jack, who had been a formidable middleweight wrestler a few years before, was like an old war horse who heard the bugle sound to charge. Steam was just about coming out of his nostrils. Forgotten was the crowd, the money, and his dignity carefully nurtured over the years. Throwing down the gauntlet, in this case his hat, was just too much. As he cleared the ropes it dawned on him, the enormity of his mistake. In the bag lying on the floor, fast disappearing beneath the feet of the angry mob, was all the money in the house that night. Without hesitation he dove into the howling crowd to recover the precious money. Grabbing it up after punching a couple of people out of his way, he spun around to finish the business in the ring that he'd started. Alas, the hat-stomping wrestler, realizing his mistake, had seized the opportunity to leave the ring in a hurry, out the other side, and was well on his way back to the dressing rooms.

Tonight the bag was bulging at the seams. I wondered how much he would steal from his partners, as there was no real way they could check on how much the gate money totaled, unless they were there to count the amount coming in.

Bert's large face showed no emotion as it gazed at the promoter. It was as if the owner was on a higher plane that ordinary mortals couldn't reach.

"Bert! Please!" Now the voice held a pleading note, gone was the air of authority. "Please! You'll kill him if you keep that up!"

"So who cares?" Came the guttural reply. "He's only a stupid Dutchman!" The mangled wrestler never moved, whether this was because he was past all movement, or like a mouse caught by a cat, he'd decided that playing possum was his best chance of escaping further punishment. If it'd been me, I believe I'd have exited under the ropes if I'd been in that shape.

"I care!" Came the surprising answer from the promoter. "I care a lot!" The crowd's screaming reached a crescendo. This inactivity wasn't what they had paid to see. Blood, action, and lots of it were Assirati's trademarks. That's why they were here in such huge numbers. Now they were beginning to feel cheated.

The promoter's answer had surprised me, after all, I hadn't pictured him as being the soft-hearted type. As a breed, promoters are usually the opposite, quite ruthless. Yet here he was, pleading for the safety of one of his wrestlers. His rating soared in my estimation.

"Why?" Questioned Bert. "Is he a fucking relative? I never knew your family was Dutch." The promoter was taken aback by the vehemence of the verbal attack. He wasn't used to wrestlers talking back. His next words restored my faith in human nature, as far as promoters were concerned.

"NO! NO! NO! He's not a relative, but I've got him booked for twenty matches this trip!"

"So what!" Came the rejoiner.

"So this is his first match in England... He's got nineteen more! If you damage him too much, he won't be able to wrestle at the other halls!"

Bert's hulking body shifted a little. I'd swear he was getting more comfortable while he weighed up the argument against his inflicting punishment and the sadistic pleasure derived from it. Then the promoter hit him with the clincher.

"Bert!" He whispered. "I promise if you let him go now, I'll book you with him on his last night over here!!" These words had a magical effect.

A big smile broke across the huge rugged face. "Okay, okay! You've got a deal!" With that he surged to his feet, but not before he'd ground his meaty fist into the Dutchman's face. He just couldn't help himself. Without a backward glance, he marched to his corner.

The referee, who had prudently stayed at a safe distance, moved in fast and counted the fallen giant out. When the count of ten was tolled, the massive Assirati launched himself into a back-somersault. This was his symbol of victory. It never ceased to amaze me the tremendous agility of this living legend. Bert left the ring with all the accolades of a triumphant gladiator.

The Dutchman, from what I could gather, could speak no English. He never spoke to anyone after the match, just packed his bag, got his money, and left the country, never to be seen in England again.

10

MAKING IT ON THE SIDE

People have, through time, tried to augment their wages or earnings by doing jobs on the side, away from their main occupation. Wrestlers are no different. If they can see an opportunity to supplement their income, most will. The only difference may be perhaps how they go about it.

Andrew Lane came originally from Wales, a son of a miner. He must have caused his family many disturbing nights. He, in some ways, was like the Gorgeous George of England, starting a trend in outlandish dress, both in and out of the ring.

The late Gorgeous George was the forerunner of extravagant clothes in wrestling. Most wrestlers before him wore mundane wrestling garb. Wrestling robes were of subdued colors and cut. He changed all that. Not only did he have a tremendous impact on wrestling, but on show business and boxing as well. Liberace was so impressed with Gorgeous George's extravagant posturing that he emulated him. In a book on his life Liberace claimed the "Gorgeous One" was his role model. Muhammed Ali also took a leaf from George's book by copying his unique style of interviews, plus being the man most people loved to hate. Many entertainers have followed in his footsteps. No one in the wrestling business at that time did quite the outlandish things he did. His dress and demeanor were unique. The impression he gave in the ring was one of foppishness, not wanting to get his body soiled by some lout, or get his beautiful hairdo mussed by a misplaced hold. In reality, he had been a brilliant amateur whose real name was George Wagner. He was as tough as they came, despite his later appearance. While a pro, wrestling under his real name, he never made any money. The shame was that after earning well over five million dollars in his career, it was reported he died broke, at quite an early age.

Lane, though not in the same class as the Gorgeous One, still must be credited with starting a trend in wrestling, and outside of it too it seems. The Punk Rockers, a case in point, dress up very much like he did fifteen years before. He was wearing makeup in the ring and dressing in very exotic robes and outfits when most English and continental wrestlers were decidedly staid. Never a big man, he wrestled in Europe for most of his career. It was only in the last few years that he broke into the American scene, where heavyweights are mostly the norm. In European circles, a smaller wrestler can be a star. In fact, two of the biggest draw cards of the last couple of decades, Jackie Pallo and Mick McManus, were only welterweights, weighing about one hundred, sixty pounds.

When I first met Lane he had been a pro for only a couple of years, but already was a controversial figure everywhere he went. He appeared to take delight in shocking people. There were stories of wild excesses in sex. He caused quite a stir with some of his escapades in a business where wild parties and orgies are the standard.

We had ridden back in the bus together, a couple of days before, where he and I had gotten into a conversation about working out. Lane told me he had some weights for sale. If I wanted to come to his place, perhaps we could cut a deal. Always interested in work-out equipment, and smelling a bargain, I went.

I arrived at his home on the day we'd both agreed upon. I was right on the time he'd said was best for him. I've learned by experience since then to call ahead and confirm that the person

EVERYBODY DOWN HERE HATES ME

I'm visiting will be home, and that they haven't forgotten the arrangement. In the wrestling business, this is a very common hazard.

His wife answered the door and gave me a blank look when I introduced myself. It was only when I explained about the weights that her face brightened up.

"Oh yes, now I know who you are, but I'm afraid Andrew has forgotten all about that!"

I guess disappointment or annoyance must have shown. I hated making a trip for nothing, or being screwed around.

"Never mind." She said. "Come on in. Andrew is filming, but I'm sure he won't mind you watching him at work."

For the life of me I didn't know what she was talking about. What did she mean by "filming"? Without any more explanation she marched into the house with me in tow. Soon all was to be revealed.

The door closed behind me and I found myself in, what looked like, a converted studio. There were some bright lights directed at the middle of the floor. Andrew was looking over the shoulder of a person, who turned out to be the cameraman, directing the camera at a couple on the floor. Actually they weren't on the bare floor, but on a carpet which was placed in the middle of the room. I couldn't believe my eyes. By this stage in my life I'd been to many places, done many things, and considered myself a man of the world. But I still wasn't prepared for the sexual scene that was unfolding right before me in the living room.

Andrew looked up and saw me for the first time, or appeared to. Knowing him as I do now, I'm not sure he didn't already know I was there, and was enjoying the sight of my confusion.

"Pat." He said. "Sorry I forgot all about you coming today." His face had a big smile on it. I was too stunned to understand his play on words, in the light of what was going on there.

"Get a close-up of that!" He said, turning to the cameraman, pointing at the activity on the rug.

My eyes instinctively turned to where his finger was pointing, taking in the scene at a glance, which wasn't difficult... everything was very graphic. It remains very vivid in my memory

The couple on the carpet were completely naked and having sex. My entrance into the room barely merited a disinterested glance from them both.

"What's going on here?" Was all I could think to say, my voice a little hoarse. I realized the stupidity of my words. It was blatantly obvious what was going on!

"Making movies." Came the quick retort. "These are some of my stars. What do you think of them? I picked them myself! Good eh?" By picking them himself I wondered briefly how he went about it. I'd heard a lot of stories that he was a bisexual, but I had discounted them. Now I was not so sure, after taking in that sly smile on his face. About him, I was starting to believe just about anything.

What was there to say except, "Yes, they're great."

"Have a seat!" Said my host. "I'll be with you in a short while. I must concentrate on the action. This is going to be the beginning of a new career!"

Slowly I sat down on the sofa. I couldn't seem to take my eyes away from what was happening on the carpet. The girl was very pretty and had a good figure — that is what was visible — since she was partially covered by the man's body. They continued with what they were doing.

Her legs were high in the air. His penis was sliding between her buttocks at a slow beat when, under the direction of cinema's newest artistic creator, Andrew, they were told to stop and hold the position while the camera took a close look.

Suddenly the door opened and Andrew's wife came in carrying a tray on which was a teapot, some cups, and a small plate of cakes. She placed the tray down on the sofa beside me with a bright smile, and asked if I'd like some tea. I couldn't believe she was so matter-of-fact about the whole situation. I was having trouble just keeping my mind on what she was saying.

"Yes please." I said. My mouth was bone dry. I had to lick my lips before I could talk.

"Milk?" She asked me.

"Yes thanks, no sugar." It was almost a typical English drawing room scene, except for the cinematography going on. His wife handed me my tea.

Andrew was talking to the couple explaining what he wanted when his wife interrupted him.

"No darling," She said. "That's not the best shot. I don't believe you're doing justice to John and Mary."

John and Mary, I realized, were the performing couple. With that she jumped up from beside me. To emphasize what she meant she pushed past her husband and the cameraman, grabbed John by the hips, and started lifting them up off the girl. Both their genitalia were in maximum view. John's engorged organ was testimony to his state of excitement.

"There," She said. "Get the camera over here." Pointing to the area she had uncovered. Then to John... "Hold it there please luv,... 'til we get a close-up."

Andrew's face showed his annoyance. "Luv," He said, his voice loaded with sarcasm. "For god's sake leave my stars alone. I'm the director here... not you!"

I could see it was time for me to go, so I stood up.

"Look, I'll come back some other time when you're less busy." I said lamely.

"What's the hurry?" Lane asked. "Stay awhile. In fact, I've got a great idea!"

After seeing this one, I didn't believe I was ready for the next.

"How would you like to be a star in my movie? How are you built?" He didn't have to explain what he meant.

"No thanks," I said. "That's all I need... My face on dirty movies all over the place!" To my ears I sounded like a prude, but it would be more than my face that would be in the movie!

Lane had an answer for everything. His enthusiasm for his new idea of me as a porno star was waxing even further.

"What about a mask? You could wear a mask! Nobody would recognize you! You'd be the first masked porno stud in the business!! By the way, let me see your equipment. Are you in good shape? What about size? That's very important!" His eagerness was contagious. Maybe, just maybe I could be a star. After all, who would know me in a mask? Then sanity returned.

Leaving my tea and cakes I headed for the door and made my escape. The weights may still be with him for all I know. I never went back to find out. Did I make a mistake? I wonder... I guess I'll never know.

11

DOWN, DOWN UNDER

One of the most powerful promoters in the world was Tim Bernard, a raving homosexual. In a business with so many tough men, he ruled with an iron hand. It was something to watch, this raving queen swish through the sweaty dressing rooms, stopping here and there to have a few words with a favorite giant of the ring. He always reminded me of Napoleon at these times, reviewing his Grande Armee.

Bernard never tried to hide his homosexuality, in fact he appeared to flaunt it at every opportunity. When asked by a wrestler if he was ever ashamed at being so blatantly homosexual, his answer was typical of the man. "When you have as much money as I have, you don't care what people think." His appearance was definitely unappetizing, spindly legs, pot belly, skinny upper body, and topped with a head that was too large for its supporting neck. His face was a pale color, mottled and flaccid. He had thinning hair on top, a grayish-ginger color with bulging eyes that peered out from behind thick lensed glasses. It was hard to comprehend that the man controlled the lion's share of a tough, ruthless, physical business. I have seen men who were fearless in the face of an angry mob, who would take on a six-hundred-pound bear, yet they would fawn, grovel, and jump at the sound of his voice. Although only five-feet, six-inches tall, his top men would sweat with fear if he appeared in the dressing room in one of his frequent rages. He controlled, used, and manipulated most of the largest, strongest, and toughest men in the business with consummate ease, loving every minute of it.

When I was in Georgia, Ron Peters, one of today's top wrestlers — then only a rookie — talked to me about how unhappy he was, because he was only making about two hundred and fifty dollars a week, which couldn't even pay his bills. He asked my advice on what he could do to improve his lot. Bernard was the promoter there, so I suggested to Ron that he talk to him and find out why he wasn't being booked in the towns that were drawing money. The next day Ron went to the office early to talk to this despot of the wrestling business. The conversation went something like this...

"What can I do for you, my boy?"

"Well Tim, I'm not making any money, in fact I'm starving to death. I'd like to have the chance to draw. Will you give me the chance?"

Bernard sat behind his huge desk looking at this tremendous athlete, one of the strongest weight-lifters this country has ever produced. The little man replied, "You don't have the experience to be a top man. That's why you're not drawing money."

"That's not fair." Ron answered. "If you give me a better position on the bill, let me wrestle better men that would help. Not only that," said Ron all fired up. "I'm being sent to the wrong towns, the small ones. I'm not being given the chance. For instance, on Monday instead of getting booked in Atlanta, I'm booked in Albany. How can I make any money there? Plus it's a long trip which costs money. Why am I always sent there?"

Looking at Peters like he was a piece of snot he just found on his favorite shirt sleeve, Bernard gave him his answer. "The reason you go to Albany is..." Bernard said. "That's my shit town. I send all my shit there." His high-pitched faggy voice concluded the conversation. Peters left like a whipped dog with his tail between his legs.

EVERYBODY DOWN HERE HATES ME

When I talked to Ron Peters he was depressed. I was incredulous. "What did you say to that? What did you do?"

"Nothing." Came the reply. "What could I do? He'd just fire me."

"Don't you see he's done that already?"

A couple of weeks later, Bernard was swishing his way through a dressing room when he bumped into Peters. Looking him up and down, like he was a cockroach that had crawled out from under the kitchen pipes in a sumptuous home, Bernard complained in his effeminate voice, "Oh my god, Peters. Are you still around?"

This time Ron got the message, leaving shortly thereafter. From what I could gather, the reason for Bernard's hatred or ostracism of the superb athlete, a man who had represented the USA in Olympic weightlifting, was he was having a fight, verbal of course, with another promoter, Greg LeGrande. LeGrande was a former protege of Bernard's. Ron was a protege of the former protege. Got it? It sounds very complex, but then that's the wrestling business!

The stories about Bernard are countless. He's a multi-millionaire, supposedly a Rhodes Scholar, who was a former groupie of the wrestling business. As a manipulator he was supreme, not only with the wrestlers, but also with the television people. Politically he is purported to have given money to the treasure chest of a past U.S. president, or so he'd boasted in the dressing rooms, telling how he'd helped get him elected.

In Australia he made a fortune by taking an almost non-existing business, run by a small clique of Aussie wrestlers, and turned it into a multi-million dollar success. From there he spread to Hong Kong, to Singapore, and even New Zealand, doing the impossible — getting professional wrestling on the government-run TV.

New Zealand had repeatedly resisted all efforts of the local promoter to get the show on TV. Bernard, instead of starting at the bottom, (pardon the pun) started at the head, (pardon the pun again) or second in command to the head man. His method went something like this I'm told...

He discovered the assistant head was also a homosexual. So Tim, with his usual flair, wined and dined him sparing no expense. He doubtlessly showered some of the expensive gifts on him that he brought back from Hong Kong. When it came to greasing the wheel of business, he was not a skin flint. Actually, he was the direct opposite — lavish. It was only in horse trading with the wrestlers that the mean petty side of his personality became apparent. Then it usually only showed when you were through, finished, and on your way out. More often than not the men in question didn't know when that moment was, only when it was too late. But by then he'd ground them into the dirt.

The secret of dealing with him was to get out before the axe fell. Then when he'd gotten over whatever fit of pique made him turn against you in the first place, he'd be ready to deal with you again. Thus starting another merry-go-round of ploy and counter-ploy. He was a man of extreme moods, going from very high, euphoria, to very low, bordering on depression. Strangely enough, when the house was packed, especially if it was a large auditorium, he would start screaming, picking on different people to vent his anger. While if things were not going too well, he would be unusually calm and have a good word for everyone.

One of my tours in Australia coincided with the same by Haystack Calhoun, a giant of over six-hundred pounds. Haystack was met at the plane by an enthusiastic Bernard. One of my funniest mental pictures was of them crossing the airport tarmac together. Haystack, from behind, looked like an elephant right down to the rolling walk, while Tim minced along side, like a Chihuahua, clutching the giant arm and peering up into the broad face, excitedly giving his star a pep talk. It was all adulation and fervor on Bernard's part — Calhoun, the man of the moment. When Haystack left, about six weeks later, another top man arrived the following day. The scene at the airport was nearly the same as the last. Chief Tomahawk was the star this time, an American Indian ex-football player who drew a lot of money all over the country because of his exciting action in the ring. As the Chief got off the plane, Bernard rushed to meet him, almost kissed him, then said, "Oh, Chief, my star... Thank God you're here! I just had that six-hundred pounds of shit over here killing my territory. You're the only one that can save everything." Then in the next breath, over his shoulder to me, "Pat, you know everybody here. Make sure Chief gets all the cunt he can handle. Get some of the Arena Rats. I'm sure you know plenty. Have a party. Do anything... Get anyone... Just make sure he's happy." Then back to Tomahawk, "You're going to love it here. Anything you need just call me." This was an open invitation to a man like Tomahawk to take advantage and go crazy. Without wasting much time, he did just that.

The first night in Sydney, Australia, we were in a hotel in Kings Cross. Tomahawk proceeded to get smashed; then for fun, throw empty beer bottles out of his fifth-floor window to the streets below. When the management came to complain, Tomahawk wanted to fight them all. Where Tomahawk went, excitement was sure to follow, both in and out of the ring.

My first encounter with Bernard was not a happy one. I was working in Vancouver, British Columbia, Canada, at the time for Gene Kiniski and Sandor Kovacs, who had bought the territory from Rod Fenton. To say they were not of Fenton's caliber is the understatement of the decade. Rod, though no saint by any means, was a man of his word, within the bounds of the wrestling business. The other pair had no redeeming features in my eyes, or in the eyes of most other wrestlers. I'd just arrived back from England when Rod sold out to Gene and Sandor because he wanted to take his terminally ill wife to Arizona. He'd been told that the climate there would improve, or make things easier for her.

Kovacs was a former referee; Kiniski, a former world

heavyweight wrestling champion. As promoters, they were the drizzling shits. To be a promoter takes a special kind of person, to be successful that is. They definitely didn't have what it took.

One morning out of the blue, I got a call from Bernard asking if I wanted to work for him. In the Vancouver territory I was hot as a firecracker, and as the TV station from there went all over Canada, I was hot over most of the country and quite a bit of the northern United States. Somewhere Bernard got wind of this, or saw me on television. He loved successes. So I'd gotten my call with an offer I couldn't refuse. He wanted me to wrestle for him in Australia for at least eight weeks. He would double the money I was making right away. And if I got over with the fans, I could make even more. Jumping at it right away, I called the terrible twosome with the news I'd be leaving in two weeks for warmer climates. Knowing them as I did, I was prepared for their unhappiness, that being their nature. But I couldn't have foreseen the degree that the shit hit the fan. They tried to lay a guilt trip on me by asking how could I do this. After all, they had put me on top. They'd made me all kinds of money. Why was I leaving? The typical attitude of most promoters was "We Own You." But that goes for only as long as you are healthy, not too wealthy, and certainly not wise. The minute any of those conditions change, out you go. No sympathy and most of the time, no reasons. All that was left was a fond good-bye, except that it was almost never fond. It didn't take me long in the business to understand this. I learned it fast as I wanted to keep my sanity, integrity, and health. I based my decisions on the foundation of self first, self second, and if there was anything left-over, self last. I confess it really wasn't that difficult for me to be that way.

The day before I was ready to leave, Kovacs called me with the startling news that Bernard had canceled my trip. He had to be joking, I tried to reassure myself. My mind raced. I'd better verify. But how?

"Suppose you won't be leaving now." He said. "We'll put

107

some bookings together right away.'' Now my guts started to tell me it was a trick.

"Did Bernard call you himself?" I asked. I kept thinking it was strange he hadn't called me. If I'd known him better I would've realized he almost never delivered bad news personally, especially if he wasn't sure of his ground. He would let somebody else do the dirty work.

"No," Kovacs replied. "It was one of his men, but I can't remember which one."

The last statement convinced me that I was getting shafted, one way or the other. The motto in our business is, "When there is any doubt, you're getting screwed."

"Hell no," I said. "I'm still leaving!" Once I'd made up my mind to go, that was it. Wrestling in Vancouver had lost its appeal since that pair had taken over. They were not only shitty promoters, they were stealing from my pay. I'd figured out they'd taken quite a bit more than was normal. Not that Rod hadn't done the same thing from time to time, but he'd done it with more finesse. Slamming the phone down, I then called the numbers Bernard had left with me. Apparently he'd done a disappearing act. Even the office in Australia didn't know his whereabouts. I knew that was a lie. I got mad because when I said who was calling, the voice on the other end got very cold and business-like. It didn't take a fool to understand that I'd become a non-person. My next call was to the airport where I was supposed to pick up my ticket to "Down Under". Funny enough, the ticket hadn't been canceled. Therefore, in my simple Irish logic, I reasoned that a smart boyo like Bernard would never cancel a man out without first canceling an expensive ticket. "Right," I said nonchalantly. "I'll be over tomorrow to pick it up, nice and early."

When I arrived in Australia, the first thing I did was to call the office. The same disinterested voice answered and got cold as before. When I identified myself, I was told the same story: that Bernard was nowhere to be found. The voice changed dramatically when I said I was calling from the Sydney airport. It underwent what sounded like an instant sex change, going from an obviously deep male voice to what sounded like a shrill female in terrible distress.

"You're where?!" Screeched the voice.

"In Sydney. Now where else would I be?" My Irishness came to the fore in moments of extreme pleasure. This was one of those moments. There is definitely a streak of perverted maliciousness in my make-up which, thank God, hasn't diminished in all my years in the business. Now it really flowed with the obvious alarm I was causing the disembodied voice on the line. It had treated me like shit up until now, or attempted to, which to me is the same thing. Putting on a stage Irish accent I said, "Bejeezus now, shuren da man himself, Mr. Bernard, wanted me over here. Didn't da gentleman leave me a ticket, bought and paid for by himself? I'm lookin' forward ta meetin' wit him. When will dat be now?"

A very pregnant silence ensued. The voice, very subdued, gave me a name of a hotel where I could stay until Bernard was found. This took six days of non-stop calls on my part, non-stop refusals on theirs. Finally when I had seen enough of Sydney, and lost my patience to boot, I threatened to go to the American Consulate about being brought out to Australia under false pretenses, as I figured that the ticket was an implied contract of sorts.

When we finally spoke on the phone Tim was in Texas, the voice claimed. Although I believed he was in Australia all along. Then he went into a long explanation of what happened. Seemingly I was supposed to have been teamed with another wrestler who had been kicked in the testicles, and he had to be sent back to the U.S. This changed everything. As I now had no partner, if there had been one in the first place, there was no position for me. When I demanded I get paid, he said he would do one better. He would book me else where. He was very upset at my using the airline ticket. So much so I believe he got his money back on it because he complained to the airlines that I shouldn't have been allowed to push the date forward on my outgoing trip. The number of tickets he was buying for wrestlers between the U.S.A. and Australia would have given him a lot of muscle with the airline in question, and he was an expert on using any leverage that came his way. Many times later I worked for him, but it was always an uneasy relationship. He's not a very forgiving person.

12

THE FIJI FIASCO

I had two weeks with nothing to do before I was booked in Hawaii. Being a man of adventure, I looked around for a place to spend that time, and to maybe have a little thrill, so I picked Fiji. What I didn't realize was I would get more than I bargained for in the shape of a shark and some former cannibals. I hired a car and took a leisurely drive around the island, drinking in its beauty.

On a lonely beach miles from the nearest town, I decided to improve my tan. The water looked so inviting I made up my mind to take the plunge and go for a swim.

I'm definitely no Johnny Weismuller when it comes to water sports. The sea was very warm and the sky a deep blue, so I closed my eyes and did my slow ponderous breast stroke. Life was good for me, not a care in the world. Forgotten was the disastrous Australian trip, Bernard, and everything. If I did think of him, it was with fondness, since he was paying for my trip. That couldn't be all bad. I opened my eyes as it was time to see how far I was from shore. I was a lot further out than I thought. Time to turn back.

I looked down into the translucent aquamarine depths. My heart almost stopped beating. There was what looked like a large gray form cruising along the bottom. My instant reaction was SHARK!

EVERYBODY DOWN HERE HATES ME

With arms thrashing, legs flailing, I aimed my body at the beach and headed for shore like a rocket. As I got closer to the sand, the water was still very deep. The shark was moving up underneath. Its shadowy shape appeared to be swimming faster, chasing me. Panic drove me frantic. Swallowing half the ocean, heart pounding, vision blurring with the strain, I was expecting to feel the terrible slicing teeth rend my flesh. Would they even find the body? Hadn't I read somewhere that sharks in this part of the world were larger and more ferocious than most? All this raced through my brain and spurred me on to greater efforts. Finally I made it to the beach. I actually did my breast stroke right up onto the sand! Lying there gasping in huge lungfuls of air, I gave thanks to the Almighty, even though I'm not a religious man. It's amazing how prayers learned in early childhood, long since forgotten, can in moments of stress return with such clarity.

The terrible pounding in my chest was slowing. My breathing was just returning to normal, when a very cultured English voice spoke right behind my ear, "I say, are you all right old chap?"

For a stunned moment I couldn't believe my ears. Was I dead? Perhaps the shark had gotten me after all. That was it... I'd been eaten alive by that monster of the deep I'd seen swimming below me, and now I was in hell. It must be hell. I was Irish, so it couldn't be heaven. And anyway, what kind of god would fill heaven with Englishmen?! Surely Saint Peter wasn't English, that would be irony indeed. It must be the devil. I knew I'd been surrounded by miles of flat sand. Nobody could have crept up on me without my noticing. All these thoughts flashed through my brain in an instant, before I rolled over on my back.

Bending over me was a tall middle-aged man, in good shape, suited up in a wet suit with air tanks on his back, and a look of concern on his face. My surprise must've registered. All I could think of was where the hell had he come from.

"Are you all right?" He repeated. "Can I be of any help?"

My voice sounded like a croak, but I didn't apologize for it. For years I'd had a horror of the water, especially the sea. I

112

had almost been drowned by a well-meaning counselor at a summer camp in Ireland. He had forcibly tried to give me a swimming lesson, but had lost me to a huge wave which had swept me out to sea. Fortunately I'd been rescued by another counselor with more brains. Now I'd just had the living crap scared out of me by a shark.

"Yes, I'm fine." I gasped. "But where in the world did you come from?" Looking around I couldn't see a house or another car or anything for miles, except the vehicle I had driven.

He pointed to the horizon where I could vaguely see a boat through the shimmering heat waves.

"That's my craft." He replied in the very English, very cultured voice, that only hundreds of years of breeding can produce. "By the way, the name is Thompson, Mark Thompson." He held out a hand to me which I shook with enthusiasm. I'd just had a narrow escape from death and my being alive was miraculous. I was starting to feel good about life again. The thought struck me that this is what makes life worth living, the brushes with danger, the happy endings. Hadn't I just outswam a gigantic man-eating shark? That was something to tell the folks back home.

"Pat Barrett." My voice had returned to normal, as had my breathing. My legs had finally stopped shaking. Then the thought hit me like a bolt of lightning, maybe he had seen the shark!

"No," He said. "I didn't see anything that even resembled one. When was this?"

"Just a few moments ago... out there!" I pointed in the general direction of the sea. Suddenly a terrible realization struck me. "Where were you swimming?" I asked, afraid of the answer. I was beginning to feel very stupid.

"I was swimming along the bottom when I first saw you coming towards me." He said. "Quite abruptly you switched around, then headed for shore. The way you started thrashing, I believed you were having difficulty, cramps or something like that, so I speeded up, just in case you needed assistance. You really looked in bad shape! I thought you might've been drowning. I was very concerned, you're a rather large fellow you know, didn't fancy trying to knock you out if it came to a struggle to save you." This he followed with a small laugh.

Laughing hysterically and rolling over on the sand, I must've presented an unusual picture to this stranger, but I couldn't help myself.

"You speeded up so you could help me if I needed it!!" I wheezed. "You've just succeeded in scaring me half to death!"

"How's that old chap?" He asked. His face showed just a hint of annoyance.

"Well, it's like this Mark... What I thought was a shark was obviously you. That's what made me turn around. When I saw you getting closer I almost had a heart attack!"

Thompson also burst into laughter when it hit him what had happened. If anyone had come along at that time they would've considered us both totally insane. There we were on an empty beach, me in just a tiny bikini, him in his wet suit and tanks, laughing our heads off.

"Well old fellow, I'm frightfully sorry for causing you so much agony. You must let me make it up to you. Where are you staying? I'd like to buy you a drink, in fact I'd like to buy you dinner."

"No!" I protested. "Let me buy drinks or dinner, or both. After all, you were trying to save me!" At this we both started laughing all over again. He wouldn't hear of me treating him. In a way I was glad. I wasn't sure I'd know where to take him for dinner, or even if I could afford it. He looked like he might have very expensive tastes and I was on a tight budget. We parted with him promising to get in touch when he finished with some business.

A couple of days later I got a call in my room. It was from Mark inviting me out that night for drinks and eats. We went to a fine restaurant and had a great meal. He was a terrific conversationalist. We'd both been to many countries and had a lot in common. It was here that Mark told me what he was doing in Fiji. His family had an import/export business of exotic articles. From what I could gather it made a lot of money, plus it also allowed Mark the opportunity to visit various countries on his yacht, which he loved. When he heard I wrestled for a living he was intrigued, or appeared to be. He never asked what I considered to be stupid questions about it. We got along like a house on fire. Politics was something that always interested me. Being a student of world history only made me a more political person. Naturally we did the unpardonable, got into a political discussion of world affairs. I believe I surprised him with my knowledge of the past. I prided myself on this arena of human endeavors.

"By the way," He asked almost shyly. "Have you met any of the real Fijians? I mean other than the ones that work in the hotels... If not, perhaps you would like to?"

Fiji's population is roughly divided into three peoples. The first, the original Fijians, are Melanesian. They were believed to be a mixture of Papuan, Polynesian, and Malay stock. They are generally a large people, most of the men standing over six feet tall, with dark skins and thick kinky beards and hair. They are known to be a mostly happy-go-lucky people; though in battle, they have a reputation for being very fierce. Under the British, I understand they have won many decorations for bravery.

Almost equal in population count to the Fijians are the Indians, who come from India. They are extremely industrious and have captured most of the small shopping and business trade on the island.

The third group is the Europeans, who make up a small minority of mostly English, Australians, and New Zealanders.

"Yes." My answer was instantaneous. I didn't need time to think. "I'd love to meet the real Fijians!"

"How about tomorrow?" My new found friend said. "They're having a party or a feast in the village in the interior where I go sometimes. Originally I would go on business, but now I like to think I'm invited as a friend.''

"Great!" I responded, hoping that I would be welcome too. I knew a little about these people and their history, just enough to remember reading that they were cannibals in the past.

We set off the next day in a hired car. I was really excited. My friend cautioned me again that these people did not have much contact with outsiders, because of the inaccessibility of their habitat, but if I followed his lead, he could see no problems.

The island was covered with thick tropical vegetation and very mountainous. Being volcanic, the mountains would rise up abruptly, giving the impression of huge green inverted ice cream cones rising from the startling blue of the Pacific. It was early in the morning and a thick haze lay over the land, adding a mysteriously eerie touch to the whole island. It reminded me of the book I'd read as a child called "The Lost World" where prehistoric animals roamed. At any moment I expected to see a tyrannosaurus come roaring out of the jungle. This was the world I was now entering.

Hugging the coast was the main road which serviced the towns that lay slumbering along the shore. This was where civilization had established itself, where the Indians lived and ran their shops and businesses. The interior was where the native Fijians lived in villages, much as their forefathers had for hundreds of years.

It was a couple of hours before we arrived, because the terrain proved to be quite difficult, and we couldn't resist stopping to enjoy the spectacular views. The village was like a scene from an old Tarzan movie. The men wore loose-fitting skirts which hung down to their ankles. The women also wore a one-piece, loose-fitting colorful garment which was tied just below the top of their breasts and fell to their ankles. They looked very relaxed and made me feel overdressed in my tee-shirt, shorts, and long socks. It looked to me like a large village with a population of several hundred. When we arrived they all crowded around to greet us. I don't believe I'll ever see so many smiling faces in one place.

From somewhere in the middle of the village came the delicious smell of cooking. My mouth started to water and my stomach growled in anticipation.

"What are they cooking?" I asked my English friend. "What kind of food do they eat?"

"Come and have a look." He said heading toward what I took to be the hub of the settlement. He seemed quite at home here among these simple people. We arrived in front of a large pit dug in the earth. It was from this the lovely aroma was coming. Over the pit were placed hundreds of large leaves, hiding from my view whatever was cooking underneath. The huge crowd had followed us and we were again surrounded. Turning to a tall native, Mark rambled off something in their language. They talked back and forth for some time, then Thompson turned to me. "The main dish will be pig." He said. "Cooked whole, under those leaves. I'm told it will be ready soon." For the life of me I couldn't figure out how they knew if they couldn't see the porker.

"God," I said. "I'm really starving!" This was the truth. I'd gotten up early, and only had a cup of tea for breakfast. The sea air and the time had developed my appetite intensely. The delicious smell was the final straw. Obviously some of them understood what I said because they all but burst out laughing. It was so relaxed there that I was really beginning to feel at home myself. Gone were my normal suspicions of strangers that always lurked in the back of my mind since I turned pro.

The feast was a great success from my point of view. There were all kinds of strange fruits and vegetables, along with green bananas, but the pork was the highlight for me. Our hosts seemed very pleased with my appetite which, even in a nation of big-eaters, is impressive.

The Fijians were exceptionally friendly, though few spoke English, or appeared not to be able to. Every now and then one of these giants would feel my arm with admiration. They were a pretty impressive bunch themselves, which did make me start to feel a little nervous. Remembering their past cannibalism, how was I to know why they were touching my arm? Maybe I'd be next on the menu, I joked with my English friend. I tried to visualize how I would look naked with an apple in my mouth. The idea certainly had no appeal!

Though I considered myself muscularly well-built at two-hundred, thirty pounds, some of these men were over three hundred and not fat! Mark explained to them that I was a wrestler. I was horrified. I'm not sure they understood what he meant, but I thought he was pushing my luck. In some ways wrestlers are like gunfighters in the Old West, once people knew what they did for a living, on came the challengers. In my experience, challengers have come in all shapes and sizes. Each had their favorite way of showing their manhood, from the simple vice-grip handshake, through wrist-wrestling, down to the old "Let's see how tough you really are..." come on. Most of the time they can be put off with my favorite get-out-of-trouble line which is, "I'm a Pro. You'll make me look bad if you beat me. Right now I'm not sure you can't!" This little line I devised has saved me from many potential conflicts, but unfortunately not all.

Sure enough, the challenge came my way once again. Not, as it normally does, with some misguided fool or braggart calling me out. No, this came in the shape of the chief of the village, who Mark told me was also chief of the regional area. I never knew exactly what that meant, the Englishman was vague. All I knew was that he was held in reverence by his people. This was evidenced by the way they deferred to him.

Dinner was finished. My belly was overloaded with all the good fare. I felt a contented relaxed mood coming over me that only good food, and plenty of it, could induce. Mark and myself were invited to the chief's house, or hut, which I gathered was a great honor. As we entered he was sitting cross-legged in the middle of the huge shack on the floor.

First impressions count with everyone, I believe, and I'm no exception. They have saved my ass many times in my life. In tight situations I've had to make hard decisions almost instantly, summing up people immediately, and acting on this in a matter of survival. My first impression of this man was of strength, but not just the physical kind. There was plenty of evidence of power in the huge bones and heavy muscular arms. No — it ran deeper than just the surface.

His smile of welcome looked genuine enough, but I'm sure I detected an appraisal in his eyes. He never spoke English. Mark obviously understood what was being said, though I wasn't sure to what extent he could converse. Turning to me Mark said the words I dreaded to hear, even though somehow I'd known they would be forth coming.

"Pat, how would you like to show the chief some wrestling?"

"No Mark," I said. "I wouldn't." My voice sounded sharp even to my own ears. What was he getting me into? I was beginning to wish he had been a shark after all. This situation could prove to be even more dangerous. My belly was bloated with about half the pig. Not expecting this situation I'd gorged myself just to show what a great fellow I was. Now it looked like I would pay the price. There seemed to be no way out. All eyes were upon me. Then I softened a little. I hadn't forgotten how he'd been nice enough to get me into the village, even though things were, in my eyes, taking a turn for the worst.

"Look at me!" I pleaded. "I've eaten too much. I'm fat as that pig!" I almost choked on the words as soon as I'd said them. After all, I remembered what had happened to it! "I don't want to start putting holds on anybody... Let alone on that..." Big bastard. The words were on the tip of my tongue, but I curtailed myself. I could never be accused of having suicidal tendencies. The chief seemed to be paying a lot of attention to our chat, for one who seemingly could speak no English.

"No, no!" Mark said. "Firstly old chap, all hell would break loose if you laid one hand on him. We'd both most likely be killed." He's got to be joking I thought. Mark must have a real twisted sense of humor. This was something I'd expect from

119

another wrestler, but not this fine upstanding gentleman. His face was totally serious, if not a little alarmed.

"Pat," He almost pleaded. "You'll have to do something to show how strong you are. Can you think of something? They're just like children, really." This said with that marvelous plum-in-the-mouth voice. "We must keep them happy, old boy!" The thing I liked was the big "we". It looked like I was going to be the patsy that'd be entertaining these brutes, not him. My bones on the line... not his. I felt like fat Oliver Hardy must have felt when he would say his famous "Another fine mess you've gotten me into." This might just turn out to be an expensive feast.

My thoughts ran wild. I looked around the big hut. It was filled with large black faces topping even larger black bodies. The only whiteness in the whole place was us. What the hell could I do without brandishing a machine gun? Then I hit on an idea. I prayed it would work.

"Who does the chief want me to wrestle?" I asked my so-called English friend. I was also beginning to have my doubts about him. Words flowed back and forth between a Fijian, who I gathered was our interpreter, and the chief. Then a tall well-built native stepped towards me. My heart sank. In the diminished light he looked enormous. I judged him to be at least six-feet, four-inches tall and weighing about two-hundred, sixty pounds. There wasn't a pick of fat on his body. He had the smooth look of a natural athlete. His abdominals were like the proverbial washboard. If he'd had a lot to eat, there was no sign of it. Thank God I hadn't had any booze. Come to think of it, I hadn't seen any, which seemed strange. Surely they weren't all teetotalers. My mind came quickly back to the problem at hand, which didn't look like it was going away. I figured he was about twenty or so, though this was definitely a guess.

"What I'm going to do," I said, taking control of the situation as best I could. "Is lay on my back. Then I want this young man," Gesturing at my opponent, "To hold me down." I figured they didn't understand what wrestling was all about, at least the kinds I was used to. My one big fear was I know *my* rules, but what are *theirs*?

It always seems strange to people that a professional wrestler talks about rules. But it's very important for me to understand what I was up against. For instance, would he try to bite me in a tussle? He did have a large mouth with huge white teeth. Would he go for a knife? To some people this was quite fair. How did he feel about things right now? Was losing face so terrible to him that he would do anything to prevent it? I knew he wasn't about to tell me, so I'd have to use my brain to get out of this tight situation. Another thing that occurred to me was what if I was in bad shape, taking a beating, how did I tell him I was ready to quit?

The thought had dawned on me to let him win. Except how could I lose if I didn't even know which way we were going to fight? If he were a wrestler putting holds on me, then I could shout that I give up, or let him pin me. Alas, he wasn't, so that was out. If he were a boxer and gave me a good punch, then I could stay down, pretend I was knocked out and get the whole thing over with.

My dilemma, as I saw it was: 1). How could I lose gracefully? 2). Would it make him happy winning gracefully, or would it spur him on to greater glory at my expense? 3). How would the chief and his cohorts view my easy defeat, with happiness or total loss of respect with all the negative consequences? Respect is in many countries more important than anything else. This appeared to me to be one of those places.

My strategy was simple in wrestling terms. As I said, I would lay on my back. He would get on top to try to hold me down. I would get what wrestlers call a top wrist lock on his arm. Next I'd throw my leg over his so he couldn't get away. Finally I'd submit him. It was that simple in theory, just as simple in practice I hoped! The chief had squatted down in the center with all his men around the hut, leaving a small area clear in front of him.

He had gotten a ring side seat. Something else I noticed was that there were no women present, though I could see several female faces at the door.

The interpreter did a good job, I guess, because when I lay down in the dirt my opponent laid right down on top of me, pressing his oversized, muscular, sweaty body on mine, making my pork dinner feel like pressed duck.

He grabbed me by the wrists with his huge hands. A buzz of anticipation ran through the men. The air was sticky with the crush of bodies added to the already intensely humid evening. He was lying so heavily on my distended stomach that I thought I was going to barf greasy pig all over him. Or worse still, I might crap right there, stinking the whole place out. I could imagine natives running to the door to escape the foul odor. At least it would solve my problem! Coming back down to earth... Lying underneath I could smell the excitement and fear of my adversary. The fact was I could also smell my own fear. I was watching his mouth intently, as being bitten was another dread. I couldn't help thinking that Fiji was turning into a nightmare in which everything was trying to bite me, first the supposed shark, and now maybe, this half-savage!

The wristlock is not really put on the wrist. With my right hand I would grasp the other person's wrist, then reach over his arm with my left, up over the bicep, then I would take hold of my right wrist with my left hand, forming the hold. The secret of this devastating move is to apply it from underneath, while you are on your back, with your opponent on top. Then push your arms up and away from you with the trapped arm inside of yours. This puts incredible pressure on the shoulder joint and collar bone. Whichever is weaker will break. The pain is excruciating from the elbow to the neck, depending on the expertise of the person applying it. Then to ensure that my adversary can't get away, remember he's face down lying on top of me, my leg goes over his. This way it's very difficult for him to turn out and get free. It's very like the feline, whether it be the noble lion of Africa or the domesticated tabby cat, that fights on its back when in real trouble. It can bring its most powerful weapons into play, its back legs, with which it can mutilate and kill animals more than twice its size. In this case I wasn't trying to kill anyone, just get my freckled Irish body out of a tight spot, and back to the good old USA, all in one piece.

Action commenced at a signal from the chief. My opponent's raw power was enormous. The fingers holding my wrists were like big vices, stopping the flow of blood to my fingers. Twisting my arms suddenly I broke free and made my move. It was now or never. He made a lunge to recapture my wrists and fell into my trap. I had him. If the truth be known, I'm sure it was he who thought he had me. The secret of this hold is not to resist or tighten up too much, to fool the other person into thinking he has the upper hand. This I had done easily because the big bastard was trying to crush the life out of me with brute strength, of which he had plenty. The difficulty for him was he had no knowledge of what he was trying to do. My problem was to keep from being damaged and having a heart attack after the huge dinner I'd eaten.

Now I tightened up and started talking to myself as I do under pressure. I don't do this out loud, but only to myself. It seems to give me added viciousness when needed. "Okay you big dumb bastard, let's see how you like this." I said to myself as I exerted more pressure. He gave a deep grunt, then tried to tear his way out. I had him well and truly for I was scared shitless to let him go once he'd been hurt. More pressure from me drew another grunt. The sweat was running down in both his eyes and mine, it must've been one-hundred-forty degrees in the hut. In the blur I could see the chief's face dimly, peering down, only inches from my face. He wanted his ringside seat, but this was ridiculous. My native's face was in the dirt. I had him beautifully, though I'm sure he didn't think it was so beautiful. In life everything is relative. I could hear my old wrestling coach saying, "Now screw it on Paddy. Let him feel some pain." His arm was bent up his back, but pushed out. The pain must've been intense, but nothing more than grunts were coming from his thick lips. Suddenly it occurred to me in a flash of insight, that this man would let his collar bone break, his shoulder be dislocated, before a word would pass his lips. He didn't know how to say "I give up." He most likely never had to. The other element was pride. These people, in the short time I had known them, had impressed me with their obvious dignity, both in themselves and in their heritage. Perhaps one afternoon was not enough time to make that kind of observation, but to this day I believe in my analysis of the situation. My actions after that thought hit me were against all the books on dirty fighting, everything I'd learned. Here was an impasse that had to be broken, or else his bones would be. I didn't believe he deserved this. He was a victim of the circumstances, as was I.

I weighed up the consequences and decided to let him go. I was new in a nasty business then. Would I have let him go if it were now? It's hard to answer if it were today, but I'm inclined to say no. I've come down a long, hard road since those days. I don't pretend to trust people now like I did then.

In saying that I let him go, it wasn't quite that simple. I first shouted to my friend Mark to explain to everybody that this was a very brave man. I could break his bones and he couldn't get away. Even to their uneducated eyes it must've been obvious that he was doomed. They were primitive, but they certainly weren't stupid. A lot of shouting went on, then it all died away. Then rhythmically they all began clapping and stomping their feet. Mark gave me the word.

"You can let him go now, Pat. It's all right."

"Well," I said from under the perspiring body between gasps, "Does HE know it's all right?!" The chief said something and the body in my arms went totally limp. Gingerly I let go then, and staggered to my feet. Everybody crowded around hugging, squeezing, and slapping me on the back. To tell you the truth, at that moment I was the proudest man in the world. The adulation

124

of these great people had an intoxicating effect.

Mark pushed through the crowd saying something in Fijian which gave me space. Then thrusting out his hand he pumped mine up and down.

"Bloody marvelous, old boy! Bloody marvelous!" That coming from this reserved Englishman said it all for me. Then he said something I never fully understood, but perhaps it's just as well. "I'm glad you pulled through for both our sakes!" Before I could ask him what he'd meant, the chief took my hand in his giant paw. For a moment I thought I was out of the frying pan and into the fire. With great dignity this giant slowly shook my hand. Everybody shouted and clapped even louder. The moment was lost to ask Mark exactly what he had meant.

Still holding my hand, the chief led me to what I took to be the place of honor. There were no chairs or tables in this huge hut, only rush mats. I was seated on the one beside him while Mark arranged himself to my right. Everyone hurried to sit cross-legged as quickly as possible. There was an air of expectation and anticipation permeating the enclosure. Not knowing what to expect, I turned to my English mentor, good old Mark, to find out. With a knowing wink and a whispered, "Wait and see, old boy..." that was the only answer I could get from him. Though we were being treated like royalty, the invitation we got was more like a command. Through the door came several women on their hands and knees, dragging a huge wooden bowl filled with a cloudy-looking fluid, and many smaller carved wood bowls obviously for drinking from. The women never got off their knees while making the preparation. When they left they were still on their hands and knees, crawling backwards.

My English friend murmured quietly in my ear, "These fellows have the right idea, eh? Keep the little beauties in their place!" Coming from him it was quite a shock. By no stretch of the imagination could anybody describe the women I'd seen as little. Also I don't know where the beauties were kept, it certainly wasn't around this hut!

EVERYBODY DOWN HERE HATES ME

The huge bowl was placed in front of the chief, who was still squatting on the ground. The exalted man started squeezing what looked like an enormous tea bag up and down in the water, which began turning a milky white.

"What the hell is he doing?" I whispered in Mark's ear, squeezing his arm at the same time.

"Take it easy, old boy!" Said my English friend, wincing. "It's Kava, brought out in your honor."

"What's it taste like?" I whispered again to Mark. I didn't know why I was whispering, except that everything had fallen silent.

While everyone seemed mesmerized by what the chief was doing, Mark explained what the liquid was. Kava is a mildly narcotic drink that's made from the root of a tree. It's pounded into a pulp, then immersed in water inside of a crude cloth bag. "Why is he still pounding it up and down?" I asked.

"Making it a bit stronger for you, old man. You should feel privileged. It all has some religious connotations, but I'm not sure what..."

I got the feeling that this was more than just a drink with the boys. What worried me was the chief. He had his huge arms up to the elbow in the milky liquid while he kneaded the bag. Next he picked up one of the small bowls, dipped it into the nasty looking substance, and to my horror, handed it to me. Now I'd been in quite a few places by that time, eaten and gotten drunk in many dives, but this was the first time I'd seen somebody with their arms in my drink. The chief struck me as being a great guy, but even in the dim light I could see he wouldn't win any awards for cleanliness.

"Do I have to?" I whispered to the man I was no longer considering my friend. "What are my options?"

By now everyone was clapping in unison, very slowly, and very loudly. All eyes were fixed on me, not with hostility, but staring never-the-less. There were at least a couple of hundred large black males crammed into the hut, and right now I was the focus of all their attention, which gave me a distinctly uneasy feeling. What would you expect with all those massive hands pounding together in the hut. The sound was quite deafening. "Yes old boy, you must drink it. I'm afraid to think what will happen if you don't... A big insult to the chief and all that."

Thompson was really beginning to piss me off. First he scares the shit out of me in the sea, then he turns a giant cannibal loose on my hapless body, now he tells me I must drink this dirty dishwater or something horribly nameless will befall me. To cap all this off I was really resenting the "Old boy" crap. My first instinct was to tell the chief to go fuck himself, but I still hadn't figured out how many of these warriors could speak English, or if my so-called English friend would turn me in. I didn't trust him anymore.

"What about this clapping? When does it stop?"

"As soon as you drink all the Kava in the bowl you're being offered, old boy."

There it was again.

"Please don't make them wait too long..."

To this day I don't know whether Mark was stringing me along. I never had the chance to find out. Closing my eyes I drank it all in one gulp. I remembered how I used to drink the senna pod tea when I was constipated as a child. I tried to earn the bribe my mother would give as encouragement to drink the dreadful stuff. Surprisingly it was not as horrible as expected, just a step below what dirty bath water must taste like. The clapping stopped. There were smiles all around. Now it was the next man's turn. The bowl went to four other people before it arrived back at me.

"Why do I keep getting the bowl?!" I complained to Mark querulously. "You haven't had a drink yet! Why me again?"

He spoke patiently, like I was a troublesome child he had to placate. "Why my dear chap? It's because they admire you. Drink up! Down the hatch!" His "dear chap" was fast becoming a real bore, as was all this shit he'd gotten me into. The clapping started all over again until I downed that one as well. Fourteen times the bowl returned to me. I've no doubt it was a great compliment, but my tongue had gone completely numb, plus I was feeling exceedingly queasy. If this was only slightly narcotic, I'd hate to see the real thing. My head was swimming. Because my tongue was now numb, I couldn't control my speech.

When we were leaving the chief tried to get me to stay overnight with his niece, who must've weighed two-hundred, thirty pounds, and was missing all her front teeth. By now I didn't care if I was roasted on a spit, boiled in oil, or buried up to my chin, I wasn't going for any more of their wonderful hospitality. It might just kill me.

On the trip home I would have assaulted Mark, except I seemed to keep floating out of the car. I don't remember saying good-bye or getting to bed.

The next day found me flying on to Hawaii. Mark disappeared to God-knows-where.

By the time I arrived in Hawaii I was dying with cramps, vomiting, and had a deadly case of diarrhea. I lost over sixteen pounds in five days. It's the first and last time I crapped my pants when trying to body-slam a wrestler. The only good thing was the other wrestler left the ring for the dressing room in a real hurry, followed by the front row. The odor was that bad.

The doctor, who was a first class sadist, laughed when I told him about the Kava scene, while poking my sore stomach with a boney hand, but he did get me well again. If I was superstitious, I'd believe it was Bernard's revenge. I never told him what'd happened.

13

BLOODY ENCOUNTERS

The Northeast of the United States is a real hotbed of wrestling. Because of its huge population and wealth, it's a promoter's dream. It's no accident that the most powerful wrestling organization in the world today is the WWF, based originally in New York, but is now in Connecticut. In the vast complex of industrial and business might, the wrestling fans that go to the matches regularly are almost uncountable. Then there is the huge number that never go to the halls, but watch wrestling religiously every time it's on TV. When something hot is brewing, like the feud between Randy "Macho Man" Savage and Hulk Hogan, with all the hoopla thrown in, the average non-wrestling fan sees how numerous the supporters really are.

It is from the northeastern seaboard that this giant wrestling promotion springboards its wrestlers and TV shows all over the world. People like Hulk Hogan, Andre the Giant, Boss Man, and Rowdy Roddy Piper are as well known in places as far apart as Kuwait, Australia, and Great Britain as they are in the Bronx. The halls are just as packed in these countries when the WWF stars arrive as they are in the Cow Palace in San Francisco or Madison Square Gardens in New York.

I was wrestling for the WWF office when business in the territory was quiet. When attendance is down, everybody suffers, from the promoters on down through the ranks. Mostly it's the wrestlers that hurt money-wise. Our expenses were always the same, whether the paycheck was good or bad. Promoters have a way of cushioning their losses. But if business stays low over an extended period of time, ultimately the office will suffer. Wrestlers are like gypsies, if the grass in one area gives out, they just move to another pasture. Wrestlers normally have no written contracts. Job security, hospitalization, and insurance for injuries are nonexistent in this business.

Boston Garden is a large stadium, and Boston fans are some of the most enthusiastic and violent. This is borne out by the fact that the ring is surrounded and covered by a large net, to stop the bottles and other objects hurled at the combatants. Plastic shields are placed around the ring perimeter to deflect BB gun pellets and various other projectiles. The first time I wrestled for the WWF office, Vince McMahon Sr. was the boss. I had only been in the country a couple of years. Being Irish in America was definitely not a drawback in the Northeast, where just about everyone is Irish to some degree. When in Boston, a very Irish city — though the Italians there might dispute that — I always got a great reception.

One of the strange things about drawing power in the wrestling business is that it's difficult to understand exactly what it is or how it works. Many men have it, some in only one area like New England. In a case like this, if they go to another territory like California, they might have no pulling power, not drawing a dime. Nobody knows why this is so, but it's a definite hazard for both wrestler and promoter. A wrestler can move his whole family from New York to California, with all the expense this entails, only to find out the fans won't pay to see him. We have a saying amongst the wrestling fraternity: "You're only as good as your last match." So you can draw in different territories, pack the halls, and be the promoter's darling, and then go to another area and lay a big fat egg. Overnight you could become a non-person.

130

When you're on top in an area, there's a tremendous amount of pressure from all directions, starting from the boss who has given you a chance, to the wrestlers in the subordinate positions, some of which think that they should be in your spot, and will do anything to supplant you. There are others who are happy underneath, but blame the top men if business is bad, because they aren't making enough money. Last, but certainly not least, there are the fans. If you don't have something special for them, they show their displeasure by staying away from you in droves. If this happened, the ax was never long in falling, with a ruthlessness and swiftness not seen or allowed in many other businesses. You could be riding high in the morning and out of work that night. No sympathy is wasted on you whatsoever from any quarter. Not to mention that the wrestlers who were happy to talk to you or joke with you, and were supposedly your buddies, suddenly treat you like you've got syphilis. Red Bastien, one of the most famous performers of the 1960's and 1970's, is a case in point. He told me the thing that hurt him most when he had to retire, due to two total hip replacement surgeries, was that the phone never rang. He was one of the most popular men among wrestlers and promoters. Luckily for his sake, he was being used by the WWF office as their public relations and set-up person for their operation on the West Coast. When I say "lucky" I mean he with his wealth of experience deserved the job. Even though I'm sure he did the job well, he was released, for whatever reason, overnight. Wrestling is certainly not for the faint of heart. For every man like Hulk Hogan that reaches the top, there are many thousands that end up broken in body and spirit, and destitute.

It was always sad for me to see old-timers come into the dressing rooms to talk to the new stars, telling stories of their days in the business that the young turks, now on top, weren't interested in. There would be smiles behind their backs when the stories of days gone by were resurrected. Sometimes the young men were just plain rude.

EVERYBODY DOWN HERE HATES ME

Contrary to popular belief, all wrestlers get hurt, knee and elbow injuries are the most common. By the time they have gone through the mill, those who have survived the emotional and physical traumas have at least one bad hip, which probably needs replacing; terrible aching knees; bad backs, stiff necks from the disintegration of the vertebrae; and damaged elbows. In some ways, people put them on a pedestal by saying "You never get hurt, do you!" If the average person takes a fall, he hurts some part of his body, whether it be a back or a leg. Then imagine if you can, a body being slammed to the boards, thrown across the ring, falling out onto the concrete floor, or worse still, onto metal chairs or upthrust fans' boots. Then tell me "You don't get hurt."

The ring is mostly boards overlaid with a thin sponge sheet. All this is then covered by canvas. Multiply the bangs taken by an average wrestler in one night by the number of weeks in a year, plus the blows administered by other wrestlers, it's a wonder any survive the first year! Actually, many do not.

One of pro wrestlers' pet hates are people who proclaim that they never watch TV wrestling. In the next breath they will start broadcasting how fake it all is, how no one ever gets hurt. What really galls the most is when these sane good folk go into elaborate detail how they strained their back as a teenager, thus preventing them from doing anything strenuous ever since.

My match that night in Boston was against a man called Claude Stevenson, who weighed about two-hundred, seventy pounds, and was an ex-boxer. Though a large man, he could move like a lightweight. I'd never seen him in the ring or met him before. I really knew very little about his method of wrestling. In those days I hadn't learned to be prudent enough to find out a little about who was going to be manhandling my body. All I knew was the office liked my style and was handling my bookings. Still being very naive, I blundered along happy in the knowledge that I was being pushed, which meant that I was being groomed for stardom, and all the benefits that go with it. The office couldn't do enough for me it seemed. I was going places. I never realized that there were equally as many pitfalls! Later I was to recall the famous ex-World Champion Nature Boy Buddy Rogers saying, "If you want to screw someone, you have to get into bed with them." Little did I know how true these words were.

That night I was on the semi-final, which meant a big step up for me. This position on the bill was second only to the main event, which translated into I was on my way up. I was assured by the promotion that before long the top spot all over the area would be mine. Just get out there and do it! Go to it! Give him hell! Let the fans have their money's worth! At that time I could've been described as young and dumb, and full of come, ready to do anything to make the grade. Little did I realize that making the grade embraced not just the physical, but also the political.

The bell rang. I charged out ready for whatever the match would bring. The stadium was half empty, though the fans were no less enthusiastic. For all that, it was still not the same atmosphere a full house would produce. I was so fired up with my own importance that I didn't understand there was a difference. For me, it wouldn't have mattered if the place were empty, I would give my all, show whatever it was that I was made of. The powers that be, of course, looked at things differently. Half-empty halls were an abomination, not to be tolerated. At the time I didn't care. I would strut my stuff.

The match was a hum dinger. Stevenson, hated by the crowd, did everything to rouse that hatred, which wasn't difficult. I was a young fresh-faced Irishman in Boston. How could I lose?

It happened at about the twenty-minute mark. I was throwing my heavier opponent across the ring to the screams of encouragement from my public, when the sky seemed to fall right on my head. Just like that, everything went black. I don't remember how or why it happened, but it seemed like a giant hammer drove me to the canvas. The count of two . . . three . . .

four... five... was echoing in my ears when I crawled to the ropes and started pulling myself up. Sweat was running down my body from my forehead. It felt strangely sticky in my eyes. For some reason I couldn't seem to open one of them. The referee was peering into my face, but everything was terribly blurred. I looked around for my opponent but he was a misty figure in the distance, who appeared to be making odd gestures out into the hall. Dimly, I could hear the crowd roaring. It was like a faraway ocean in a wild storm, crashing in thunderous waves. There seemed to be a lot of faces looking up at me, with their mouths open, from just outside the ring. For the life of me I couldn't understand what they were saying. The bell pealed and the announcer's voice, he sounded miles away, shouted above the roar. I wasn't able to figure out where I was, or for that matter, what I was doing there.

"The winner... Ladies and Gentlemen... The match being stopped because of a cut eye... is The Destroyer!"

Cut eye? What cut eye? I still had difficulty understanding what he was talking about, but I vaguely knew it must have something to do with me. My hand went to my head and felt both eyes, first the right one, that was okay, then the left. Something was very wrong. My eyebrow, or just below it, felt weird. My eyelid was not exactly in the right place. It seemed to be hanging down somewhat. I focussed on the hand that had felt my eyes. It was covered in a thick red fluid. Blood. But surely it couldn't be mine. I didn't feel any pain, just a numbness above my left eye. I was also becoming aware of a numbness in my jaw, on the right side, but I didn't relate one to the other.

Above the tumult a voice shouted, "The stretcher is here! Come on Paddy. Lay down here. We'll take you out!" My protests were stopped by the referee who said, "Pat, that eye is bad! You're going to need a lot of stitches. We'll get you out of here quicker."

I kept thinking where am I? What town? I couldn't remember how I got to wherever I was that night. I knew I wanted to get

134

back to the dressing room and see what damage had been done. I climbed onto the stretcher and was carried to the back of the hall, toward the dressing rooms.

Suddenly everything stopped. The mob had closed ranks in front of my stretcher bearer and we could go no further. The incredible press of people was unbelievable. Everyone in the place wanted to get close, to get a look at the fallen, bloodied Irishman.

The face of an old woman came into view. She must have had the strength and stamina of a war horse to have fought her way to my side through this mob. She stared at my crimson drenched body, then at my face, which was a mask of thick congealing blood. Laying there helplessly staring up at this old woman, I waited for the sympathetic touch of her hand, and the kindly word from my angel of mercy, who had risked life and limb to be by my side in my hour of need. With a movement so fast, it belied her age, she thrust out a scrawny hand, scooped up a handful of the thick gummy substance that was on my cheek, then to my amazement, stuck her fingers, substance and all, into her nearly toothless mouth. The whole world stopped for what seemed like an eternity, while I stared in total fascination at this old hag bent over me, with her red dripping fingers in her mouth, like one of those witches in MacBeth foretelling doom. Then she scooped up another handful of blood from my body.

"God!" She said in a shriek heard above the uproar. "God! I can't believe it!" Still holding her bloodied hand over her head. "It's real blood! I swear it's real!" She swung around waving her fingers for all to see.

A terrible rage welled up inside of me. At that moment I could easily have wrung her scrawny neck. As if in a dream, I felt my hands reaching for her. Fortunately my stretcher lurched forward and she was lost in the crowd.

My trip to the hospital followed so quickly, they must've had an ambulance waiting, which is unusual at wrestling matches. I wondered about that later. They carried me into the accident room, from there into a small operating theater, where I was left, still in my wrestling trunks. How long I was there, I can't remember, but it appeared forever before the white-coated figure of a doctor arrived.

"Well," He said. "And what have we here?"

I choked back a caustic reply. What did it look like he had there? Mother Goose? The joy that flooded over me at seeing help quickly vanished. I knew by now, all I wanted to know about doctors. Hadn't I met enough of them in my career? But I was assuredly in no position to be a smart ass right then.

"A wrestler, eh?" He said, looking at a chart in his hand. "Had a bit of an accident?" He asked with a slight sneer, or maybe I was overly sensitive right then, but somehow he didn't come across as any Dr. Kildare.

I still said nothing. I could sense this was going to be a long night. By now it must've been after midnight, and I was stiff from lying on the table where they had placed me. I felt like I had a giant pounding hangover. I was getting cold, the blood and sweat had dried on my skin.

"Nurse! Bring our patient a mirror and let him get a look at the damage he's done!"

I couldn't believe what I saw. My face was a crimson mask with lumps of congealed blood matting my hair. One eye seemed to be higher on my face than the other. Then I realized why. A long gash was running across the top of my eyelid, causing it to droop. This gave me the appearance of Charles Laughton in the "Hunchback of Notre Dame". Gone was the clean-cut, fresh-faced Irishman. Staring back at me was something out of a horror movie.

"Then clean him up so I can get a look at his eye, it seems a bit nasty."

The nurse was a very matter-of-fact, no-nonsense type, as are so many when on duty. My observation has been that nurses, airline hostesses, teachers, and prison wardens are all the same type. They want to control people. Their attitude generally is

136

don't talk, don't move, don't make waves, and don't make the place untidy.

My head by this time was throbbing. The doctor came back to get a second look.

"Ah," He said. "You certainly did yourself some mischief with that eye." I wished he didn't keep referring to what I did to myself. "It's going to need some stitching. Let's see now... How many would do?"

While he was talking I got the impression that I was a piece of inanimate beef about to be dissected and no answers were expected.

Finally he straightened up. "Well," He said. "Pat, is it?" I nodded.

"You've got a pretty bad gash there that's going to take a lot of sutures. It's a tricky one... Going to take a lot of expertise if we are to preserve your good looks!" This was the first time he sounded a bit human. "You don't want to end up with a permanent squint!"

Now, in all of my life, I've never met anyone who wanted a permanent squint. Why should I be any different?

"Look Doctor, do whatever you think is necessary to sew me up, but would you please get on with it?" The moment I said that I could've bitten off my tongue. I was in a very vulnerable position to speak to anyone like that, especially to the man who had the power to give me a permanent squint!

"Right!" He said briskly. "Let's get on with this right now. Nurse, get me the equipment I need." Then peering at my eye again, he said the words that told me he hadn't missed the command I'd given him, nor the edge in my voice. My feeling was that I was about to pay for that.

"Don't bother with an anesthetic, nurse. It won't be necessary. We have a very tough wrestler here, I'm sure he won't mind a little pain. He's used to it, right?" They looked at each other the same way people do who are enjoying an inside joke at someone else's expense.

EVERYBODY DOWN HERE HATES ME

I was on the horns of a dilemma. He knew it, so did I. Obviously it was a game that bastard enjoyed playing. It took forever while he worked on my face, a very painful forever, while he kept a running commentary and conversation about wrestling, travel, all kinds of topics. I guessed he was trying to keep my mind off of what he was doing, but I still felt the pain. By now the wound was cold. The adrenaline had subsided, or done whatever adrenaline does after it's of no further use by the body.

Finally the job was finished. He stood back with a critical eye to examine his handiwork. The nurse stood beside him.

"Beautiful... Beautiful!" He murmured. Modesty was not his strong point, that's for sure. "Nurse, bring Mr. Barrett the mirror, let him see how he looks now." The doctor looked from me back to her. "Hurry! I want him to see how nice I've been to him."

I was definitely interested in seeing how my face looked. In my mind's eye I could picture a big jagged scar running above my eye, looking very sinister. I was pleasantly surprised. He may have been an asshole by temperament, but he was a main-eventer as far as the stitching goes. The job was beautiful, the stitches small, neat, and close together. It was impressive, especially as I've seen sutures done all over the world, by a variety of doctors, on a variety of people, and on various parts of the body, but none as good as this.

"Well, Pat, have I done a good job, or not?" He was standing there with his hands washed and stuck in the pockets of his white coat. The Beast (I'd named the nurse for myself) was standing in her customary behind-his-shoulder position, stone-faced as ever.

"Doctor," I said gratefully. "You're an artist."

"Well now," He said. "I got my practice suturing from your fellow countrymen. I've honed my skills on many a thick Irish head, not to mention other parts."

"How's that?" I asked. I was feeling much perkier now, after looking at the job he'd done. I'd forgotten the pain and agony for a while. My mind started calculating how soon I could get back in the ring again... A couple of days, providing they were small towns that didn't have a commission, or worse still, a commission doctor. In the big cities the Boxing and Wrestling Commission insisted on a doctor being in attendance, but in the smaller towns the promoters could get by without one.

"Weekends, when your Irish friends here in Boston..." He made it sound like I knew them all personally. "...Get to drinking, the fighting starts. That's when I got my practice." Now he was all business again. "I don't like that crack in the head you got." He said, as if to say maybe I did. "So I'd like to do a couple of tests. It must have been some blow... to do that kind of damage, especially on a hard-headed Irishman!" It was difficult to know if he was joking or not, whether he really felt that way about the Irish. He was not trying to be my favorite person. I've never had the awe that most people have for doctors. To me, they do a job for money. Some do it well, others do it better, and some are hopeless just like any other profession. But I never got the feeling that just because they were fixing my wounds or ailments, that it gave them license to treat me like crap. I've seen many that should've been wrestling instead of doctoring.

One commission doctor that comes to mind was taking the heart beat of various wrestlers on the card. He was listening to mine when another wrestler crept up behind and started tapping on my back with his finger. The doc almost jumped out of his skin!

"What's wrong?" I asked.

"You've got a double heart beat. That's what wrong. I've never heard anything like this before!"

"Is it bad?" I asked innocently.

"Bad?" He said. "You can't wrestle with that! You'll have to go straight to the hospital for tests."

The joke had gotten out of control as far as I was concerned, in fact it was backfiring.

"Look," I said. "It's just a joke." I realized he must've known what was going on all along, and was now turning the tables on us.

"What do you mean it was just a joke?" He wasn't smiling. What made me nervous was he had the power to stop my wrestling that night, and a lot of other nights as well, permanently if he so desired. Right then it looked like he did so desire.

I explained what we'd done. The other wrestler had, by now, made himself scarce.

"I don't believe you." He said. "I'm not letting you wrestle tonight, and that's that." Here comes the big crunch. "You won't wrestle again until you prove to my satisfaction that you are fit!"

"Don't move Doc!" I screamed, my face only inches from his. "Just stay there, I'll be back in a minute." I rushed out of the dressing room into several others, panic in my heart. He just didn't look like he was bluffing. Finally I found the other man involved and dragged him back to my room.

The doctor was talking earnestly to the booker. A booker is the man a promoter uses to match wrestlers against each other, then he makes a booking date for the men, hence the name "Booker." And, of course, he had the power to cancel my matches. Tonight he was looking more unhappy than usual. They both looked up when we arrived back.

"What's going on Barrett?" Asked the booker. "The doctor tells me you have a medical problem and you can't wrestle tonight. Is this right? Why didn't you tell me?" His voice was all ice.

"NO!" I shouted. "It was just a bit of fun. Look, I'll show you what happened." Turning to the other wrestler I demanded, "Show him what you did!" The wrestler kept a poker face.

"I've forgotten what you wanted, Pat. Tell me again."

My face must have been a study. I could feel my blood pressure rising until it would blow the top of my head off. Now I really would have a medical problem!

"Listen Fuckwit, if you don't stop screwing me about, and

140

he stops me working, I'll kick the shit out of you right here and now. Understand?''

Now I don't know whether I could've kicked the shit out of him or not, but at that moment my fury was such I would've attacked King Kong himself!

"Okay, okay!" He said. "Here's what I did. . .'' Tapping me on the back.

"Get your stethoscope and listen!" I ordered the doctor, half frantic with worry. I knew that once my name got on the commissioner's bureaucratic list of unfit wrestlers, it would take a stick of dynamite to get it off. Reluctantly he put it to my chest, listened briefly, then looking me in the eye, said two words.

"Fuck you!" Then stuffed the scope in his pocket and left the room.

I was shocked. Who would expect a doctor to talk to a potential patient like that? The booker gave us both a cold look then hurried after him. The room erupted into laughter, myself included. Everyone was laughing at how the good doctor could be taken in. Me, I was laughing with relief. I realized how close I had come to the worst thing that could happen to a wrestler, outside of death, namely being out of work. My faith in doctors diminished after that even further.

The tests the Boston surgeon wanted consisted of simple multiplication, repeating various words that the doctor thought of, then counting from one hundred backwards, quickly. I asked what this was all about.

"You've taken such a crack on the head that I'm afraid there might be damage to the brain or internal hemorrhaging."

I laughed at the idea, but he cut me off.

"It's no joke, put that idea out of your head! I'm afraid you might have had a bad concussion, not just from whatever you were hit with, but I noticed you have a slight lump on the back of your skull. . . most likely from where you hit the ground. What I'd like to do is keep you for a few days for observation. How do you feel about a spinal tap?"

EVERYBODY DOWN HERE HATES ME

"Listen Doctor, I don't mind staying overnight, but I'm not staying any longer, so you can forget that. You've done a great job on the eyebrow. I really feel terrific, but a little rest would be nice."

"If I don't persuade you to stay for the observation, what about the spinal tap? It would give me a better idea what's going on in there." He said, tapping me lightly on the back of the head.

"Sure." I said. "You can do that. What's a few taps on the spine to a wrestler who had taken kicks in the back for years?"

I noticed he looked a little puzzled at my answer, but then he was all business again.

"Nurse!" He said to the battle ax, who always seemed to be at attention. She definitely looked like a full-blooded Viking warrior, with breasts.

She made me take off my wrestling trunks and boots, gave me a fast no-nonsense wash, then got me sitting up on the table with my knees drawn up and my head bent over them, hugging my legs with my arms. I couldn't understand why all the preparation just for a few taps on the spine with a rubber mallet. I imagined it would be something like what the doctor gives your knee when he wants to test your reflexes in your leg. The position was quite comfortable, even though my back was bent over like a hoop. I could hear all kinds of clinking going on behind me, but I didn't pay much attention. Great lethargy was now taking hold of me after the long and eventful day.

My mind had drifted to the fact that no one from the office had come to see what was happening. I didn't expect sympathy, but I could've died for all the attention I was getting from them. If nothing else, I was to learn something very important that night. Never let a doctor, or anyone else for that matter, put me in a position of weakness or vulnerability, without the full knowledge of the ramifications of what was going to happen.

My eyes were closed. I was just on the threshold of that lovely state of mind where one is poised between sleep and some strange world, aware that everything going on is miles away, and doesn't affect one at all. I love that feeling, and try when I achieve it, to hang on as long as possible before sleep claims me.

Suddenly I was attacked from behind, at my lower back, by an alien with a laser beam so hot it froze my whole being. I couldn't make a sound, the pain was so excruciating. I hadn't expected what was happening. My God, I was in a hospital but had the doctor gone mad?! Was he trying to butcher me? Gritting my teeth, I could feel my lips pull back in an animal snarl.

"God damn! God Dammit! What the fuck are you doing?!" I tried to curtail my bad language. My feeling is that the overuse of it shows a limited vocabulary, but right then it was all I could say.

Dimly I became aware of hysterical sobbing that appeared to be coming from someone nearby. This couldn't be from me, unless I'd become a ventriloquist. I could distantly hear myself cursing and swearing, but this was definitely sobbing, and furthermore it was female.

Slowly twisting my head I saw a sight never expected in my wildest dreams. The Viking nurse was leaping and hopping around on one leg, throwing punches at my shoulder. My first thought was she had gone mad. Why, I couldn't understand. Then slowly all became clear.

As the mist of pain cleared, I realized that in my anguish, when the hypodermic had entered the spine, or wherever it goes in a spinal tap, when the pain had hit, I had reacted blindly at whatever was causing my agony. My hand had hit the warm flesh and had gotten a death grip on the inside of the victim's ample thigh, right above the white stockings she was wearing. If it had been another time and place I might've appreciated the sight of two full-bodied legs enclosed in white stockings, held up by a garter belt. In this case all I instinctively wanted was to inflict as much pain as possible on whoever was torturing me, just as an injured wolf bites at his tormentors.

As quickly as it started the pain stopped. I released the nurse's leg. I watched as she stumbled around the room sobbing and holding her injured leg while the doctor followed, trying to console her. What could I say that would make her feel any better? Anyway, I wasn't feeling too friendly myself to anyone right then.

She left the room a few minutes later. I never saw her again, but I bet the next spinal tap she attended she stood a respectable distance from the patient.

The problem for me had arisen out of my misunderstanding of what the doctor wanted to do. In Ireland we don't call the procedure of withdrawing fluid from the spine, a spinal tap. The name used is a lumbar puncture. Had he mentioned that, I would have known the danger involved. The blow on the head must have dulled my wits somewhat.

I stayed overnight. In the morning a couple of Australian wrestlers brought my clothes, which had been left in the dressing room. The hospital asked who they should send the bill to. I gave them the New York office address.

After I got back to my hotel I gave a lot of thought to what had happened, and more importantly, why. It was the beginning of my understanding of the machinations of the wrestling business.

Two weeks later I got Stevenson alone in a dressing room. He was sitting with his back to the door when I came up behind him with my shillelagh in my hand. The shillelagh, for those who are not Irish, is a knotty wooden club made from the Blackthorn tree. It's very tough and hard, not something the average person wants to be hit with!

Tapping him gently on the side of the head I told him not to stand up, not to even move. He was visibly shaken at the position he was in. I should never have been able to get that close to him without his seeing me. He swore that he hadn't used a knuckle-duster, brass knuckles, or anything but his fist to give me a fourteen-stitch cut over my eye. Then tapping him not so gently again, I told him that if or when we wrestle again, we would wrestle. As I talked to him I kept getting madder and madder as I remembered the pain and agony the man had put me through. It was only the voice of one of the wrestlers telling me to take it easy that brought back my sanity. Seemingly I was tapping him harder on the head all the time, as if to emphasize my point. I told Stevenson the name of the game is wrestling, and if he resorted to punching me with brass knucks again, I would bury the shillelagh in his head, and he wouldn't even see it coming, just as he hadn't seen me this time.

A few weeks later, we were back in Boston in a tag match. He had a partner and so had I. The place was packed to the rafters with blood-thirsty fans. All of them looking for a repeat performance on someone — I don't think they were particular on whom. Yes, the old wrestling adage "All that's red turns to green" was proved true once again.

14

THE JOKER'S WILD

The wrestling business isn't all grim. I wouldn't want anyone to believe it is. A lot of wrestlers have a comic side to them and are great practical jokers. But sometimes the jokes get out of hand, people can and do get badly injured.

Joey Heart, one of the greats on the American pro scene, poured gasoline into Jake "The Lumberjack" West's inhaler during a match. Jake had severe asthma, which was worse after a match. One night West rushed into the dressing room, his lungs screaming for air. Grabbing up his inhaler, he gave himself a big blast in the mouth. His face turned purple. He almost died as the fumes took hold of his already-tortured lungs. West didn't see the funny side of things and vowed vengeance. A few weeks later, he went to the hall where Heart was wrestling. He told the security cop outside if he heard any loud bangs not to worry, because he had some cherry bombs and wanted to pull a joke on one of the boys. What he had, in fact, was a loaded double-barreled shotgun, which he pulled on Heart. Now Heart had a lot of balls, and was not easily frightened. He didn't believe West meant business. He just laughed and turned his back, calling West's bluff. He couldn't comprehend that the Lumberjack would seriously try to kill him. To prove that he was serious, the infuriated Lumberjack turned the barrels on Heart's wrestling bag, which was sitting on a table in the middle of the room. Slowly and carefully he pulled the trigger and blew the bag to pieces. There were wrestlers hurtling all over the place to get out of the line of fire. I was told the sound and effect of just one barrel going off was deafening. Heart, who was all attention now, crept to the door, white as a sheet. This probably saved his life. West told me later while we were in a show together in Las Vegas, that it was the sight of fear on Heart's face that stopped him from pulling the other trigger. The bag, I'm told, was more valuable than just the average, with socks and trunks in it. Seemingly some of the wrestlers had put their valuables, watches, rings, etc. into it for safe-keeping during the matches. The reason they chose this particular bag was it had a lock on it. As you can imagine, there wasn't too much left. Whatever remained was scattered all over the dressing room.

* * * * * * * * * * *

Slasher Carloni was a natural prankster who would do anything for a bet. While working in New York, he went into a restaurant with his arms pushed down into his pants, the empty sleeves of his overcoat tucked into the pockets. While sitting there, looking very forlorn as only he could, a waitress approached him. He told her he was waiting for somebody. The waitress later approached him because he was still alone and hadn't ordered. He said he would like some food, but because he had no arms he had to be fed. He couldn't understand why his friend was late, but he was sure he would arrive. That was why he was waiting. The soft-hearted waitress fell for his story and offered to feed him. After much cajoling, he allowed himself to be swayed. Carloni was more than happy to let her, but she didn't know this. He was a consummate actor. The boss came over to see what was happening, as it wasn't every day one of his staff started feeding the customers. When he saw the state Slasher was in with no arms, he was very sympathetic. He was also curious. How did Carloni lose his arms, or was he born that way? This was all that Slasher wanted. He started on his heroic tale of how he'd lost his arms in Korea, leading his platoon in a desperate charge against hordes of Chinese that were encircling his men, about to wipe them out. He was a gifted story teller, his listeners were spellbound, the waitress was occasionally at the point of tears.

After an excellent meal, fed lovingly, forkful by forkful, it came time to pay. He told them to get his wallet out of his pocket. The boss wouldn't hear of it, in fact he was offended, and insisted on giving Slasher the meal with his compliments. "Any man who would give his arms for his country, saving his men from certain death by knocking out so many machine gun nests will not pay in my restaurant." Nothing was too much trouble. What was a lousy meal to a man who'd done so much for his people? There were tears in Slasher's eyes as he thanked everybody all around.

Carloni's ride to the matches had arrived. He climbed into the automobile with difficulty, the boss opening the door for him, even getting a kiss from the waitress. The other wrestlers in the car, used to his crazy pranks, didn't bat an eye.

If he'd left at that point everything might have been all right. They would have been happy in their ignorance. Slasher being Slasher, he had to do the job all the way. A joke was not a joke unless the recipient understood what was happening. As the car drove from the curb, Carloni had the driver stop for a moment. He then leaned out of the window and waved good-bye. The boss' mouth dropped open, rage written all over his face. He charged at the car screaming obscenities, not caring how many large men were in it. The driver hit the accelerator and roared away, leaving the unfortunate proprietor shaking his fist and jumping up and down. It was a horrible joke, but then wrestlers have a very basic sense of humor, if not downright cruel. God help any unfortunate amputee that went into that restaurant after Carloni. I can imagine the treatment they would get!

15

ON WITH THE SHOW!

My first look at Frederick Apcar was outside the dressing room at the Coliseum in Las Vegas. He was wearing an expensive tailored leather jacket when he approached me with the line, "My name is Frederick Apcar. I want you to be in my show." Looking him over, all I could think of was here comes another fag, only this one has a French accent. I wonder is it real or just a cute gimmick?

My match was finished. I was heading for the showers when he stopped me by stepping in my path and waving his card under my nose. Although he was not pushy, he was insistent. He wanted me in his new "Casino de Paris", which was opening in about six weeks. Would I like to be a gladiator in it? Definitely this sounded like a come-on, an original one I must admit. In my career as a wrestler, I've had many passes made by homosexuals. Never have I wanted to punch, kick, or beat them up. They have their way and I have mine, besides females have always been my passion.

Apcar, to me, was a perfect gentleman while he tried to explain to me, whose mind was on a cute little fan that was making eyes in my direction, what his show was all about.

Dimly I remember saying something like "Yes, okay. If I change my mind, I'll call you."

EVERYBODY DOWN HERE HATES ME

He pressed his card in my hand and told me to call collect. That I never forgot, it was so rare in the wrestling business.

A couple of weeks went by. I never gave him or his talk of a show a second thought. I was in a dressing room in California when I overheard a conversation that made me sit up and take notice. Seemingly Jake West, (formerly known as The Lumberjack) had flown to Las Vegas to do a job in the Dunes Hotel. He was a gladiator or something like that. The conversation was disjointed. Everything was vague. Suddenly I remembered the whole conversation I had that night I was in Las Vegas. It all came flooding back. Maybe Apcar was genuine after all and not just a fag on the make. Hopefully I hadn't thrown the card away. When my match finished, I showered as fast as I could and raced for home.

Shortly after I was on a plane to the most famous gambling town in the world, not knowing what to expect, but always ready for adventure.

I was met at the airport by a limo, whisked to the Dunes Hotel and Apcar's office. I was given the V.I.P. treatment by everyone I met, the chauffeur, and numerous secretaries. It was heady stuff. Apcar was charming as only a Frenchman can be, except this time he was very business-like as well. When I heard the proposition, excitement built up inside of me, but I tried not to show it. It was time to bargain. I found out right away that inside that velvet exterior was a tough cookie. Would he pay more than was already offered? Sorry, that was impossible. We went back and forth on this, but he was adamant. The show was on a tight budget. Much as he would like to, it was impossible. It was then that I started to realize why Apcar was in the position he was, producer of one of the most famous shows in the world. I was discovering that he was turning out to be a very canny businessman, and not at all soft as I first thought. Then I saw a photo of his family, wrong on two counts.

We agreed on the terms. I was in along with two other wrestlers, Jake West and Robert Duranton. Did I know the latter?

Yes, I'd met him in England a couple of years ago. Apcar explained that he and Robert had grown up together in France, and had been very good friends.

Duranton was one of a kind. From the French body-building point of view, he had been close to perfection before he took up wrestling. Picture wide shoulders, great legs, not a deep chest but adequate, a very strong-looking muscular neck, a handsome face crowned with a mane of hair, and completely crazy. His ego more than matched his physique. Charles deGaulle could've learned a thing or two from him. I was a Pygmy ego-wise in comparison. Little did I know then how it would eventually bring about the end of the show for us.

Jake West was completely different, tall and cadaverous, especially by wrestling standards. He'd once weighed about three hundred pounds and looked terrific at that weight calling himself "The Lumberjack." His appetite for drugs and young girls was stupendous. He once told me if a promoter gave him enough money to live on, and supplied him with girls, he'd work for nothing else. It's also said he kept an arsenal of weapons around him. While wrestling in the Midwest, he would drive down the back roads lobbing grenades into farmers' front yards just for kicks. But, as I said, he was now a shadow of his former self due to drugs, girls, and a lack of eating.

Frederick Apcar must've been crazy to have put this volatile mixture into his show, but then I suppose this is what made him a great producer. He took calculated risks. He is recognized as one of the greatest in show business. I think perhaps in this case he'd made a mistake, the risk not calculated enough.

We'd started rehearsals for our fight scene, which lasted about sixty seconds. The whole show ran a couple of hours of non-stop action. Apcar convinced us that though we'd been hired to do a fight scene only, we would enjoy doing other things as well. One must appreciate the genius of this man. He convinced three cynical wrestlers to take on other things that were not in our contract. He had us do acts that were completely alien to

151

our nature. For example, he had us dancing with men who were dressed up as women. We were also in a car chase scene. Only two of us worked every night. So long as two showed up, any two, it didn't matter, the bosses were happy. I didn't realize, for a long time, the jealousy we incurred. We were the envy of everyone in the show. Everybody else worked seven days of the week, with no respite. Dancers were particularly overworked, underpaid, and abused. They had so many people over them who could fire them, or get them fired at a moment's notice, it's a wonder they had any self-esteem at all.

The car was a wooden affair that was on stage atop very tiny heavy wheels. It was positioned in such a way that it appeared to the audience to be in the middle of a road. The background was projected on to a screen in front of us. Every night two wrestlers would climb into it and maneuver it across the stage, trying to keep it lined up with the road which was moving at high speed. I remember the first time in the vehicle I almost got car sick. I just looked at the screen and thought to myself, I'll never be able to do this. Jake, who was very tall, would sit cursing the people in the show, as he tried to get his large frame to pilot this very low car in cooperation with Duranton or myself. The car itself was quite heavy with small iron wheels, very low slung, like a sporty MG convertible. When we started learning to move it into place, Jake's big feet were constantly getting under the wheels. The cursing would be directed at whoever his partner was at the time, the Frenchman or myself. We both thought this was great fun and went out of our way to make sure the wheels did run over his feet.

I had decided I wanted to be in this show very much, enjoying the different things I was seeing and doing. Not so for Duranton, who seemed to hate the whole thing from the beginning. I couldn't understand why. It was only when he was leaving that he passionately explained to me how he felt.

"In this show I am nothing!" He shouted in a fit of frustration. "I am a piece of shit in a shit pile! Nobody recognizes me! In

France,'' He said drawing himself up to his full height, his thick French accent becoming thicker, "I am somebody. When I walk down the street, people stop and point, 'That's Duranton, the famous wrestler!' But here I am just garbage!''

There was no use pointing out to him that there were good sides to the show. No long distance driving every night. No injuries. No worrying if the people were coming to see you, or if the house was full or empty. We had a consistent paycheck coming in. No fans trying to kill us or smash up our cars. No calls to wives from female fans at midnight, telling of rendezvous' that might never have happened. This was a nice break for two years. All these things meant nothing to him. At the end of a year, he left for France. If Apcar had socialized with him more, perhaps he might've stayed. As Duranton left, the show folded for us as well. The Dunes could or would not hire someone to take his place. Hotel officials maintained it was too expensive to pay everyone for the rehearsals that would have to be done. I didn't want to face working seven nights a week with Jake West, and to give the devil his due, I'm sure he felt the same about me. Wrestlers do not make good companions to each other. The end result was we all left. Sometimes I believe the Dunes heaved a sigh of relief. Though they are used to temperamental people, I don't believe they ever experienced anything like us!

A third man was involved in the car scene, who was one of the stars of the show. Physically, he was a small man, but he made up for his lack of stature with his Napoleonic ego. In this scene he was an escaped prisoner who would climb down a prison wall, then rush and jump into the back of our open car. One of us was supposed to catch his outstretched hand as he launched himself through the air. When the wheels would run over Jake's feet, he would become so incensed that he would completely ignore our unfortunate third man, who would still heave himself enthusiastically at the vehicle. The end result was the poor bastard would fall flat on his face. The audience thought this was all part of the show. I think they enjoyed it. From the star, all you got was weeping and gnashing of teeth. I believe if he'd been bigger and stronger we would have had a fight on our hands, he would become so enraged. Fortunately prudence prevailed.

We managed as the weeks went by, to iron out the difficulties. Jake, who had two left feet, even managed to learn to dance a passable Tango to "Hernando's Hideaway" with the gay dancers. This was also something we'd been conned into. You could always tell the nights when wrestlers were in the audience. At this point there'd be extra loud hoots of male laughter, followed by lewd personal suggestions that could only have come from someone in our business who knew us well. Most times the dancers we were with would just giggle and whisper, "Your wrestling friends are back... They're very naughty!" But there were some that got quite upset, some of the remarks were quite explicit. The scene visiting wrestlers loved the most was the orgy, where we laid around half-naked, surrounded by topless girls caressing our bodies. I don't know what made me do it, but one night when I knew several of the boys were watching the show, I slipped a small vibrator on stage. This was difficult to do as I only had on my gold jock strap, which was my entire costume for this scene to hide it in. I'd been planning it for some time, to give the boys an extra thrill.

While I was laying on a couch one of the show girls would do a slow exotic dance in front of me, then turn her back and sit slowly down at my side. This girl had a beautiful bell-shaped bottom, one of the nicest I've ever seen. It would pass so close to my face I could've stuck out my tongue and licked it. Oh, I would've loved to have done that. I always wondered how she would react if I goosed her. As she sank to the point of no return, I decided to do one better. I slipped the vibrator between her marvelous cheeks. She sank right down on it till it disappeared. I couldn't believe what was happening. There was no response from her... nothing. She seemed oblivious to what I'd done. I decided to go the whole hog. I switched the machine on, my hand now also between her cheeks. For a moment nothing happened, then she exploded upwards like a Polaris missile being launched. A shriek came from her that would wake the dead, and certainly could be heard all over the theater. I hadn't expected her to sit down so far, or to react so vehemently! It went right into her ass, she told me later, almost making her piss. The whole show stopped for the longest second of my life. Everyone, the audience and the people on stage were looking in her direction and mine. Finally, it seemed like a lifetime, things started moving again. I quickly hid the vibrator back in my jock strap. The girl sat down with a shocked look on her face. The audience, thinking it was part of the show, applauded. I could hear the hoots of laughter coming from the wrestlers. They had known, seeing the faces of the company on stage, that it was not a normal occurrence. The girl's face, they told me later, was a sight to behold. Not being able to help myself, I took a quick bow in the wrestlers' direction. This fact was not lost from the stage manager's beady eyes. I could tell by his face he couldn't figure out what had happened. I wasn't about to tell him!

I hurried past him fast as I could, to get rid of the vibrator, pretending I didn't hear when he called my name. Funny enough, he never came near our dressing room at any time, no matter how we screwed up. I believe he thought we were wild animals, and to go into a wild animal's lair was out of the question. The girl never told the management what happened. She said she'd hurt her knee on the way down, and got a reprimand for making such a fuss. She was a real trouper, coming to talk to me about it a couple of shows later. She said she still wasn't sure what I'd done, but it was the weirdest sensation, coming so totally unexpected. When I explained, she had a good laugh. Then she stunned me by wanting to borrow the vibrator to try it on another girl in the show. I put a stop to that idea quickly. I caused enough waves, no need to push my luck.

Dress rehearsal night was all excitement. I'd never seen anything like it before. Back stage the tension was all around me. I was not picked to dress, but Duranton was.

EVERYBODY DOWN HERE HATES ME

The seating was full of all kinds of people, from Apcar, to the bosses of the hotel, to visiting bigwigs from other hotels. I didn't know before that night what a dress rehearsal really was. I'd never given it much thought, not being in contact with this kind of business. Everything so far had gone without a hitch, which in a show that size was incredible. I don't know how much it cost to put on, but it was in the millions.

Now came the part where Duranton was supposed to chase one of the male dancers through a door. The Frenchman was supposed to run on stage through one door, as the dancer would exit through another. For some reason Duranton had trouble figuring out which door was which. I watched with apprehension as the moment came closer. The slightly-built male dancer came shrieking through his door, all dressed up as a prostitute, right on cue, along with five other dancers. There were altogether six exits and six entrances. So far, so good. They stopped for a couple of seconds, supposedly looking for the cops, then rushed to exit out the door beside the one they had entered through. Suddenly my worst fears were realized. The door from which Duranton was supposed to appear remained shut, but the exit door at the rear of the stage burst open, as if by a whirlwind, smashing the unfortunate dancer right across the stage, to land in a screaming, shaking, kicking heap, arms and legs up in the air, the pink dress wrapped around his head.

Like a giant blue Juggernaut, Duranton appeared, with a wild look in his eyes. I could see by the intent look on his face that he'd made up his mind to pick the right door, and to be through on time, but alas it was definitely not to be. There was a stunned silence. You could've heard the proverbial pin drop. Suddenly the dancer burst into tears. I hadn't seen a male cry for a long time. I felt a bit embarrassed.

Out of the audience jumped the choreographer, who was in charge of this part of the show. "You stupid, stupid man!" He screamed at Robert. "Can't you ever get it right?"

Duranton, who'd been looking at the dancer on the floor with

156

consternation, turned in some surprise. He had tried so hard to get it right, this verbal attack shocked him. Then his face changed. I wasn't sure what would come next, but my heart had almost stopped. I knew that look. The Frenchman looked the choreographer up and down slowly, then started unbuckling his belt. "He wouldn't!" One part of my mind said. But the part that knew him well recognized that he didn't give a shit, once enraged he was capable of anything.

I watched with fascination as the scene unfolded. That stage I'm sure had seen many strange and wonderful things, but it would never see anything stranger. He had gotten his zipper open now and was pulling his pants down. The place could've been empty. There was complete and utter silence. Even the choreographer was staring with his mouth open. Duranton's pants were dropped to his ankles, followed by his underpants. Then he did it. Half bent over and reaching back with both his hands, he started to spread the cheeks of his ass open.

Looking backwards, he shouted with his marvelous French accent, "Fuck you! Fuck you! You little queer cocksucker! You know what you can do, Cocksucker? You can kiss my asshole! I am sick of you and the other cocksuckers here, with all the fucking whores who work here as well!"

I looked around. People were stunned. People I'm sure who five minutes before, if you told them that they would be shocked by something that would happen on stage, would've laughed at you.

Suddenly Apcar came alive. He'd been this man's boyhood friend. I believe he had an admiration for his physique and temperament. My suspicion was he was a closet fan. I venture to say the next few minutes would change that forever.

Apcar shouted something in French to his friend. His face had a pleading expression. I don't know what was said, but it made not a bit of difference to the enraged French wrestler, actually it only seemed to infuriate him more.

Duranton turned to face his old friend. "Fuck you too, Apcar!"

157

He shouted. "Fuck you, what have you done for me? Brought me and my wife, who is a saint — not like these whores that show everything to everyone, and fuck anybody — to this place. You have not once invited us to dinner at your house. So fuck you too! I do not need this!"

There was a stunned silence. Duranton had turned full face to the audience. His clothing was still around his ankles. Everyone could see that not only did he have a good body, he'd been runner up in the Mr. France contest, but he was quite well endowed, and the outburst hadn't made anything smaller. By this time I was sunk down in my seat, trying to pretend I had no connection with him. Out of the blackness a voice abruptly cut through the silence from a couple of rows back and boomed out loud and clear, "That's it Duranton baby! That's it! You tell those queer sons of bitches! You don't take any shit from nobody!"

Horror flooded all over me. I'd often heard people say, "I wish the ground would swallow me up." Well, that's how I felt right then. I knew that voice. Jake West was three rows in back of me, leaning back in his seat, big feet on the back of the chair in front of him. To cap it all off, he was puffing away on a joint. I didn't have to be told what it was. I'd seen him roll enough of them, plus the sweet smell of grass was in my nostrils. He's the only person I know that would've had the balls to smoke a joint at that point in time.

What followed was utter chaos. I picked that moment to skulk out, unnoticed. There was no way I was going to be associated with West or Duranton by the show business people. I was expecting a lynching, and I didn't want to be a party to it, if it could be helped. The show went on. Apcar managed to cool Duranton off and led him away. There was a definite chill backstage, for the first couple of weeks. I believe if we had not been in so many different parts of the show, we would have had our contract terminated. By conning us into doing more than the sixty-second fight scene, which could easily have been dropped, the show was stuck with us. It would have cost too much to train new people to do our parts at that point in time. Thankfully, the memories of show people are short. Everything was okay after a while.

To the end of our stay there, I got the feeling we were viewed with suspicion. Wariness would be a better word. Rather like you would view a pet viper that a friend had left with you, after you'd been told it loves people.

16

MONKEY BUSINESS

The shouts and screams were getting louder. I couldn't understand what in the world was going on. In the wrestling business, such noises are common place, but I didn't expect to hear them in the comparatively sane atmosphere of the Dunes hotel.

Striding to the door of my dressing room, I flung it open, not knowing what to expect. The view from the landing outside was panoramic. The dressing room we three wrestlers shared was perched high up behind the scenes giving us a clear view of almost everything that went on backstage. My gaze was drawn to the totally unexpected, violent scene below. Rolling on the ground, thrashing madly and punching at himself, was one of the many stagehands that helped to keep the famous show, "Casino de Paris", moving with military precision. What really intrigued me was that he was surrounded by a variety of people, stagehands, dancers, show girls, artists, dressers, all manner of show business entities, who were trying to hold him with little success. All the weird screaming and grunting was coming from him; intermingled with cursing and swearing that a longshoreman would've been proud of. I was sorely puzzled, recognizing the man on the floor as one of the stagehands by his all-black outfit. It was my belief that they wore strictly black so they couldn't be mistaken for anyone else, especially the homosexual male dancers who were in the show. Maybe I was imagining it, but stagehands went out of their way to be what can only be described as extremely macho. They walked around backstage with a distinct gait, like so many peacocks strutting their stuff, or the cowboys one sees in the old movies. Their cold steely look telling the whole world that they are men to be reckoned with. This particular hand, for I recognized him now, was one of the more truculent types. I had seen him throw his weight around a couple of times. He looked like a cross between John Wayne and Jack Palance. What puzzled me was that he was the last person I would have expected to go crazy, or even show signs of being unstable. Belligerent, yes, but crazy, no. Yet here he was frothing at the mouth, eyes wide and staring, rolling around trying it appeared to do mischief to himself. In the meantime the crowd had grown. But what struck me as strange were the actions of some of them, especially the ones close to him. They were making what appeared to be frantic grabs at his body, then jerking their hands back as if they had been burned.

I started to think that maybe he was having a fit of some sort. I hadn't seen that type of thing since I was a child, and even then I couldn't remember it clearly. But from what I could recall, it was a similar kind of situation, with the man on the ground thrashing around in a frenzy. Leaning over the bannister, I watched the whole proceeding with interest. I couldn't say I was sorry it was happening to this particular stagehand. I had had a run-in with him while I was waiting to go on stage one night. His name was Jeff, and he considered himself to be pretty tough.

The night our animosity started I was standing in the wings when I felt a sudden movement behind my back that shouldn't have been there. My instinct for self-preservation is very acute, so I jumped forward and whirled to meet whatever the threat was. It was Jeff practicing his karate punches, and the sudden movement I felt was a punch he had thrown at the back of my head. I knew, or at least believed, he had no intention of hitting me, but it was his off-hand attitude that did not endear him to me.

"Scare you, Paddy?" He asked, with a sarcastic smile. "How come a big tough wrestler like you scares so easily?"

This coming from a lot of other people wouldn't have bothered me, but his manner raised my hackles instantly. Then to add insult to injury he said, "Just as well, I don't really mean business! You'd be so easy to deck, it would be a sin!"

Madness welled up inside of me. My heart was beating fast. I wanted to smash him, but at that moment my call came to go on stage. I was so mad I couldn't even talk, but rushed on to do my tango with a male dancer. I knew in my heart of hearts I was overreacting, but he had that effect on me.

If anyone had suggested a year before that I would be dancing with a male, let alone with one in front of an audience, I would've told them they were crazy. Yet here I was, a pro wrestler, rushing away from a confrontation with a man, straight into the arms of another — so I could dance with him. My world had definitely turned upside down.

My duties during this part of the show were to dress up as a policeman in the old-style uniform and dance "Hernando's Hideaway" with a male dancer dressed up as a prostitute. Even under normal conditions, it was tough for the partner who had to dance with whichever wrestlers worked that night. We were not the smartest movers in the world when it came to dancing. It was something we never really got used to — male dance partners, and dancing a dance like a tango where a partner had to be held close at times. That night my mind wasn't on my work. I was still rankling at Mr. Macho, and it must've been apparent to my dance partner. During the dance, he would spin under my arm which was raised high, while he held my hand. Then we would come together in a close embrace for a number of steps, cheek to cheek. This always brought howls of laughter from the audience. I never figured out if they just enjoyed the scene of men dancing with each other, or whether our obvious clumsiness compared to the grace of the male dancers made it funnier.

As my partner spun under my arm, he squeezed my fingers in a vice-like grip, I supposed to get my attention. Or maybe he was a sadist? But for whatever reason he did it, he definitely got my attention. Spinning around to face me, still squeezing my fingers which were trapped by his, he kissed my ear.

"Come on big boy, pay attention, and don't forget to hold me real tight, love." He couldn't have picked a worse night to do this. This was the straw that broke the camel's back. All my pent-up frustrations at the stagehand burst forth. Pulling my hand violently out of his grip, I reached around the dancer with both arms, just under his short ribs, locked my hands, and squeezed hard and fast.

"Is this tight enough, love?" I hissed back into his ear, but I don't think he ever heard me. His eyes were bulging, his mouth was open wide in a soundless scream, with his hands clawing at my arms. Before I relaxed my grip, he suddenly found his voice, which came out in a high-pitched shriek that shocked me back to my senses. I was aware of all the dancers' heads jerking around in my direction, but I must say they were all troupers. They never even broke stride, even though my partner was screaming like a stuck pig. Then I relaxed my hold which gave him the chance to tear himself away from my clutches. Shrieking and sobbing he tore off stage, leaving me dancing on my own. The old maxim of the show must go on came to me, so I whirled by myself in unison with the other couples until the end of the dance.

Before I was finished on stage, remorse took hold of me. I felt I shouldn't have vented my spleen on the poor man, even though he hurt my fingers, maybe he was trying to get my attention. Then my vindictive side questioned his right to hurt me, whatever the reason. If he wanted my attention, there were other options.

When the curtain came down to thunderous applause, I was sure the public had no idea that what had happened wasn't part of the show.

I charged off stage looking for the stagehand to have a show down, but he'd disappeared. The stage manager tried to talk to me, obviously wanting to ask questions about the incident, but I brushed him aside and went back to the dressing room. About fifteen minutes later I was feeling very relaxed, when there was a knock at the door. Duranton was reading a French newspaper in one corner when Bruno, the head male dancer, entered to complain about my conduct with one of his men. By that time I'd simmered down completely and would've been more than happy to apologize. Unfortunately for Bruno his next scene in the show was as Caesar, and he was dressed for the part, from the laurel wreath on his head to the toga wrapped around his body. To make matters worse, he was Italian, and looked the part of a Caesar to a tee. When he started to demand an apology, it was too much for Duranton, who started laughing.

"Look at heem, Pat!" He said. "Not only does he dress like Caesar, but he's beginning to believe in the bullsheeet!" Bruno, who was straight as a die, and didn't really deserve the treatment, tried to retain his dignity. By now Duranton and I couldn't help ourselves, and we were laughing so hard we couldn't hear a word he was saying. As he became agitated, his English got worse. He started shouting in broken Italian. Between the broken French, the broken Italian, and the hysterical laughter, the unfortunate man forgot everything he wanted to say. He collected what dignity he had left and departed, not getting any satisfaction from me.

All of this came back while I watched Jeff rolling and screaming on the floor. My unforgiving Irish nature was glad to see him in that position, but I was still intrigued at what was wrong.

Suddenly, from under his arm, a small devilish red face appeared, snapping and biting like crazy. It looked like something from out of a nightmare. From its lips the screams were pouring forth, adding to the madness of the situation. Jeff definitely wasn't

164

having convulsions, but perhaps it would've been better if he had. What was giving him fits was a young orangutan. I'd recognized who the owner of the little red face was. But why were they in conflict? This particular orangutan was only a baby, and a lovable one at that. Everyone in the show found it irresistible with its ugly little face, big eyes, and gentle manner. It was hard to imagine that this was the same animal. It had to be, there was only one that size in the show.

When Jeff rolled over I got a view of the situation. The baby had him grasped firmly with both its arms and legs, while Jeff was desperately trying to hold its head away from his body. Jeff was punching its head, when he could, with his other hand. Strangely enough the punching seemed to have no effect, which surprised me. This was a big, fit, strong man used to karate. Finally sheer weight of numbers overwhelmed the fighting orangutan. But it was game to the end and didn't go easily. It took five men to pull the infuriated little animal off, and take it away squirming and screaming. I found out later what had happened.

Every night, twice a night in fact, the little orangutan would be held by a stagehand at the stage door, waiting for its turn to go on. People passing by would pet the adorable little creature. If it really liked you, it would give you a special big hug and a kiss. That night it was Jeff's turn to hold it, but for some reason it didn't want to go on stage. The girl who handled it in the show also had to handle two baby gorillas, plus a large female orangutan. Grabbing it in the usual manner, she tried to pull it from Jeff's arms, but it refused to let go. She pulled harder, but it only hardened the animal's resolve to stay put. The girl lost her patience and panicked. She should've already been on her way with the animals. She could hear her cue music, so she shouted at Jeff to give her the damn animal. He tried to tear it away from his body, but to his surprise he had no success. The creature clung to him like a limpet. Then he lost his temper and made the mistake of slapping it. That's when all hell broke loose.

EVERYBODY DOWN HERE HATES ME

The placid baby went berserk and tried to bite his face, while emitting high-pitched screams. From there it was all downhill for the stagehand with this little demon trying to bite anywhere and everywhere.

It was two weeks before I saw Jeff again, but he was not the same man. His right hand was in a cast, broken on the head of the orangutan. But it was more than his hand, his spirit was crushed. The dancers, especially the male ones, teased him unmercifully about trying to have it off with animals, especially ugly, unwilling ones. As for me, for once I was kind, particularly since I had enjoyed watching the fight, but I wanted to know what happened to the karate. This, for some reason, upset him very much. From that day on, he never spoke to me. All I can say is he was a very poor loser. As for the baby orangutan, it went back to its winning ways, hugging and kissing everyone who would let it. While I remained in the show it never went berserk again.

17

SOUTH OF THE BORDER

I woke instantly and leaped straight out of bed. Someone else was in my hotel room, someone that had no business being there! When I was a kid in Ireland I slept so soundly it was like I was dead. But since turning pro that has all changed. Now it takes very little to wake me. I don't know whether this is just a normal transformation, or whether the wrestling business had done this, from the years on the road worrying about some crazy fan getting to me when I was unaware. When people accuse me of paranoia about nutty fans, I just point out what happened to John Lennon. I know he didn't get it in the back, but I don't believe in making it easy for anybody to nail me. Now here I was in Mexico of all places, standing naked beside my bed, trying to see in the dark, knowing there was someone in my room. Someone who had not been there when I went to sleep.

My trip South of the Border actually started in Las Vegas. The promoter came to see me while I was working at The Dunes' "Casino de Paris". We struck a deal that sounded good to me, so as soon as my contract was finished at the show, I packed my bags and headed South.

On my first night in Mexico City, Lutteroth, the promoter of all Mexico, took me to the huge Mexican arena to familiarize me with the local style. It also gave me a chance to see my

167

opposition in action.

The first match I watched was a six-man tag. After seeing that fray my stay almost ended before it began. Two men on one team were holding one of their opponents outside the ring, whaling away at him. One of the partners of the man being held jumped over the ropes from the ring apron, charged across the ring at breakneck speed, away from where the three men were, bounced off the ropes to gain momentum, and charged toward the three. Just before reaching the ropes, he jumped clean over them with his arms held out in front, fists clenched, just like the classical pose of Superman in mid-flight, ten feet in the air. In the meantime, the trio had their backs to him. The man's intent was obvious, dive onto the struggling bodies and deliver a blow to the back of the heads of his opponents, thereby gaining the release of his partner. Alas, it was not to be. As we say in Ireland, there's many a slip between the cup and the lip. Just before he struck them, an irate fan jabbed a lighted cigar into the leg of one of the wrestlers. The wrestler yelled and threw his body violently away from his tormentors, which made all three shift completely out of Superman's line of fire. It was almost like watching a comic strip, with the man in midair trying to get back to where he came from. This also was not to be. He hit the concrete with a terrible impact, face first, then skidded along like one of those jets making a belly-flop landing on an aircraft carrier. Everyone jumped to their feet, cheering or booing, depending on whose side they were on. The two men whom he'd tried to hit dropped their victim like a piece of crap and started kicking him brutally. He never moved. They then shifted their attention to the two remaining men who were going at it in the ring. They left the senseless man where he was. Even from the back of the arena my years of experience told me he was unconscious. A stretcher was brought out from under the ring by a couple of seconds, who then lifted the inert body onto it, and rushed him to the dressing rooms.

They passed Lutteroth and myself on the way. I got a good

look at him. He was a real mess. His forehead was already grotesquely swollen, making him look like a creature from Mars. His nose, chest, and belly looked like raw meat. Blood was pouring from his mouth where a piece of tooth was sticking through. His nose didn't look very healthy, and it was bent out of shape. He hadn't regained consciousness as he was hurried past me. He looked about twenty years old, reminding me of myself when I first started, only he was lighter, about one-hundred, seventy pounds.

Turning to look at the promoter, I found he was watching the action in the ring with interest. It was as if he hadn't seen the body that had just passed by.

"Mr. Lutteroth," At the sound of my voice, he turned toward me with an inquiring look on his face.

"Yes, Pat?" He waited for me to speak, giving me his full attention.

"You don't expect me to do crazy things like that, I hope." I had to be careful, I didn't want to screw up my deal in Mexico, neither was I a kamikaze wrestler! If that's what it took to make money here, then it was north of the border for me.

"No, no, Pat." He reassured me, giving me the full benefit of his charm. "You just wrestle like you always have."

"But what about the man they've just carried out? You said to watch the style in Mexico, and become familiar with it... Is this the normal style?"

"Pat," He said. "You must understand that these men you are watching now, the man on the stretcher, they are all preliminary men. They all know I am here tonight so they try extra hard. They want to be noticed. But I assure you wrestling is at a high standard in this country... You'll see."

During my first match there my nose was smashed so badly that both my eyes almost closed. As a last resort, after all else had failed, the doctor stuffed my nose with bandages to stem the flow of blood. I couldn't believe how much bandage can be pushed up into a nose, but it seemed like yards of it. From that

169

first day, every time I wrestled in Mexico City, my nose would bleed profusely. I put it down to the high elevation. It didn't matter what I did to protect it, the first time I got hit on the nose the bleeding would start.

Two weeks into my stay I got a kick behind the testicles which dropped me to my knees. After the match I still felt very sore between the legs, but then every night something is sore when you wrestle, so I didn't pay much attention to it.

I woke up at about six in the morning with what felt like a watermelon growing from my body. In the night a lump about the size of a big fist had grown right where I was kicked. I felt like I was on fire, dying of thirst, sweating and shaking. I headed for the bathroom, waddling as best I could. Suddenly my legs felt wet, I thought I had pissed myself, but it wasn't that. The lump had burst and was draining down my leg. I rushed as fast as I could to the toilet, where I squatted and let the pus and infection drain out. The stench was terrible. I could barely stand it, but I had no option. I didn't know where to get help, when I tried using the phone nobody answered.

When the draining had finished I tore up a towel, put it between my legs, and put on a clean pair of underpants. I didn't have the promoter's phone number, so I had to wait for the office to open to get help. In the meantime I went to the only other person I knew in Mexico. That was Danny Hodge.

Hodge was the World's Junior Heavyweight Champion at the time. He was the only gringo wrestler, other than myself, in Mexico. He was from Oklahoma and hated every minute he'd spent in Mexico. He had nearly died himself, with a particularly devastating case of Montezuma's Revenge, just before I arrived. It had taken three weeks for him to get rid of the bug, even with antibiotics and a doctor's care. We were virtually prisoners in the sense we depended on the office to do most things for us.

Danny was a super person, as well as a super athlete. He had represented the USA in both amateur wrestling and amateur boxing. He had freakish strength, far out of proportion to his

170

two-hundred, thirty pounds. His favorite demonstration of strength was to snap the handles off any pair of pliers that the fans would give him.

Danny rushed right out into the street looking for a drugstore to get me some bandages. He was gone for some time. I was beginning to think he had gotten lost. He then came back chuckling to himself.

"I've got the perfect thing, Paddy, to put on that hole." He laughed to me, although I thought it was no laughing matter. It was still draining, but not at the same rate.

"What's that?" I asked. I was a little upset with him laughing. I was feeling quite sorry for myself.

"This!" He said, pulling out a box from a brown paper bag. "What is it? Come on, cut the bullshit! Where are the bandages?"

"Here! These are better than bandages!"

I couldn't believe my eyes. Had he gone mad? What he produced was a large package of Kotex, sanitary napkins.

"Pat, it looks like you've developed a cunt, and these are the best things for that!"

Then the funny side of the whole situation hit me, and I started laughing. I felt so weak and sick I had to sit down, while I shook with both laughter and fever.

Here I was in Mexico, feeling like my last days were upon me, looking for sympathy, and this ape was handing me a box of Kotex. As it turned out, they were a great idea, absorbing the crap that never seemed to stop draining.

Finally I got through to the office and Lutteroth. After he listened to my story, the first thing he asked was, "It won't stop you from wrestling tonight, will it?"

"I don't know. The way I feel right now, I haven't got any energy or strength."

There was panic on the other end, then he said, "Look, you're in Monterey tonight for TV. Catch an early plane there. There's one in an hour and a half. I'll have the local promoter call a good doctor to see you. They have really good doctors there,

171

the best in all Mexico.''

I knew this was bullshit, but then there wasn't too much I could do. I knew if I went he would get me a good doctor. It would be in his interests to get me well as soon as possible. In my short time in Mexico I'd become a big hit, especially in Monterey. For some reason the people there liked me, more importantly, they came to see me. Relief sounded in Lutteroth's voice when I agreed to go.

My trip was a nightmare. I don't remember too much of it, but I arrived feeling like death. The local promoter met me himself, his face showing great concern. I got the feeling he was a genuine person. Later on, he proved me right.

I was rushed to the private home of a doctor right away. He was a small Mexican with a large moustache. Without a word he took me into a tiny surgery and gestured for me to take my clothes off. Then he put me on the table with what looked like leg rests on it. Where had I seen something like this before? Then it hit me. It was an examining table for pregnant women. I'd really come a long way, first wearing Kotex, then lying on my back with my legs up in the air on a gynecology table.

He disappeared between my upraised legs. I could feel him touching places that I didn't let men touch. I was now cold and had the shakes, even though the surgery room was quite warm. Then he reappeared with a cabinet and started picking up surgical instruments.

"Are you going to cut?" I asked.

He looked at me with a smile and said "Si."

"Will it be a big cut?" I asked again. It was a stupid question, I knew it, but I couldn't shut up, I was as nervous as all hell. It wasn't everyday I let someone cut between my legs. Big cut, small cut, there wasn't anything I could do right then, whatever he did.

The doctor had in his hands a kidney shaped dish, lots of cotton, and a scalpel. No hypodermic, so I guess it's pain city again. As it turned out, there was very little pain. My rear end

172

was already so hot and sore that I never felt much. Although the fact that he was out of sight, between my legs, behind my testicles, and cutting with a knife was disconcerting to say the least.

I hoped this man was not a wrestling fan that didn't like me. The thought boggled the mind, the position he was in, the situation I was in. I found myself having a conversation with him. He didn't say much, just bobbed up every now and then and smiled. Then he disappeared back down between my legs.

After what seemed a lifetime he reappeared, went over to another cabinet, and returned with some large pads which he taped to my body where he'd been cutting. Then he gestured for me to get off the table, and he proceeded to do a thorough examination, taking heart beat, blood pressure, looking in my mouth, and taking my temperature. Then away he went, out of the room, only to return with another man who turned out to be an interpreter, left by the promoter to take care of me.

He told me what I'd already suspected, that the doctor couldn't understand English. All that conversation was wasted. When I was ready to leave, the interpreter explained the doctor's diagnosis was that I had an infected bruise of a non-specific origin which, he believed, would not be gotten rid of with antibiotics. He had cleaned out the wound, but I must be careful in the future of getting hit in that area. It could erupt again, he said. I would probably have to have surgery later on to clear it up properly. He gave me a couple of types of capsules to take, told me to drink lots of water, no alcohol, and have plenty of rest. Everything he said was right on. I had to have major surgery in New Zealand later that year, for it had developed into a fistula which, fortunately, did not touch any vital parts, but only by a hair's breadth.

In the time it took for me to get better, I'd lost fifteen pounds in two weeks. All I know is I felt lucky in meeting a doctor who obviously knew what he was doing.

Business as usual, I got back into the swing of traveling to

the various towns and cities. Something that bothered me was
the number of cigarette burns that covered my body, especially
in Mexico City. I can count on one hand the burns I'd gotten
in other countries in a year. But here I seemed to get at least
a dozen every time I wrestled... very painful ones too. They
take a long time to heal, especially when you are sweating,
wrestling and training everyday. By the time I was in Mexico
a few weeks, my skin was a mass of small round raw patches.

I discovered the reason for my problem. At ringside in Mexico
City were five businessmen who came to the matches every week.
I'd noticed them many times, always in the same seats, always
well-dressed and very prosperous looking. They really came to
my attention one night when I was walking around the ring during
a match, taking a breather. I was keeping my eye on the referee
who was counting me out, when a foot tripped me. I didn't fall,
but staggered while trying to regain my balance. It made me look
silly, which brought gales of laughter from the five business-
types, for it was one of them that owned the offending foot. From
then on, I kept them under quiet surveillance.

My next match in the city was hot and heavy. I was rolling
across the ring, away from my opponent, who had just tried to
land on me from the top rope. There was a flicker like a fire
fly arching through the air that found its way to the mat and
landed right under my back. In the excitement of the match I
only felt a slight sting and knew instantly what had happened.
The bastards, I thought. No wonder my skin is getting like
hamburger. They were obviously experts at placing lighted
cigarettes under my body with just the flick of a finger.

Rage suffused my whole being. I wanted to jump out right
then and smash them in their fat sweaty faces. But of course,
that was out of the question. The last thing I wanted was to spend
time in a Mexican jail on charges of assault. I'd already lost
enough weight! I knew that with patience my time would come.

At the same time I had a run-in with the boxing and wrestling
commissioner, who was constantly interfering with my matches,

just making a damn nuisance of himself. For some reason he took a real hatred to me, pushing his head through the ropes during my matches, and shouting God-knows-what in my direction. I still didn't understand very much Spanish, but it didn't take a genius to know he was being a shit. Then he would lecture me in the dressing room, through an interpreter, or try to. I guess I fueled his hatred by bending down in front of him, during his tirade, after taking off my trunks, and giving him a big Irish moon, ostensibly to take off my boots.

Mexico City was not the only place I'd had problems. Acapulco, one of the most beautiful places in the world, nearly cost me my life.

During a tag match, while my partner was battling an opponent outside the ring, a small Indian rushed from the crowd with a club and tried to brain him from behind. Without hesitation I lunged forward, grabbed his up-turned arm with my right hand, and wrenched the club out of his hand. Then using my left hand, I jabbed him in the guts, and went behind and started to choke him with his own club, which I thought was poetic justice. Just before my victim lost consciousness, out from the crowd came another Indian, charging in my direction, only this one was carrying a gun that looked absolutely huge. What really scared me was that he was trembling with rage or fear. I couldn't tell which. By then it really didn't matter. The important thing was that the pistol was pointed straight at my head, with the hammer back.

Ducking behind the limp body of my Indian gave me time to survey the situation. To say that I was scared was an understatement. I knew right away they were together. They looked like two peas in a pod to my eyes. The second one was screaming something in Spanish. His eyes were bulging. He held the gun out in front of him with his arms stiff. The weapon looked like a cannon. I imagine the fans were still screaming, though I could hear nothing. For me, the whole world had narrowed to that dark hole that kept pointing in my direction.

My partner was beside me now, looking stunned. He was a Mexican wrestler who could speak English.

"Do something!" I shouted. "Say something to that son of a bitch with the gun! If he keeps pointing it at me I'll kill this mother!" Alluding to the body I was still holding between me and what I felt was certain death.

My partner got his wits about him and started shouting something in Spanish to the second Indian. At first, whatever he was shouting didn't seem to be getting through, but then I saw comprehension dawning. My partner moved slowly toward the man with the gun, which was still pointing shakily at me. Keeping his movements very slow, he stretched out his hands toward the Indian, palms up. Then he was beside the gunman and started talking away at a furious rate. He grasped the nearest arm gently but firmly, and swung it away from me toward the ring. My eyes followed it. At the same time I tried to watch the Indian's face, which was turned toward my partner. They were in a deep conversation. It looked like an argument to me. Whatever was being said seemed to have a calming effect on my assailant. Our wrestling opponents had come to the inside of the ropes and were staring down, watching the scene with interest. They were both pointing and laughing, obviously enjoying my discomfort.

The Indian let out a burst of Spanish, as if to emphasize something. His arms jerked up with the effort. Suddenly the gun with the hammer cocked was pointing unintentionally at the two wrestlers in the ring. In fact it was wavering between the two. If my position hadn't been so precarious, I would've died laughing right there at the instant change of expressions on their faces. It was a mixture of horror, surprise, and terror all at once. Hesitating for only a second, they turned and bolted from the ring, heading for the dressing rooms. This was the best bit of teamwork I'd seen the pair do all night! I later learned that they'd grabbed their clothes, without showering or getting dressed, and left the arena. I guess he'd made believers out of them, even if he hadn't meant to.

My partner straightened out the situation. It seemed the two Indians were undercover police, though what they were doing at the wrestling matches wasn't clear. The one I had choked got carried away with the tactics of my partner, hence the club.

What I found out later was that the state where Acapulco is has more murders a year than all of Mexico put together. So I was lucky again. Obviously policemen who worked in conditions like that would not lose any sleep if they shot a gringo, accidentally or not. I didn't tag much with that partner again. I must say he had a lot of guts. A week after I left Mexico, I was sent a newspaper clipping. My partner had been stabbed through the heart and killed by fans who surrounded him as he was leaving the arena. He was a brave man, too brave perhaps. He didn't deserve to die like that.

So here I was in my hotel room in Monterey, naked as the day I was born, peering through the darkness, trying to see who was there besides me.

I could barely make out the outline of a body now standing a short distance away from the side of the bed. Backing around and away from the outline, I made it to where the light switch was and turned it on. There standing in the light was a quite attractive woman of about twenty, very pretty, and about medium height. She didn't have a weapon in her hand. It seems a bit silly now, in the cold light of day, that I was scared to death. But I'd been through so many hair-raising experiences with nuts in the last ten years, and Mexico more than most places, that I wasn't taking any more chances than necessary.

She didn't appear nervous, which also surprised the hell out of me. I gave the clock beside my bed a quick glance, my God, it was 4 a.m.! Whoever this was, it wasn't the maid! Finding my voice I asked what the hell she was doing in my room, scaring the crap out of me at this hour. How did she get in? For a moment I'd forgotten that I was in Mexico and she might not understand a word I was saying.

"Please, Señor Barrett, don't be mad at me." Her voice was husky and warm. She was certainly attractive, but I was still very wary. "I'm a friend."

"A friend?!" I asked. "What the hell kind of a friend creeps into a person's room while they're sleeping? I've never seen you before! Who the devil are you?"

"Please!" She said, stretching her arms out and taking a step toward me. "I'm a friend, a... how do you say it... a fan of yours... I wanted to see you very badly."

It was then that I realized that I was standing by the door, with one hand gripping a chair, the other one still on the light switch, completely naked. As I glanced down I realized that I was looking in good shape after a restful sleep, also her presence might have had something to do with it. Well, if she came to see me, she was certainly getting an eye full!

I calmed down a bit once I was sure she wasn't carrying a weapon. Her English was quite good, though she was obviously Mexican.

"Okay, you'd better tell me what's going on." I sat on the chair, turning the back toward her. It would be handy if I needed it. After all, it was only a girl in my room, and quite a pretty one at that. One part of my brain told me to relax. The other part, wanting to preserve life and limbs, reminded me that in the past I'd been kicked, hit with bottles, stones, and other objects, threatened with knives, razors, guns, and all manner of dangerous weapons. And all of this had not been by men. Some of the most fanatically dangerous people I'd met were women, so I wasn't taking any chances. Without bothering to get dressed, I listened to her story. It didn't look like it bothered her, that I'd no clothes on, so it didn't bother me. Plus she'd already seen everything of me there was to see, so it would be like shutting the gate after the horse had bolted.

It turned out she had watched me on TV for several weeks, and had liked what she saw. She couldn't get to the matches because she always worked at night, but she'd wanted to meet me very badly.

"How come you always work nights?" I asked, trying to weigh her up, suspecting the answer already. Her poise at seeing me naked led me to believe she was either a nurse, a saint, or a hooker. She didn't fit the Florence Nightingale look, nor my image of Joan of Arc.

"May I sit on your bed, Señor Barrett? I'm a little tired."

"Yes, of course." I replied. I still wanted to hear what she had to say for herself, but I wasn't going to lower my guard too easily. "But stay where you are, at least for the moment." I said. My mind was racing over all kinds of probabilities as to why she was in my room. I wasn't necessarily going to believe what she was about to tell me. Looking at me with big, beautiful, brown eyes that were the picture of innocence, she told me her story.

"I work in a house, mostly entertaining men in the evening."

No need to tell her I was aware how hookers operated generally. I just let her talk. "I watched you last Saturday on the TV." She turned on the full power of her eyes. "You were so good! I decided to come and see you. So I found out where you were staying." All the time she was talking she was sitting with her legs swinging, showing no trace of nervousness or shyness. She certainly had balls, not physically I hoped, but balls nevertheless.

"How did you find out where I was staying?" Was my next question.

"It was really easy." Again the smile that could melt ice. She came across quite nice, a very pretty girl. I tried to kick myself mentally, I didn't know enough about her to start thinking like that.

"I have, how you say it in English, connections." She struggled with the word, but got it out.

Suddenly the thought struck me. I reached back and tried the door. It was locked firmly. The lock looked intact. How did she get in I wondered. Glancing over to the window I saw it was

179

closed, plus I knew she could never have opened it without my hearing. So how did she get in? Knowing there was only one way to find out, I asked her.

"It was very easy."

I wished she didn't lean back like that, it was very difficult to concentrate with more of her leg showing and her breasts pointing at me that way. She seemed proud of herself.

"Well then, how?" My voice was taking on an edge again. I must keep control of matters, which is difficult being naked in front of a stranger, a beautiful one at that. I didn't want to play silly buggers at this hour of the morning.

She lifted up her hand, which was clenched. I hadn't noticed it before. I must be slipping. Then she opened it. Nestled in her palm was a key. My God, she had the key to my room, but how?

"Who gave you that, and why?" Hotels, even in Mexico, weren't supposed to hand over room keys to strangers. What she said next blew my mind away.

She got it from the hotel clerk downstairs. I was stunned to think the clerk would hand over my room key to a stranger. "Why would the clerk give you a key?" I asked. She started to laugh as if I was some little boy asking a silly question.

"Because I paid him!" Came her answer. "It cost me an American dollar bill."

The implications of what had happened hit me instantly. My life was worth one lousy American dollar, not a very high price. After all, she could've wanted me dead or maimed or whatever.

As it turned out, she was a great person, and I was very lonely. A man lives not by bread alone. She made me an offer I could refuse that night. I was really too shook up to consider any offers, even if she was pretty. I still didn't trust her. A couple of days later, I went to her work place, where I was made welcome by all the girls. Everything was laid on free gratis. They showed me a great time.

Since that episode in Mexico, I never stay in hotels or motels without first testing windows and putting a chair under the door handle. I want to live to a ripe old age, at the very least, give myself an edge.

Strangely enough, about a year later, something similar happened to me in Tennessee. I had checked into a hotel about 2 a.m. I had an overnight bag, so the night porter didn't come up with me. I opened the door and turned on the light, the switch was just inside the door.

A voice rose up from the bed, a quiet voice, but one not to be ignored. There was a man lying in my bed, staring, with a pistol pointed right at my chin. He slowly cocked the hammer.

"Can I help you?" That's all he said. A few words they may have been, but the rock-steady gun spoke volumes.

"I... I... I'm s-sorry." I stuttered. Funny, I never had a stutter before. "It must be the wrong room!" Slowly and carefully I backed out and closed the door. Rushing downstairs, I didn't wait for the elevator. I used the stairway three at a time, my bag swinging at my side. I charged to the desk.

"What the fuck's going on?!" I screamed. "I almost got killed up there! There's a guy in my room with a gun! What's happening?"

The desk clerk turned white and jumped back from the counter.

"I don't know!" He shrieked nervously, looking at this two-hundred, thirty-five-pound wrestler who had gone mad at the most inopportune time, namely when he was on his own at 2 a.m. He backed up to the pigeon hole rack, trying to put as much distance between this lunatic and himself. "What room did I give you?" He squeaked.

Slamming the key on the counter I told him. Fear still kept my heart hammering in my chest. Glancing at the key, then at the guest register book, he gave a start.

"Yes, I made a mistake. I'm very sorry. I see what I've done."

His abject apologizing had a somewhat calming effect on my jangled nerves. Since when would anyone expect to have a gun pointed at them when they open their hotel room door? That's only supposed to happen in the movies.

EVERYBODY DOWN HERE HATES ME

"Okay, tell me. How did you screw up?"

"I've never done this before," he pleaded. "In all my years in the hotel business... Never!" He was almost talking to himself, shaking his head in disbelief.

"Right. So you never did this before... Did what?"

Looking down at the counter he explained. He got the number of the empty room from the book, then reached to get the key from the pigeon hole, except he must've looked away at the crucial moment, or gotten careless. Anyway, in reaching back he must've picked the wrong hole, gotten the one above the one he intended, consequently giving me someone else's room key. Oddly enough, the man whose room I entered never complained or made inquiries. The hotel wouldn't tell me who he was, so I didn't pursue it. Now I have two phobias, entering and staying in rented rooms. I always knock before opening the door, and I always jam a chair under the door handle once inside. People have looked at me strangely when I tell them this, but my philosophy is, better to be a live coward than a dead fool.

Finishing up in Mexico was somewhat of a relief. The week before I left Monterey, where I was one of the most popular wrestlers ever, a fan shouted from the bleachers above me in English, "Señor Barrett! Please! I would like a photo. Look up, please!"

Feeling in a benevolent mood, knowing I was leaving the country for good in a short time, I turned my smiling face to the people above. God, I should've known better!

There was a sea of brown faces looking down. A hand belonging to one of them held not a camera, but a can, poised over my upturned head. Instantly I reacted, accelerating forward, but alas, too late. I didn't know what it contained, but I knew for sure it bode me evil. Piss cascaded all over me, soaking my hair, my shoulders, my trunks, and my boots. Right then I wanted to run back out of the safety of the tunnel, claw my way up to the bleachers, and inflict punishment on the piss-pouring gentleman. Discretion prevailed. If I tried I might end up covered with a lot worse. If I'd any doubts about it being piss, they were soon dispelled when I entered the dressing room. Roars of laughter greeted me as the other wrestlers saw my predicament. Some even jumped around the room holding their noses and shouted "Piss! Piss!"

Looking at all the grinning faces I thought to myself, it's just as well, I wasn't looking for sympathy. If I had wanted that, I'd have to go elsewhere, there was none here.

Entering the shower with as much dignity as I could muster, wearing everything, including my boots, I washed. Word spread rapidly. Wrestlers from other dressing rooms would suddenly appear solemn-faced to gaze at the piss-covered gringo. As soon as they disappeared from sight, shrieks of merriment would erupt, and I'd hear crashing and banging as they fell over the place in their hysteria.

Then the comic nature of the incident hit me as I got out of the shower, and saw the pride of Ireland in the full length mirror, looking more like a drowned rat than anything else in the world. That's when the other boys came around, slapping me on the back, still laughing uncontrollably. Up until that moment I'd always felt like an alien from another planet. Now I was one of them. If I'd only known it would take a can of piss!

My last night in Mexico City was a special hair match. I was against a man called El Nazi, who came from God-knows-where. He most certainly wasn't German, but I guess all Nazis aren't.

The rules were simple. Whoever lost the match, lost his hair. I'd no intention of returning to the states bald. They had a barber ringside, ready to do the job. Looking him over carefully, he didn't strike me as being another Vidal Sassoon, and I do like my hair.

The auditorium was packed to the rafters. Sitting at ringside were my cigarette-throwing friends, smirking and shouting obscenities.

I'd not forgotten them by any means. Though I was able to cut down the number of cigarette burns by carefully watching,

EVERYBODY DOWN HERE HATES ME

I was never able to eliminate them altogether. They were too expert.

All the time in that country I'd tried to figure a way to get back at these bastards without getting in trouble with the police, who are not at all sympathetic to wrestlers brutalizing fans.

The match was going well with the Nazi in full retreat, when I knew how to get my revenge.

Most of the people came to the matches dressed for a wild and wooly night, in other words, not in their best finery. Not so, these five guys. They were always dressed to the nines, like five peacocks, obviously a very proud, affluent bunch.

The bout was about halfway through according to the clock, when I noticed the one in the middle, who seemed to be the ring leader, lighting up a cigar. This was too much. Cigarettes were bad enough, something would have to be done, and fast!

I knew what was on the evil bastard's mind. This was to be his coup de grace. A lighted cigar placed on the right area of my body would make a marvelous farewell burn. But I was on to him.

My opponent heaved me across the ring. As I flew through the air I desperately tried to watch the five banditos in front. Sure enough, over came the cigarettes like so many mortars, heading in the general direction of where my body was going to land. Right there, in amongst them, was the cigar, leaving a trail of sparks like Haley's Comet.

Twisting in midair, I managed to change direction somewhat. But I couldn't avoid them all. I felt one hit, but I considered myself lucky the cigar was lying intact. Its huge glowing ember still alive.

My nose, in the meantime, was doing its Mexico City usual, bleeding all over the place. I sucked the blood up through the back of my nostrils, into my mouth, until my cheeks were bulging.

Then I made my move. Grabbing the cigar in my hand, I rolled swiftly onto the floor, right in front of my would-be tormentors,

184

taking them completely by surprise. I can still savor the following moments.

Holding the cigar by the unlit end, I ground it into the crotch of my friend in the middle. Phase one went perfectly.

He tried to jump to his feet, but I got my hand in his big sweaty face and shoved him back down like the bag of shit he was. Now for phase two...

Pursing my lips, I started spraying first the one in the middle, then on either side, with a stream of red gore. They didn't have a chance to get away. I splattered them from their faces down to their beautifully tailored suits. Covered in the blood I'd stored, they were stupefied. This was so totally unexpected that it left them paralyzed, which added to my satisfaction. They couldn't even get out of their seats to retaliate, that is if they'd wanted to. I was heading back to the ring. The referee had forgotten to count. He was also enthralled by the event. Then obviously realizing his dereliction of duty, he started to count from the beginning. In the time remaining I decided to take a respite. That's when I had my second revenge of the night. The worm had turned!

Rushing up behind me was the commissioner, the bane of my life. I'd forgotten about his bad habit of interfering in my matches. Like the proverbial bad penny, here he was again.

His hand descended quite violently on my shoulder. He intended, I believe, to spin me around and do God-knows-what. So I helped him by turning fast, at the same time bringing my fist shoulder level. I connected right on his chin. If ever a punch should be called beautiful, it was this one. It was like slow motion. His eyes were glazed. The mouth which had so many times given me abuse went slack. Spit flying from one corner soared in the air. His arms dropped and his knees buckled. He was like a puppet whose strings had been released by the puppeteer. It was so easy it was almost pitiful. I had knocked him out with that one short sharp blow to the jaw. It was really poetry to my eyes. Maybe not to his, though I doubt he even saw it coming.

The count had stopped again as the bewildered ref watched the new turn of events. Leaving him lying there, I entered the ring fast and continued on with my match. It really wound up as an anti-climax. The people in the audience being a sadistic bunch had obviously enjoyed the special attraction of the businessmen with the blood on their nice, light-colored tailored suits.

Now they were treated to the spectacle of the commissioner being helped, by two brawny seconds, back to the dressing rooms.

Even taking the hair from El Nazi didn't get the reaction it would have normally. I was right about the barber, if that's what he really was. He butchered El Nazi's hair. Maybe he didn't like Hitler.

Back in the dressing room, the commissioner had a minion come in and tell me I would never wrestle South of the Border again. I was so happy to be leaving I sent a return message.

"Tell him I will hold him to his promise, and he can stick Mexico up his ass!''

18

THE PARTY POOPER

When Timmy O'Mally and I became tag partners in the great Northwest, I knew right away we could get along, but just how well I couldn't envision. In many ways, though we were both Irish, he was the total opposite of me.

After a match was over we didn't socialize much. Now and again we would have lunch together, or perhaps a workout, otherwise we kept things mainly on a business level. Most times we would go to a town separately, that way we didn't get on each other's nerves by over-exposure to one another. As a team we were drawing well. Fenton, the promoter, should've been happy, but for some reason he didn't like O'Mally's style and talked about getting someone else for me to tag with. I finally convinced him to leave us together. That didn't stop him bitching to me about how O'Mally held us back. I respected Fenton's business acumen, but in this case I believed he was wrong. Even though Timmy wasn't as spectacular in the ring as I would've liked, he had an air of innocence about him, especially for a pro wrestler. The fans really liked him, and in our business that was very important. Nobody could do a Sleeper Hold like him, and the fans loved that. Normally he appeared to move a bit awkwardly, but when slipping the Sleeper on he was poetry in motion.

EVERYBODY DOWN HERE HATES ME

In private life he was a lonely man, going through a divorce that had a profoundly hard effect on him. He didn't sample any of the gorgeous young females that hung around the wrestlers just waiting for the word to take care of his wants. I tried several times to fix him up with someone nice, but he always backed away.

There was a party on in town that I was invited to by some fans, and they asked me to bring Timmy along. Sometimes they could be boring, then again they could be wild as all hell. I agreed, but first they had to promise to have a six pack of Mackison's Ale there. The reason was simple. Timmy didn't drink under normal circumstances, but he did love a bottle of Mackison's, and I thought it might loosen him up.

On the night of the party we arrived to a packed house. The place was really jumping with drunks and semi-drunks, already spilling out onto the lawn and driveway. We had difficulty finding a place to park, but finally I squeezed my car into a spot down the street, a short distance from the house.

The wine and beer were flowing, the food abundant, so much so that I must've put on five pounds in very short order. There were cheeses and salami, all kinds of summer sausage, cold pork, ham, turkey, everything to tickle the palate. My friends had not forgotten the strong ale, which had been hidden so nobody else got their hands on it. I was drinking Guinness, which was also laid on in my honor.

Things were going terrific. I was chatting up a scrumptious blonde and doing fine, when I heard a shrill voice lift in anger. Looking around to see what was happening, I suddenly got a sinking feeling. The screeching was coming from a skinny, pimply faced girl who had O'Mally bailed up against the wall. She was poking him in the chest emphasizing some point she was making. Although I couldn't understand all that was being said by her, I could smell trouble. Letting the blonde go reluctantly, I pushed through the crowd that was beginning to collect. I couldn't comprehend what the problem was.

188

My Irish partner was a very non-threatening person, to say the least, especially outside the ring. With women he was always a real gentleman, with that old world courtesy that is seldom seen nowadays. I was nonplussed at the confrontation that was obviously brewing.

Arriving at the scene I took the whole situation in at a glance. One very drunk girl was harassing a polite, semi-drunk wrestler. Now lots of people have a problem with that scenario, but it happens more often than not, though the drunk was not always a girl. Wrestlers, by no means saints, have for the most part learned to curb their volatility with people outside the business. Lawsuits have seen to that. Many pro wrestlers have been abused by all kinds of people telling them they are jokes, actors, and fakes, etc.

Timmy was the last of the old-world gentlemen. As I listened I started to get irritated. This pimply faced girl was reviling O'Mally, standing on her toes, calling him a fake in a stupid business. She was telling him she'd seen him on TV, seen his lousy hold which she didn't believe in anyway, all the time emphasizing her point with a stiff finger to the chest. He was smiling benignly down into her face, saying little, but I could smell trouble.

The trouble was not with the girl, but with the other people that surrounded her and Tim. That was the reason he was not defending his position. He was just making conciliatory noises. His obvious meekness was starting to inflame some of the others who were her friends. I had found that if I was being badgered about the business, the best thing to do was to get on the offensive with a verbal attack, ask what they did for a living, etc. to throw them off balance, then move away. These people were mistaking kindness for weakness, and they were getting bolder. The fact that they had had a lot to drink didn't help matters.

Moving to the attack I told the girl that she was a real killer diller, and it would make us look bad if she beat either or both of us, we'd be out of the business. The idea was so ludicrous that it got a good laugh and some of the group started to drift away.

"Come on Timmy, let's have another drink."

"That sounds like a fine idea." He said, starting to move away with me. At this, the skinny girl came alive and grabbed him by the arm, her face suffused with anger.

"You chicken shit bastard!" She screamed. "You lousy no good chicken shit! You have your friend to help you!" We were both taken aback at this attack. "You couldn't put your lousy hold on me, you big shit! You're nothing but a jerk! Do you hear me? A stupid jerk!!"

She was so worked up, she was literally stamping with rage. The whole thing would've been funny except by now a large crowd of drunks surrounded us. I was beginning to feel like General Custer must've felt at the Little Big Horn just before the last charge.

"We must be going." I said to Timmy. "Let's get out of here."

This was met with howls of protest from those gathered around. The sweaty faces were laughing now, but it was an ugly laugh. Looking around, I couldn't see a friendly face anywhere.

"All right little lady," Said my friend in that voice that struck terror in my heart. It was that smooth soft voice he always used before putting the Sleeper on his victim. I don't believe he was even aware of what he was saying. This was his little routine, a bit like a cat twitching its tail and whiskers before it pounces.

"Try doing it to me!" She said turning her back squarely to him. "Bet you can't put me out, you fake!"

I don't know what the girl was drinking, but it would be marvelous stuff to give an army going in to do battle! It seemed to make her absolutely fearless. But that is one of the problems wrestlers have with women, especially at parties. They feel safe in saying anything they want. Men are usually more cautious.

Grabbing O'Mally's arm fast, I tried to stop him. But it was too late. He clamped his left arm around her neck from behind,

190

then brought his right arm up to the side of her head, then locked his left hand into the crook of his right arm, putting the right hand on the back of her head. Moving backwards, he simultaneously bent over her body. This was a move I'd seen hundreds of times before. She was taken by surprise. His speed of movement was so deceptive that it looked like slow motion. I'd never seen his retribution done any quicker.

No one ever got away once the move was initiated. Usually with an opponent he would duck under the outstretched arm in front, then move quickly behind to put on the hold. This arrogant drunk made it even easier by turning her back. Her body went totally limp. The crowd around us went silent, though the music and noise from the rest of the house still continued. Conflicting emotions surged through me. On the one hand, I was not happy about him putting a hold on a woman, even one as objectionable and belligerent as this one. This was not from gallantry. She deserved everything she got. What did disturb me were the ramifications. This person could mean a lot of trouble. The other side of the coin was that she was going under easily, so it would all be over quickly and we could get our asses out of there.

Suddenly she came alive. I couldn't believe my eyes. This had never happened before, nobody had ever started coming around like this and I'd seen many tough men succumb. How could this be possible? The violence of her sudden movement nearly knocked Timmy off his feet, but he recovered his balance quickly. She started kicking frantically, thrashing around like a mad woman, her arms reaching upwards and backwards, her clawing hands desperately trying to tear at the face of her assailant, which was out of reach. All the while her gaping mouth emitted horrible sounds of choking and gagging, intermingled with half-sobs and screams.

Suddenly it hit me, what had gone wrong, why this skinny girl wasn't laying on the floor asleep, with her tongue hanging out, causing no more trouble. Instead she was bucking like a bronco in Timmy's hold. That was it! She was able to move around in the crook of his arm because the triangle he made with his body was too large for her slender neck. So instead of his bicep and forearm pressing on the nerves on the side of her neck, thus rendering her harmlessly and blissfully unconscious like it had with everyone before her, she had twisted around in the hold and was now being choked senseless, which was not a pretty sight, hence the barfing and kicking.

The crowd around us had swelled until the large room was nearly bursting at the seams with sweaty-faced people trying to get a look at what was going on. Grabbing my friend by the arm again, I put my mouth close to his ear and begged him to let her go, but again, it was too late. He was past the point of no return, nothing short of maiming would force this usually placid man to release his hold on the wretched girl who brought all of this down on herself. By the looks of things, to my experienced eyes, this was about to be the focus of a general donnybrook with, I suspected, Timmy and myself in the center...

Shouts of "Let her go, you madman!" were ringing in my ears when I was jostled violently from behind by a surge of people. Was I imagining it, or did I get punched in the back at the same time? Whether by accident or intent, the blow to the back was a definite warning sign that the natives were very restless and getting worse.

As I turned my head to see who might be taking cheap shots at me, I heard someone close by say, "Oh my God!" in the tone of voice that I knew could only mean more trouble. Looking around quickly I realized my worst fears were justified. In fact, things had escalated even more than I'd expected. The trouble-making girl who wanted to test the Sleeper Hold was not yet asleep, but in her wild struggles to escape the steel bands that were choking her breath from her body, she had pissed herself. Urine was spraying the floor in an uneven pattern under her thrashing limbs. Some of the crowd was caught in the spray, causing them to fall back in horror.

It was this falling back, causing mass confusion, that probably saved our hides. Grabbing Timmy by both cheeks and jerking his face around until it was only inches from mine, I shouted at him.

"God dammit Timmy, she'll die! LET HER GO... NOW!" My words seemed to get through to him for I felt his arms relax.

Taking her now limp body, I thrust it toward some of the people who'd been the most vocal.

"Get some cold water for her now," I commanded. "And give her plenty of air. She'll be okay." Inside I was saying a silent prayer for both her and us. Taking my partner by the arm I started for the door. Using the confusion caused by both the urinating and my thrusting her body into their arms to decoy their attention, we began our escape. With my outthrust arm as a battering ram, we burst through the melee into the night air outside. For a moment I couldn't remember where I'd parked the car, but the howl that went up behind our backs sharpened my memory. Throwing our dignity to the wind, we sprinted down the driveway until we reached the vehicle. As we opened our doors out of the house spewed forth a mad screaming mob. I didn't remember there being so many people at the party, it looked like thousands. All levity gone, this wild screaming horde was thirsting for our blood.

The car was jammed closely between two other cars, so I had to back up as best I could to get enough room to get out. Fear gripped my stomach like a band. I knew we'd be shown no mercy. Even though we might do some damage before we went under, the result was inevitable. There were just too many of them, plus sitting in a car was not the best position to try to protect oneself.

Cursing, sweating, and swearing I willed the car out from the small space at what seemed like a hundred miles an hour, leaving some bumper behind. As we shot out bottles and beer cans started to rain down on the roof. One bottle smashed on the windshield, but fortunately did no more damage than a few scratches. As we accelerated down the street, I looked in my rear-view mirror

193

and saw people rushing to their cars. Those bastards really meant business. Swinging wildly around a corner, I took evasive action, driving madly down back streets, becoming completely lost. Finally I felt we were in the clear and started slowing down, still keeping a wary eye on my mirror.

Relaxing somewhat, I turned to Timmy, who was sitting unconcerned in the passenger seat watching me. This was too much. I had to say something. He looked so maddeningly free from all worries while I felt like an overstretched piano wire, ready to snap. "Didn't you realize she was choking?" I snarled. We'd had a very close call and he didn't seem to be aware of it. "You could've killed her!" I wasn't so much worried about her, I felt she deserved everything that happened to her. God knows how many people she'd made miserable before this. Maybe, in the future, she'd learn to keep her big mouth shut. But in my mind I was upset that my partner had put our lives on the line. Being wrestlers I'd learned we could expect no mercy from a mob, in actuality, not from anyone!

Looking at me with that quiet Jesus Christ expression that I'd learned to hate, Timmy said in his soft Irish brogue, "You know Paddy, me boy, it's not good for you to get yourself so upset... You'll have a heart attack if you're not careful."

If ever there was a time for me to have a heart attack, it was then! I could feel my eyes bulge with suppressed rage, my heart was pounding so much I couldn't speak. I wanted to beat him over the head with my bare fists, or better still, a club.

Pulling the car violently to a stop at the pavement, I turned to face him, prepared to scream abuse at his stupidity. He met my gaze with a disarming smile that stopped the speech in my throat. I found myself at a loss for words. Then everything drained from me, the hate, the fear, and the rage. I found myself starting to laugh, not hysterically, but uncontrollably nevertheless. My body was racked with laughter, deep shuddering bursts exploded forth filling the car.

"Timmy," I said between gasps. "What am I going to do

with you? Your damned calmness under fire will be the death of me!''

Our partnership lasted for a long time by wrestling standards, and to this day I remember him with a fondness that I don't often bestow on many people.

19

THE SAMOAN

He is one of the legends of the pro wrestling business, both in and out of the ring. From Samoa, the land of natural fighters, came this huge charismatic man. I first met him in England where he had just arrived from Samoa, by way of New Zealand. Hearing laughter coming from the audience, I was very curious to see what was causing the hilarity. Frivolity was not the normal reaction displayed in a wrestling hall.

Peter Fagasa, the Samoan, was draped between the top ropes making up the ring corner, the back of his neck on one side and his ankles catching the other side, virtually becoming a human hammock. He looked like he didn't have a care in the world. The fans were laughing at the sight of the huge bronzed wrestler's mode of relaxation.

As the bell went for the next round, he jumped lightly from his perch to the canvas, in a motion that was as smooth as silk. At that time he weighed in at two-hundred, seventy-pounds and could move with the speed and grace of a man half his size.

I had just returned to England from the USA and was looking forward to letting the fans in Europe see the greatly improved Irishman in action.

After his match, the promoter asked if I would give Peter a ride back to London, which I was happy to oblige. I was intrigued by this man. I had never seen a Samoan wrestler before, plus his unique and original style fascinated me.

On the way back we picked up a few beers to drink on the trip. I figured it would help to break the ice, and he seemed happy at the idea. He had a broad handsome face topped with shoulder length curly black hair. His large white teeth were in an even larger mobile mouth. He came across to me as good-natured, ready with an easy smile. Our conversation was relaxed. We talked about our careers and where we would like them to go.

He had started wrestling rather late in life, in his mid-thirties, when a lot of wrestlers are already on the ash heap because of injuries. Though not overly tall for his weight, about five-feet, ten-inches, he exuded great power and balance. He asked me many questions about the USA and seemed interested in breaking in over there. But the overall impression I got was he had a lack of ambition.

We arrived at his flat in high good humor, brought on by good fellowship and a liberal amount of booze. I was invited in to meet his wife and daughter, and to have a little supper.

His wife was a very large powerful woman weighing about two-hundred, fifty-pounds. There was nothing timid about her. She greeted me warmly and begged me to stay and eat. It was now after midnight. I hadn't eaten anything substantial since about 3 p.m. The thought of a snack was very inviting. I certainly wasn't expecting the gargantuan meal that had been prepared and was obviously waiting for the royal master!

There was roast pork, chicken, ham, cooked green bananas, and potatoes, with side dishes I'd never seen before. All of this at 1 a.m.! I was almost overwhelmed. I had a very healthy appetite and I figured I would give a good accounting of myself. Just as I was prepared to eat, his daughter came in from her room. The way she greeted her father was so effusive it was obvious she adored him. She was about seventeen years old and came across as being shy and reserved, completely the opposite of her father and mother. As it turned out she was his most ardent fan, going to the matches whenever possible, writing articles about him for the many wrestling publications and thus helping to boost his career. It was a lovely family scene with this genial Polynesian prince, master of all he surveyed.

I saw him a few weeks later wrestling in a preliminary match. What struck me was his apparent laziness in his wrestling. Even though he exuded talent, all he seemed to want to do was to roll around the ring and act the clown. This was a big disappointment to me. I'd taken a liking to him and couldn't understand his lack of desire to succeed at his chosen profession. He was quite content to just clown through his match. Being such a powerful brute, his opponents could do little with him, whether he wanted to wrestle or not. Talking about his match afterwards, he laughed at my suggestion that he should be more aggressive in the ring.

"Hey, brotha!" He said. "You take life too serious. Let's have something to drink!" I was starting to realize his drinking appetite matched his eating one. We parted that night without the subject being broached again.

One night I was invited to a party where there were several wrestlers. One of them was Peter, and of course his wife and daughter. The party was in full swing when I heard Rea, Peter's wife, shouting in broken English and Samoan. There was no mistaking her voice. The shouting seemed to be coming from upstairs.

As I pushed my way into the hallway to see what was causing the furor, a female body came hurtling down the stairs, head over heels. It was a young blonde woman, quite attractive, though at that point in time she really didn't look her best. Standing at the top of the stairs was Rea, with an angry scowl on her face, gesturing wildly after the body that lay in a heap on the ground, moaning. Behind her was Peter with a broad grin on his face, appearing to be enjoying all that was going on. This was my first inkling that all was not right in paradise.

Afterwards Peter told me what had happened. The blonde and he had found a cozy little walk-in closet where they could steal a few kisses and a grope, when Rea started looking for him. With the sure sense that must've come from years of practice, she pinpointed their hideout and found the culprits. Jerking the door open, she literally caught Peter with his pants down. Taking the situation in with a glance, she snatched the girl by the hair, and dragged the unfortunate female out of the closet. Ignoring Peter who was busily pulling his pants up, Rea started slapping her with a meaty hand. Then picking up the half senseless girl, Rea bodily threw her down the stairs.

Peter was laughing about it when we talked. He thought it was all a great joke, laughing loudly, slapping his thighs at the same time. The poor little blonde girl had been hurt quite badly, but there was no remorse from either Peter or Rea. While he was telling me the story, Rea came into the room. She joined in on the laughter, especially when he started extolling her physical prowess.

This was the first sign of cruelty that I noticed under the smiling faces. I filed it away for the future. It was to save my ass years later.

My first match with him was almost a disaster. He wouldn't get up and move around. I tried almost everything, but he would just roll out of the ring, walk around with a big smile on his face, and get in just before being counted out. Maybe what I couldn't do physically, I could do mentally. Pushing my face close to his I called him a dumb Samoan. It was said not with conviction, but with the intent to get a reaction from him, and with pure frustration.

It was as if lightning had struck. He roared from the canvas and attacked with a viciousness that even surprised me. As I got to know him better I realized that underneath that big bluff smiling facade, lurked a different person, a very basic primitive one that would kill without a qualm when aroused. From being the hunter, I suddenly became the hunted. I had to use all of my wiles to stay out of real trouble.

I never saw him in England after that.

EVERYBODY DOWN HERE HATES ME

Peter Fagasa moved on to France, where he was a sensation. His wrestling style was changing.

The next place I met him was in Hawaii. He and the family greeted me like I was a long-lost brother. There were many feasts and booze-ups. In Hawaii being Polynesian was a great asset. With his talent now manifesting itself more and more, he was like a god. People would crowd around him in the streets, mobbing him wherever he would go. Somehow he didn't seem contented there, mainly because his career appeared to be going nowhere. That was because when he first had arrived in the islands, he was teamed with another Samoan. The Samoan populace turned out in mass to watch them wrestle. His growing reputation had preceded him. During the action, their fans, taking exception to the tactics of their opponents, rioted and smashed the auditorium. When thousands of Samoans riot, it's something to behold. The huge men and women were breaking chairs and doors and frightening everyone, including the promoter, the police, and the other fans. So from that day on, Peter's doom was sealed. No longer were he and his partner pushed into the limelight. In fact they were rarely ever teamed together again.

When I arrived on the scene, Fagasa poured out his tale of woe and asked if I could get him booked in San Francisco, as I knew the promoter there. Because I liked him and appreciated his talent, I made some phone calls to get him booked on the mainland. In this I was successful.

When I arrived in California about a week after him, he was already being groomed for the main events. How it came about was strange.

The promoter, Roy Shire, didn't know what a Samoan was, even though I tried to explain it to him on the phone. He came into the dressing room and said that the Cow Palace was filling up with fat Mexicans. To emphasize his point, he maintained that they were the biggest Mexicans he'd ever seen. He even commented that their hair was quite curly. What really shocked him about these giant Mexican men were they were wearing skirts and had their hair drawn up in buns.

Peter, who had been listening to the dialogue, drifted outside into the auditorium to have a look at these seemingly strange Mexicans. Coming back into the dressing room, he pulled the promoter aside and informed him that these "fat Mexicans" were in reality his people, Samoans. Roy and he went out together to have another look. The Samoans went crazy. Here was their hero in the flesh, the man who had been featured in the James Bond series, who had even fought Bond hand to hand!

By now his style of wrestling had changed. He'd gotten very ambitious — the goading of his wife and daughter was paying off. He was now a superb performer. On the West Coast he was a huge success, not just with Samoans — of which there are a great number — but with the general public as well.

His habits outside the ring hadn't changed, he lived as hard as ever, maybe even harder. Drinking and women were his life. And he had found a ready partner for his cavorting in wrestler Ray Stevens, who is another legend in the business, both on and off the canvas.

Ray has the appetite for living of at least three men. He would arrive at the matches unshaven and hung-over from a night of debauchery. Laying on his stomach, he would have one of the men massage his back for as long a time as they had, or until they got tired. Then he would shave and shower and be ready just in time for his match. It never ceased to amaze me how he would transform the minute he donned his wrestling gear and entered the spotlight. Suddenly he would come alive, climb into the ring, and wrestle like he'd been in bed for twenty-four hours. If the truth were known, he most likely had been, but certainly not sleeping! These two men were the bane of Shire's life. He was always worried that something would happen to one or both of them. Rea was also going crazy. Her dreams of his success became nightmares as he stayed out night after night, eventually coming home to their apartment hung-over, exhausted, and smelling of sex.

EVERYBODY DOWN HERE HATES ME

The Fagasa family were now living in a rented apartment in Hayward, California. Stevens lived just up the road from him, so their get-togethers were very frequent.

One night it was too much for poor Rea. Peter woke up with the premonition that something was wrong. When he tried to move, he found that his balls were in some kind of vice. He thought for a moment that he was having a nightmare and swore to himself to mend his ways. It was worse than a nightmare — it was Rea. She was kneeling between his legs, smiling down into his face. It was the same smile he'd seen many times before. She had a large meaty hand wrapped around his balls and was squeezing with all her considerable strength. Even though he was in agony, he started to surge up, making a swipe at her head.

"No, no, Peeta!" She said. "You lie very quiet and listen to me." It was not the words that stopped him, but the large, very sharp knife that she was holding in her free hand, its edge poised under his testicles beside the trunk of his body. He froze, almost swallowing his tongue. Even though he'd gone to bed dead drunk, he was now suddenly cold sober.

"Are you crazy, Rea?" He said. "Put the knife down and let my balls go!"

"No, no Peeta," She crooned. "You've fucked around too many times, last night was your last! I'm gonna make you a steer instead of a bull." This was followed by her hysterical laughter.

He started to get up again but felt the knife nick his skin. He knew Rea was quite capable of doing everything she threatened. He begged and pleaded, threatened and demanded, but all was to no avail. Then when he finally realized there was no escape from his determined wife, he asked her what she wanted, how he could make things right.

"Peeta," She said. "Nothing you say or do can change my mind. I'm gonna cut your balls off and send them to that little Mexican horse you been seeing." ("Horse" was her word for "Whore", her own style of broken English.) "I don't mind you fucking her, but you a stupid man... You spend all your money

202

on her! Why aren't you more like Pat Barrett? He fucks them, but he doesn't spend his money . . . He spends theirs!'' This of course was not true, but I did have a reputation for being thrifty.

She had made every endeavor to remind him of this when we were together. He would laugh heartily at the time, but as I got to know him I realized he took it all quite personally. He kept watching me, especially when we were drinking. He would remember past injustices, real or imagined, and mull them over in his mind.

When he was in Japan he got into a fight with another wrestler, Billy Robinson. Billy was one of the best men in professional wrestling to come out of England, a hard tough competitor, feared by many on both sides of the Atlantic. Robinson had been ribbing Peter for a long time, with Fagasa just laughing it off. Both of them had been drinking as friends when the Samoan reminded Robinson of how he thought all Samoans were stupid and slow. Billy, who was never one to shirk a fight, said that's how he felt, so what. Peter said it didn't matter, then when Robinson relaxed, he punched him through a glass panel in the hotel.

Billy was no push-over and rushed into the fray. Grabbing Peter's arms under his armpits, he prepared to drop back into a suplex. This maneuver would've finished the fracas right then and there. Robinson, the better wrestler and in extremely good condition, looked set on demolishing Fagasa. By dropping back into the suplex, a wrestling maneuver that would've taken the Samoan high in the air, then brought him crashing down on his head, he hoped to finish Peter off quickly. Even a man of Peter's strength wouldn't have survived that! The only thing he forgot was that Samoans have a secret weapon, their teeth. Peter was no exception. As his feet came off the ground, he opened his cavernous mouth wide and secured a mouthful of prime English cheek that would've done "Jaws" proud.

Clamping on tight, he was in the process of tearing off a man-sized chunk of meat from the Englishman's face. Blood was everywhere. Robinson released his hold and tore himself free.

EVERYBODY DOWN HERE HATES ME

Three other wrestlers, who'd been enjoying the spectacle, stepped in and separated them. Robinson went to the hospital. Peter had another drink to wash the blood down. This was fighting Samoan-style, no holds barred and he was an expert at it!

Now here he was in California, in a different kind of struggle, where he had a lot to lose. Finally, after what seemed like a lifetime to Peter, but was actually a couple of hours of alternative crying and threatening, Rea told him what she wanted. Never once had her hands relaxed on either of his testicles or the knife. Her orders were that he was to give up the Mexican girl he was seeing so much of, and cut out his drinking, at least at the nightclubs. If he wanted to drink, why not do it with his loving wife and daughter?

Peter, full of remorse for his wayward life, begged forgiveness and promised to be faithful for all eternity. The fact that his wife had been drinking beer and held a razor-sharp knife behind his balls might've helped. He also knew that Rea, in her present state of mind, was ready to do major surgery without an anesthetic.

"All right, Peeta." She said. "I let you go this time, but remember. . . No more fucking around with that horse!" Laying down the knife, she smiled. "You a good man, Peeta. . . Just get led astray too easy. Give all you money to those Mexicans, you finish wrestling, you have nothing!"

Checking to see that the knife was out of her hand, Peter came up off the bed with a roar. Snatching the knife up, he broke it in half, hurling the pieces away from him. Smashing Rea in the face with a thick muscular hand, he knocked her off the bed. She jumped to her feet and tried to escape, but he smashed her again. He was bellowing like a mad bull now, at the top of his lungs. Rea ran from the room, down the stairs, and out into the early morning dawn, with Fagasa in hot pursuit. The blows she had taken would've knocked the average man out, but she was made of pretty strong stuff. She was a princess of Samoan royal stock. Fighting ran strongly in her blood. She and Peter had

204

battles all around the world. I found out later it was part of their way of life.

Crawling under a truck in the parking lot, she hid from him while he rampaged naked through the parked cars, shouting in English and Samoan what he would do to her. It was only when the police arrived that he calmed down. Then, and only then, did she crawl out from under the truck, contrite and naked. He was so well-known and liked that no charges were pressed. The happy couple was last seen that morning entering their rented apartment, still naked, laughing and giggling like naughty children.

When I saw her a couple of days later, she laughed at my expression when I saw her face. It was still bruised from the heavy-handed slaps.

"Me and Peeta have a lover's quarrel, Pat." She said. "Nothing to worry about. He a stupid man, always blow his money... not like you. You very careful. Not stupid. You not let girls take you for everything, not like Peeta!"

All through this Peter sat with a beer in his hand and a big friendly smile on his face. Somehow I felt I would pay dearly for this comparison at a future date, but it would be at a time of his choosing, I was sure of that. I was beginning to know this man. And it made me very uneasy.

20

BARING IT ALL

While in Florida I had a lot of fun. I really enjoyed myself and made a lot of friends. I'd met some people who belonged to a nudist colony and was invited to spend a weekend with them.

Now the state of being nude was no problem for me, especially in front of other people. Half my life was spent nude or semi-nude in showers, dressing rooms, gyms, or on stage in The Dunes of Las Vegas. I did a fight scene wearing only a little gold jock strap, leaving my bare ass hanging out at the back. So going nude was no cause for alarm in my mind. In fact, I relished the thought. Men are definitely shyer than women, when it comes to taking off their clothes. I've been to countless parties where stripping was the norm. The thing that struck me most was how uninhibited the fairer sex could be in comparison. I was brought up to believe that women are shy about their bodies. Anyone that believes that should be a wrestler for awhile. It would quickly dispel that notion. I've often wondered why men are less eager to strip. I believe it's because they are "penis conscious". The first thing most men do in a gym is look at another's penis when they are naked. You can see them doing a mental calculation or comparison, whatever you care to call it. Is his bigger than mine? I bet mine, which is smaller now that it's relaxed, gets just as big as his, which is twice the size.

Yes, I went through all of that years ago. Now I know what I've got. I'm happy with it. Though I will admit, if I had a couple of inches more — just for show — it would be nice. I can see myself in the dressing room of a new territory, taking off my pants slowly, while I'm still sitting down, then my underpants. Next, I'm standing up in my full glory. Nine inches swinging gently from side to side as I head toward the toilet. All eyes riveted. Alas, tis but a dream.

So here I am at the nudist colony, naked as the day I was born, and ready for a swim. Maybe it was the wrong day, but I'd expected nubile young things romping around on the beach with full breasts, tight buttocks, and sparkling eyes. I'm not saying that beauty was all I was interested in, but I must confess, after years of looking at cauliflower ears, scarred foreheads, and broken noses, beauty is always refreshing. Today was not the day for me to find what I desired. On the contrary, I've never seen so many large vicious scars in my life. It looked like most of the female forms on view had been used for Japanese bayonet practice, over and over. The only thing that saved the day was my companion, who was quite lovely. She helped me make it through the distraction of all the awful bodies.

I'm not a brilliant swimmer by any description. I never actually learned the art until I was twenty-four. After I had come to the USA a friend of mine, Jack Bence, taught me to swim in a kiddie pool in Atlanta.

My main problem had always been trying to float. Everyone who had endeavored to teach me, and over the years many had, repeated the same thing. "You must learn to float. Come along now, it's easy." It was never mastered — at least not by me. For twenty-four years I'd tried unsuccessfully to swim, to no avail.

Jack Bence, an American I'd met in England while he was wrestling over there, took me under his wing. We met again in Georgia, the first place I wrestled in the USA. He was an excellent swimmer, had gotten medals in the Navy for saving

207

drowning sailors, four or five I believe. His credentials were impressive. He'd invited me to a swimming pool outside Atlanta, owned by an old friend of his. It was a private pool, but I would have no problem getting in Jack told me. His old friend loved the Irish.

When we got there I couldn't believe the sign that was on the front gate. "Only Clean White Gentiles Allowed" it read.

"Is this for real?" I asked Bence.

"Sure it is!" Came his reply.

At that moment I was attracted to an argument that was going on. A man, who looked seventy in the face, but only fifty in the body, was telling a group of people, a man and his wife, and two children, that they couldn't become members. He was saying that even though they maintained that they weren't Jews — only Italians, they looked Jewish to him — and as he owned the club, they couldn't come in. It was final. No Jews allowed. I really felt sorry for the people. It was a hot muggy day. The kids looked especially hurt. I remember thinking "welcome to the real world!"

His antipathy to them was contrasted by his warm welcome to me. The owner couldn't do enough for us. Seeing that I was Irish, he made me a full member, no charge. When I brought up the membership limitations, especially about race, he would brook no argument.

I remember his saying "If government passes those new laws forcing me to take people I don't want into a place that I paid for with my sweat, then I'll close the club, build high rise offices, and sell'em, before I'll allow them to tell me what to do!" As we all know, the government did pass those laws making discrimination illegal. I heard the old fellow did as he promised and closed up shop, built the offices, and sold them.

Jack's first swimming lesson began with his instruction to lay face down in the kiddie pool, with my eyes open, then practice breathing, while doing the breast stroke. This might be why, even now, when swimming I don't have much power in my legs, but can pull myself through the water with my arms for hours.

The looks we got from some of the mothers, at first, were highly suspicious, but Jack was one of the best "pussy pacifiers" in the world. He soon had them eating out of his hand. Between the two of us, we must've nailed half the young mothers in the club. I even learned to swim!

When I first saw the lake at the nudist colony, I wasn't at all happy. Even though I could now swim, my distrust of large bodies of water was so ingrained, as to be almost pronounced. It will probably stay with me until I die. The water, to make matters worse, was dark and forbidding. It was impossible to see more than a few inches into it. I decided to stay sunbathing on the bank as long as possible, until the heat and teasing from the girl I was with made me take the plunge. Suddenly there before me, some distance away, was what looked like turtles bobbing on the surface. My nerves were a little on edge, so the thought of turtles swimming that close didn't help. I'd heard all kinds of horror stories about snapping turtles and the damage they could do to the unwary. The thought that froze my blood was wondering how well they could see in this brackish water, or did it matter? Did they snap first and ask questions later? At the thought of this kind of drastic and unwanted surgery my cock shriveled up completely.

"Are those turtles?" I shouted at a passing nudist, thinking of the stories I'd heard about the large size of snapping turtles and their ferocity.

"No, no," He said. "They're alligators."

At first I thought he was joking. Florida, I knew, had an over abundance of the brutes, but I felt sure that a club like this would figure some way to keep the animals out. Now I'm quite conscious of how a wrestler is expected to be fearless. But in this case, I'm sure I didn't hide the quaver in my voice. Bathing suits are not armor. It's amazing how even more vulnerable the lack of one makes a male feel. At least it did me!

"Aren't they dangerous?" I queried, trying to edge toward

shore without being too obvious.

"No." Came the answer. "At least not if they're under eight feet long, then they might be nasty... especially the bulls... especially during mating season."

All kinds of questions tumbled out of my mouth. "Is it mating season? How will I be able to tell if it's a bull?" I'd never thought of researching the gender of alligators before. Somehow I felt sure they would object. "How do you know how large the animal is from this distance, if most of it is under water?"

"That's easy, measure between the eyes." Came the laconic reply from my new informant, who was now some distance from me.

I edged closer to the shore. All the while squinting, trying to get a fix on the alligators, of which there were about six from what I could see. The trouble was the brutes wouldn't stay still, just kept disappearing, then reappearing at another spot, which didn't help my nerves.

I might've started swimming again, except at that moment Sherri, the girl that brought me to the club, had chosen to swim up behind my back. While underwater she reached up with her hand and grabbed my shriveled cock. She grabbed me with her fingernails, not hard enough to damage, but hard enough to almost give me heart failure. I let out a yell heard all over the grounds, slapping and kicking at the water. I scrambled up on the bank, losing whatever dignity I may have had.

All I could think of was one of the alligators had mistaken my "friend" — the one I'd brought overseas with me; the same friend who'd been in places braver men feared to go — for a small fish or worm underwater. He was about to be torn off my body and devoured. I know my cock had been devoured many times by open mouths, some caressingly, some hungrily scarring, whether by intent or just carelessness. But never had the thought occurred to me before this, that it would end up inside the belly of an alligator.

Roars of laughter came from everyone around. Though they

210

couldn't have known for sure what had happened, they put two and two together when they saw Sherri's smiling face surface behind me.

I lay panting for breath on the bank. If I could've gotten hold of her at that moment, I'm sure I would've committed murder. She, being no fool, stayed in the water laughing. I was not about to go in again. Afterwards I saw the funny side of things, but I stayed on dry land for the duration. I also learned a lesson. Fear could and did wipe out all rational thoughts from my mind and leave me a gibbering idiot for a moment. It was very disconcerting.

My grand finale at the nudist club has me puzzled to this day. We had gone into the dining room to have lunch when we were approached by a committee member. He told us we must wear something around out genitals while eating our food there. I couldn't understand this. Perhaps I like food more than most people, but the sight of other people's genitals doesn't put me off my lunch. Why should mine put them off? Especially as I felt mine were cuter than most. Still they insisted on enforcing the rule. That was what we were told none-the-less. I noticed he was wearing a towel around his waist, as were most of the club members in the restaurant. A loud argument followed which drew the attention of other committee members. Soon I was surrounded by a sweating crowd who were adamant that I put something around my loins or I couldn't stay in the dining area. The committee members who had arrived in a hurry at the sound of the altercation were all still naked, having come running when things got heated. It was difficult for me to be serious when I kept seeing genitals waving around as their owners became more vehement. That was the straw that broke the camel's back. It was a not-so-fond farewell that I bade to the camp, particularly as I told the president to stick the club up between his ample buttocks. That was when I was escorted naked to the front gate by about twelve committee members, and told not to come back. Imagine being ejected from a nudist camp for refusing to wear clothes! I've never been to a nudist camp since.

21

ONE FOR THE ROAD

When I was first told that Dick Carlson was a great cocksman I found it a little hard to believe. It was just that he didn't look like a man who could successfully seduce women — well maybe a certain kind — but not your down-to-earth smart business types — never. But the number of different types he collected boggled the imagination, high-bred, low-bred, smart, simple, everything in between just as long as it wore a skirt. Dick aimed for them all. To me, his line was so obviously that, just a line. But it seemed that women of all ages, looks, and creeds swallowed it hook, line, and sinker.

I introduced him to an airline hostess I knew in Australia. She was as hard-bitten as it was possible to get, and always reminded me of that old song, "Hard Hearted Hannah." Really a very pretty girl, she was used to all kinds of men chasing after her. She used them any way she wanted, then discarded them like a half-smoked cigarette. I knew her through a friend of mine and watched with fascination as she cannibalized her different dates, very much the same as the Black Widow spider devours its mates.

Carlson was a six-footer with a slight stoop. He had bleached blond hair, a nose like W. C. Fields, the ingratiating manners of a used car salesman, all packaged up in a rather smooth unathletic-looking body. Not what you'd expect a wrestler to look like, and certainly not the Don Juan type.

Despite all this, his record with the ladies was impressive. I'd known him a few years earlier, down South. He came from Tennessee somewhere, a small town close to Chattanooga. The man was an expert with the good-old-boy bullshit.

He arrived in Australia about a month after I did. As this was my third trip there, I was beginning to know the country better than the natives. In my previous trips down-under I'd made a lot of friends. The Australians, to me, are some of the greatest people in the world. They try not to work too hard, but they play for keeps. They make sincere friends for life. God help the person who makes the offer lightly to an Aussie of "Why don't you come and stay with me sometime?" One day, maybe twenty years down the road, along will come your Australian friend of your wild youth. You've left him behind years ago in your memories, while you've settled down to a humdrum existence. Suddenly he's ringing your doorbell and extending his hand saying, "Good on 'ya mate! Ya told me ta come and stay . . . Here I am!" And he's as wild as you remember him, maybe even more! Your wife meanwhile is looking at you with that, you-knew-people-like-this-before-you-met-me expression on her face.

Dick heard I had many friends amongst the local airline attendants, so he asked would I introduce him to a good-looking Aussie girl. My mind went to Jane, the hard-hearted Hannah. I'd just seen her the night before demolish her escort at a party. She left with someone else without telling her date. The poor man wandered around the rest of the evening looking for her. What a match that would be, Jane and Dick! Talk about clash of the titans!

It was arranged. They met a few nights later at the matches in Sydney, where I made the introductions. It was a couple of weeks before I bumped into them again. I was busy in western Australia, which is really beautiful country, vast golden beaches bedding up to a marvelous deep blue ocean. What I couldn't believe was Jane's transformation. She was eating out of his hand. She was not the same girl that I knew. She was like a lamb with a "Yes, Dick" here and a "Yes, Dick" there. Gone was the shrew, in its place was a sweet young lady.

Even my friend Gary remarked on it. Gary was in the management side of the airline that employed Jane. They had known each other for years and she was a good friend of Gary's wife. Dick and Jane had gone out together for about a month before Carlson got into a spot of bother with the office and was fired. Gary called me up. He sounded very upset. Carlson was going back to the states, but that wasn't what was upsetting him. Jane was leaving for the states as well. I guess he didn't want to lose a good hostess. Not only that, she was selling all her goods and chattels, that included her condominium, which was in a very elite part of Sydney.

I called Dick to ask what had happened. I didn't care what was going on with him, or her for that matter, but I was nosey.

The scoop was that he was going back to Tennessee, taking Jane with him. In fact, he was going to marry the little lady. I had a good laugh. In my eyes they deserved each other.

Shortly afterwards I left for New Zealand and forgot all about them.

Some months later, when I was back in the states, I got a call from Mary, another Australian airline attendant and a friend of Jane's. She said she was in the USA, and would like to look Jane up for a visit. Was I interested in going along? My answer was immediate. I definitely wanted to see Mrs. Carlson, to see what time and the South had done to her, or what she had done to them and Dick. Remember she was a tough cookie in her own right!

We arrived at the house late on a chilly autumn evening, only to find no one at home. Mary said Jane was most likely still at work. She had the address. We could go there. What I couldn't figure out was what kind of work would anyone do in the square at 9 p.m. in a southern town?

My mind raced through all kinds of different things she could do, from fishnet stockings to pushing dope. As it turned out, it was none of those. It was still a shock to see that feisty good-looking girl that I remembered, working in a little mobile hot dog stand. What really stunned me was her appearance, she'd aged about twenty years. Her skin looked wrinkled and tired, nothing like the fresh-faced girl I knew in Australia. She was so happy to see us it was pathetic. Why did I keep thinking of the story "The Taming of the Shrew"? She kept side-tracking any conversation about Dick, who was away wrestling. We had a few drinks while she had a good cry on Mary's shoulder, then left the next day. I never saw her again. But I heard through the grape vine that she finally packed her bags and left for Australia, leaving her money, which was invested in the farm, behind.

Dick and I met in Florida a few years later. With him was a stunning blonde beauty he called Sam. Why in the world she had a name like Sam, I never knew. She was really gorgeous, one of those high-bosomed, high-assed blonde girls, with beautiful blue eyes, that are the dream of so many men.

Pulling him aside, I asked what ever happened between him and Jane.

"Divorced." He chuckled. "The southern air wasn't too good for her."

"What happened to her condominium back in Australia?"

"Well," He replied succinctly. "She had to sell it so we could buy my farm."

"What farm?" I asked. I had no compunction about asking personal questions. If he didn't want to tell me, I knew he wouldn't. He was no shrinking violet.

"My farm!" He answered. I noticed he didn't say 'our'. "You know... where I live in Tennessee."

"Oh, well, what happened to that? Do you still have it? I mean, didn't she make you sell it to get her money back?"

"No! No." He laughed so hard I thought he'd choke. "She was in a hurry to get home to mother. She just left me the whole lot!"

Seeing as how I introduced them, I should have felt some remorse, but I'd learned by then to save my pity for those who deserved it. He didn't seem sorry either — that was not his nature — but then he had Sam to console him.

Sam drove with him to all the shows. The sight of her beautiful body would cause men to stop and stare, every time she got out of the car. Dick enjoyed the sensation she produced. He would take great delight in fondling her voluptuous ass seemingly absent-mindedly in front of people.

On the way to Miami there was a toll booth we passed through going to and from the show. At night there was an elderly man who collected the money. He knew most of the wrestlers by sight, and always had a friendly word for the boys.

Dick was going through this particular night about 2:30 a.m. in high good humor, with the beautiful Sam, who by the way, had just turned eighteen. The old duffer made a lewd remark about her, how beautiful she was, and what a lucky man Dick was, obviously overwhelmed by her good looks and the fact that she happened to be stroking Dick's leg sensually when he looked into the car.

Carlson asked how long it had been since he'd had a good climax. This remark was met with a toothless laugh.

"God, it's been so long I can't even remember what it's like!"

"Can you still get it up?" Was Dick's next question.

"Hell no! It done shriveled away!" At that remark Dick looked at Sam with a smile.

"What do you think, honey? Can you do anything for him to make his life a little happier? Think you can get it up?"

Most girls would've been offended. Not Sam. She was a swinger, loving the effect she had on men. She languorously got out of the car and walked straight into the toll booth. Before the surprised toll collector could collect his wits, she had unzipped his pants, taken his cock into her mouth, and started blowing him.

One of the wrestlers timed the act. Forty-five seconds, from the time she ducked her head between his legs, to the time he let out a shuddering cry, and nearly collapsed at the same time. Carlson told me later he thought the old fart was going to die, right then and there, but apparently he was made of sterner stuff.

They drove away laughing, leaving the old-timer gasping for breath, not believing what had just happened.

This went on for several weeks, with Sam doing her thing in the toll booth on the old collector. Suddenly he disappeared. No one could explain where he went. In his place was a much younger man who said he knew nothing about the old man's whereabouts.

Dick's stay in Florida terminated and he moved on to greener pastures. Sam also disappeared, never to be seen around the wrestling halls again.

About six months later I was driving to Miami one afternoon, when lo and behold, there was the old-timer collecting tolls again. He recognized me right away. We exchanged some pleasantries, then I asked him where he'd been all this time. He seemed reluctant to talk about that. Sensing a story here, I probed a little deeper.

"Have you seen Sam recently?" I asked, hoping for a reaction. Consider now, how many men are lucky enough to be blown by a beautiful girl while on the job, especially a man that looks like him! He really was no enchanter.

His manner became very furtive and evasive. "No." He said. "I haven't seen her for some time." The words were so dragged out I knew I'd hit a nerve.

"Do you miss her?" I leaned out of my car, pressing for an answer. "Well, yes and no." Came the reply reluctantly.

He was so ill at ease that I just knew there was something he didn't want to tell me. That only hardened my resolve to get to the truth, whatever it was.

"Well, yes and no." He muttered, his voice was so low that

I almost couldn't hear it. The road was empty, nobody else was at the toll booth. If ever I was to get to the bottom of his disappearance, now was the time.

"What do you mean, 'yes and no'? I would've thought you'd really miss her, I mean she was good, wasn't she?" I realized I was twisting the knife a bit, but I couldn't help myself.

"Yes," He said. "But she also got me into a lot of trouble, though she didn't mean to!" He added hastily.

"Hold on, let me pull out of the way." I wanted to hear this, so did everyone else in the car. It sounded like the makings of a good scoop and I didn't want to hold up traffic. I pulled my car over to the side, got out, and walked back to the booth.

"What happened? How did she get you into trouble? Has it got something to do with your not being around for awhile?"

"You said it!" He blurted out all his pent-up emotions, which were surging like a swollen river bursting its banks. "What happened was I started telling the other guys in the company, and a few friends, about this beautiful blonde eighteen-year-old that was giving me head every week while I was on the night shift. At first, they thought I was just joking. Then when I got mad because they wouldn't believe me, things got serious." All four wrestlers, myself included, crowded around the toll booth. "My boss thought I was hallucinating, so he sent me to a psychiatrist for an evaluation. The doc insisted I get some time off... Maybe I was overworked. He put me on medication. I had to attend special psychiatric treatment sessions. That's when they figured I was cured. They put me on the day shift, because they thought the strain of night work was too much. Sooooo, here I am. I think I'm lucky they didn't lock me up!"

That's why he was reluctant to talk about it, he didn't want to go through all that again.

He was able to laugh about it all when I saw him a few weeks later, but he always asked if I'd seen her.

Before I left the Florida area a referee came up to talk to me, just prior to the matches.

"By the way, do you know that old guy who runs the toll booth? He says he knows you and several other wrestlers."

"Yes, I know the guy. Why?"

"Is he all there?" The referee asked, touching his head.

"I believe so, but why?"

"My wife and I drove through here with another wrestler today. We stopped at the booth. The guy recognized the man I had with me. He seemed friendly enough, then he looked at my wife and right out of the blue he asked, 'Is she a good blow job too?' I almost died. The wrestler with us went hysterical in the back seat, but he wouldn't say why. What the hell's going on? Is he punchy or something?"

"Let me ask you something..." I countered. "Is your wife blonde?"

"Yes." Came the reply.

"Has she got a good body?"

"Yeah," He answered. "What the hell's that got to do with anything? I don't see..."

I cut him off in mid-sentence. "Bear with me for a minute. Don't get mad, all will be explained. Does she have blue eyes and is she young?"

"Yes she has blue eyes, she's fairly young, but what the hell is going on?"

I could see he was getting very annoyed, but I couldn't help myself. I was enjoying the moment, making him wait. I believed I knew what had happened and why. I told him the Sam story. At first he didn't believe me, then I could see comprehension dawning on him. Fortunately he had a good sense of humor, and so it seemed had his wife when he told her the story. She had heard the question asked at the toll booth and had been just as mystified as her husband. We all had a good laugh.

22

ARENA RATS AND
OTHER FANATICS

I've compared notes with musicians, football players, baseball players, and others about fans and how crazy they can be, but I can only talk about the fans who follow wrestling. The main difference, I believe, in wrestling fans and others out there is that wrestlers go out of their way to incite them, thus making them even crazier. This, I freely admit, is like pulling on a tiger's tail, only it's more dangerous. Once you get them mad, how do you cool them down? I've done this myself when I've wanted fans to hate me. Sometimes in interviews on TV I would tell people that I've been in communication with my mother in London. I said that she'd told me that if I couldn't beat the bum I was going to wrestle next week, she would come over from London and personally beat the daylights out of both him and me. For quite some time, while I was doing these kind of interviews, she was the most hated woman in America. The truth is she is only five-foot and half-an-inch tall, very kind and gentle, and couldn't bring herself to hurt a fly. On one of my trips back to Ireland I told her about my interviews and the hate mail I'd gotten calling her all kinds of names. She just smiled, obviously not believing a word. It was a good thing she never read any of the mail I received, she wouldn't have thought it was so funny.

While I was in Fort Lauderdale, I was watching two heels at

work on two other wrestlers. "Heel" is the name given to wrestlers that blatantly break the rules, thus becoming the object of the fans' hatred. Suddenly from the back of the hall a young man streaked forward to the ring, spun through the ropes, and attacked the heels, two of the biggest, strongest men in the business, Bobby Duncan and Bob Roup. Bobby was playing football as well as wrestling, and must've weighed two-hundred, eighty pounds in shape. Roup had represented the USA in amateur wrestling, in the Greco-Roman style. This requires great balance and strength on your feet. It is one of the toughest forms of the sport. To get into top shape required by this style of wrestling, a man has to be tough mentally as well as physically.

Against these giants went a one-hundred, fifty-pound fan, who with no hesitation, went straight into battle. No knight of yore ever attacked greater odds, or fought with more vigor, in defense of a fair maiden. Except this fair maiden happened to be a two-hundred, forty-pound wrestler.

It was a tag match, which means four wrestlers were involved, but no more than one man from each team was supposed to be in the ring at the same time. The heels were naturally double-teaming one of their opponents, much to the dismay and rage of the onlooking fans, when this young knight went into action. Unfortunately the dragon, in the shape of Roup and Duncan, was too large and too tough to be subdued by the brave knight. He did get in a couple of punches before he was seized by first one, then the other wrestler. They took turns in throwing punches at him, savoring the moment and taking their time. They were going to teach him a lesson he wouldn't forget, bearing in mind that he could've had a knife or gun in his hand, as some wrestling fans do. He put his head down to protect his face, consequently taking most of the blows on the top of his head. Before they were finished his body had gone limp. Then he was flung, barely conscious, through the ropes onto the floor, where he was picked up and dragged to the dressing rooms by first-aid men. Looking at how his limp body was dragged away reminded me of the bull at the end of a bull fight. One-hundred, fifty pounds of dead meat. I followed the two men who were carrying his mutilated body. In my years of wrestling all over the world, I've never seen lumps like those he'd collected on his forehead, the top, and back of his head. The lumps stuck up through his hair like small round horns. There must've been at least thirty of them! His lip was split. One eye was closed. I almost felt sorry for him, except that he had no business jumping in the ring.

Many of the boys have been damaged by irate fans, even killed. It isn't unusual for knives and guns to be produced in the audience of the matches. In a way the wrestlers were lucky. If he'd had a weapon, they would've been in real trouble. With the atmosphere in the hall reaching a fever pitch, they should've been on the lookout for trouble-makers like him. They had been careless. Also if he had not been handled swiftly and ruthlessly, he could've been followed by half of the audience. As it was, the temperature in the hall must've risen thirty degrees by the end of the match. The two heels had to be protected by guards and other wrestlers when they left the ring.

In the meantime the young man had regained consciousness in the dressing room and was preparing to go to the hospital when I got a chance to talk to him. His wife was crying pitifully at his side while she lovingly caressed his forehead. The lumps were what fascinated me. I could barely take my eyes off them.

"Why," I asked, "did you do such a stupid thing? You jumped into the ring with two men that were both twice your size and trained wrestlers as well!" I was perplexed as to what his motivation could've been.

He looked at me through his one good eye, then shook his head ruefully, and incredibly he grinned. It must have hurt like hell, but he was game. "Well, I was sitting with my wife Helen, watching the two SOB's beating on my favorite wrestler, Mike Graham. She was getting madder by the minute at their tactics, and that dumb referee didn't seem to see anything. Suddenly Helen shouted at me, 'Are you going to let them murder him?

What kind of a man are you?!' The next thing I knew, I was in the ring, fighting for my life. I don't even know how I got there. I don't remember leaving my wife... nothing."

Helen broke into deep shuddering sobs that racked her whole body. I felt pity well up inside for this woman who had inadvertently put her husband's life on the line.

It was my turn to shake my head. "Well, I guess you learned your lesson. Bet you won't do that again. I suppose you won't even be back to the matches."

Without hesitation he answered, "I'll be back next week, if they let me in." Then he paused. "Yeah, I'd do it again, if they was beating up somebody I liked." He said it with such conviction that I had to believe him. The conversation was cut short by the arrival of the ambulance.

When he was loaded inside, his young pretty wife threw her arms around him and gave him a big hug and a kiss. She whispered in his ear, "You were wonderful, baby!" I helped her into the ambulance to be beside her husband in his hour of need. I was deeply touched. Perhaps his crazy attack was not in vain. It showed what some people would do for love. It was wonderful to see how she appreciated his amazing act of foolhardiness. Saying good bye, I jumped to the ground and turned to help close the door. His wife was right behind me. To say I was surprised is an understatement. I was shocked. "Aren't you going to stay with your husband?" I gasped, gripping her arm. "You can ride in the ambulance. He needs you."

"'Course not!" She snapped. Her eyes now dry, flashed fire. "He'll be okay, he's tough. Anyway I wouldn't miss this last match for the world!"

Turning, she waved farewell to the ambulance, then without another word, headed back to her seat.

The last view I had of her was when she was jumping up and down beside the empty seat that had belonged to her husband, screaming abuse at the men in the ring.

EVERYBODY DOWN HERE HATES ME

* * * * * * * * * * *

Fans have also tried many different ways to get into the dressing rooms. Many women make the direct approach by offering sex. There is a fascination among fans to see what goes on behind the scenes. If dressing rooms open directly onto a hall or corridor where fans have access, whenever a door opens it's immediately blocked by crowds of curious, eager faces dying to see what's happening within.

There was the fan who came up with an ingenious way to get inside. The promoter was making his rounds checking to see if all the men were present, when he noticed a very unfamiliar looking figure sitting in a dressing room with a mask on. He couldn't remember having a masked man in the matches, so he went to the Booker to check. The Booker lines up the men in the matches to make it interesting for the public, and books the dates.

"No." Replied the Booker, looking at his booking sheet. "There's no masked wrestler on the card, but let's go talk to him. Maybe he's here by mistake."

"Who are you?" The promoter asked.

"Me?" The voice asked from behind the mask.

"Yes, you." The Booker chimed in, in a not-too-friendly voice.

"Nobody." Came the reply.

"What do you mean 'Nobody'?" The Booker's voice had risen somewhat, attracting the attention of a couple of wrestlers. The figure on the bench was now surrounded. "If you're nobody, what the fuck are you doing in the dressing room wearing a mask?"

"I just wanted to be with the wrasslers!" Came the surprising answer. "I'm a fan and I couldn't get into the dressing rooms any other way, so I made this mask. Then it was real easy!"

There was a stunned silence, then pandemonium. It was like a room full of bears finding a skunk in their midst. In this case

224

the skunk didn't last too long. He was snatched off the bench, lifted shoulder high by two large men, then rushed to the back door which was held open by a uniformed security guard. The masked intruder was hurled through the door into the back lane, where he bounced on the concrete before crawling away into the night. As everyone headed back to the dressing rooms, the guard called out quite cheerfully, "That's the shortest professional wrestling career I've ever seen!" The boys broke into laughter. Good humor was restored. As for the fan, I often wonder what story he told his friends. Over-reaction by the wrestlers? I just think of what happened to John Lennon.

* * * * * * * * * * *

When I think about fans, I consider all the different kinds of folk who attend the matches on a regular basis. Some of the more interesting, especially from the wrestlers' point of view, are the girls or women who hang around. In fact, some aren't more than mere girls, who are in almost all the halls waiting to succor the wrestler of her choice. They are called "Arena Rats" by the boys, though I think this is a harsh name for most of them. There are some who deserve it. They come in all shapes, sizes, ages, and social backgrounds. The one thing they have in common is the love of wrestlers. The good part about these women is they will take care of a wrestler's sexual wants without all the maddening games normally expected to be played by horny males.

One wrestler, Jim, was a big man, even by pro standards, and considered himself to be quite a ladies' man.

He was giving a certain young lady his best shot. After all the foreplay he knew turned a woman on, some oral sex thrown in to warm her up, he performed a session of sex she wouldn't forget. As he reached the crescendo, she was moaning with delight. He was congratulating himself on being a superstud. Just at the moment of his climaxing, she tightened her legs around his heaving body, grasped him passionately in her arms, then whispered in his ear, "Oh Jim... Jim... please tell me something..."

"Yes." He groaned. "What do you want, baby? Anything." He thought that more than likely she wants to hear him say "I love you." Well, he reasoned, he would tell her that, if it made her happy. He would give her some encouragement. "What do you want to know?" His voice was a hoarse whisper, thickened with passion.

He was so close he was falling over the edge. Her hot lips were pressed close to his ear. She murmured these words, "I want... Oh, Jim... Tell me, is wrestling all fake?"

Somehow, he told me, it was never the same after that.

* * * * * * * * * * *

Gregory Neilson had very little patience with people in general, but with foolish belligerent wrestling fans, he had none at all. I'd heard stories of how he'd called pugnacious people into the ring. Those stupid enough to get in never lasted too long. He reminded me of a praying mantis. That is an unfair analogy in some ways, but he had a lot of the same qualities. His arms and legs were long, lean, and muscular. His weight was a deceptive two-hundred, thirty pounds, which is not large in the heavyweight division. His reflexes were incredibly fast. Just like a praying mantis, his arm would shoot out and snatch a limb or a head, whatever was within reach. His face never changed expression while he was inflicting pain and damage. By most people he was considered quite good looking, with an angelic baby face. His fair hair, what was left of it, was cut very close. He looked more mature than his years from a distance. This prompted fans to tell his opponent to "Finish off that old bastard!" Wrestlers dreaded those words. It meant that Gregory would step up the pace of the match and get even more brutal. He was in fantastic shape. There were very few men who could keep up with him. His eyes were the coldest blue I'd ever seen. They never smiled. As time went by I got to know him quite well. We were swapping jokes in a pub when I noticed that even though he laughed, his

226

face never changed. In my mind he was the perfect fighting machine, no wasted motion or emotion. I don't believe he ever hesitated when it came to violence. Neither did he have any remorse. He eventually wore a mask and had great success with it. It hid his balding head, and accentuated his athletic body.

I had the misfortune of wrestling him in a town which was predominantly Irish. I had lots of fans there who automatically hated anyone I wrestled. They believed I could and should beat anyone in the world, especially this old man who, though they didn't know it, was the same age as I. Things were not going too well, in fact, since the beginning of the match I had been in trouble. It was apparent to all. Tonight, in the front row, sat a very loud fan, quite a big lad, who looked like he could handle himself in a fight. He was on my side and made no bones about it, so much so that his remarks regarding Neilson had gotten quite personal, about his breath, his love life, his mother, anything he could think of. As the match progressed, this fellow took to jumping out of his seat, threatening to do all manner of things to Gregory. Neilson had, up to this point, totally ignored him, which seemed to infuriate the fan even more.

In England, wrestling is in the form of five or ten-minute rounds, similar to boxing. I prefer the American style myself, wrestling until a submission or a fall is taken, or the time limit expires. A submission is when one wrestler gets a bone-breaking hold on another, which forces him to give up. In this case I was content with the rounds, for it gave me a breather, only one minute, but it's amazing how much you can recover in even that amount of time. Sixty seconds are better than nothing!

It was during this brief respite that the beefy fan in the front got really excited by my performance. He jumped up and rushed to Neilson's corner. Then turning to look at me, my new-found friend shouted above the noise of the crowd, "If you can't beat this old bastard, I'll have to get in and do it myself!"

Gregory was seemingly paying no attention to him up until this point, but I knew better. Nothing escaped the notice of the perfect fighting machine.

It doesn't pay to be unaware of what's going on around you in the pro wrestling business. Even now I don't sit comfortably in a restaurant unless I've got my back to the wall. I want a clear view of everything around me. This way chairs or bottles won't get smashed on my head from behind. It's been called the "Gun Fighters' Position" I'm told, from the era of Doc Holliday. I can sympathize with the feeling.

Neilson said nothing but walked from his corner to the center of the ropes, sat on the middle one and pulled up on the top, then gestured for my vocal friend to enter. The challenge was obvious. For a moment I thought the fan was going to be foolhardy enough to get in. If he had, I had no doubt he would've lasted only as long as Neilson wanted him to.

If a fan jumped into the ring, most wrestlers finish him off as fast as possible, doing whatever is necessary to smash, pulverize, beat or maim any person crazy enough to enter the lion's den. The wrestler is the one with everything to lose, namely their living and their standing amongst other pros. In a situation like this, the pro takes a terrible risk. If he doesn't beat the fan decisively, everyone turns against him including the promoters. People who don't wrestle can be awkward to handle. They always do the unexpected. It was the measure of Neilson that he never rushed to finish a job like this. He took great delight in playing them like a fish, letting them think they'd gotten away, then reeling them in, making them look stupid. He would hurt just enough, but not too much, then make them scream in a submission hold so the referee would have to stop it.

The fan quit his tirade for a couple of moments. I watched with interest. My minute's rest was up. No interruption was going to come from me. I needed all the time I could get. Then with the universal gesture of his middle finger, the man turned his back on the ring, with great dignity, and returned to his seat. Then in a loud voice heard above the laughs from the delighted audience, he concluded "I don't waste my time on old useless men. Let Pat finish him off!''

My heart sank. Action was about to be resumed with this fighting machine, who was now madder than a rabid dog in water.

Neilson glided across the ring, his face betraying no emotion. He started stalking me. Perhaps if I could stall a little, the seething rage would subside. I knew instinctively there was violent rage behind that marble facade. Wrestlers dread the advance of age, hating younger wrestlers full of piss and vinegar. To be called an old man when you were still young and as talented as your opponent was just adding insult to injury. Finally I couldn't, in all decency, keep backing away. I had my image to live up to, "The Fearless Irishman, always ready for action."

We hooked up, which means we locked arms, supposedly going for the best hold. I was really on the defensive, trying only to protect myself. My erstwhile friend, in the meantime, was back in his seat, wearing a self-satisfying smirk. I began to believe he'd had a little to drink. Didn't he realize how close to the brink he'd come? Now I was the one who was going to suffer. I hated him, almost wishing him dead.

Gregory's arms were like steel bands. He had me in a side head lock, making me see the milky way and millions of swirling stars in my eyes. He turned me around in the center of the ring, dragging my reluctant body behind. Was I imagining it? No. The hold was beginning to loosen. I could move my head somewhat. Putting my right arm around his waist, I hurled him toward the ropes. Maybe he was getting tired. Who knows? I wasn't going to look a gift horse in the mouth! My wish was that he'd give my head a break, though not the kind of break he'd been trying to give it a few seconds earlier! Gregory flew from my arms like an arrow. I marveled at my strength, my recovery. He bounced from the ropes at incredible speed, even for him. Coming from a shoulder tackle, at his speed, if we hit it would be extremely painful for me. I steadied myself for the impact, but he missed, only by a hair's breadth. Neilson ran right past at top speed to the other ropes. Turning my head, I followed him with my eyes. Then it came to me, an inkling of what was about to happen. He wouldn't, I reassured myself, but deep down inside I knew he would. Just before reaching the ropes he tripped, or seemed to trip, which sent him hurtling head first between them. As he went through, his hand snatched at the middle rope, momentarily holding on long enough to turn his body around. His feet barely seemed to touch the floor. He was going backwards towards the front row at incredible speed.

Those who regularly sit in the front row of wrestling matches learn to watch, very carefully, what's going on in the ring. They become quick of mind, their reflexes sharpened by years of experience. Large bodies have been known to come out over and under the ropes, taking all that is in their way, tables, time-keepers, seconds, and unwary people with them. The breed of person who sits in the front row is usually an alert and watchful animal. At the first sign of trouble it assumes the defensive posture, covering the head, putting both feet up in front of their bodies, or both. There's always the option of making a hasty exit out of harm's way. This, to them, is all part of the thrill. It enhances the experience I believe, because the same people usually sit in the same front seats, in the danger zone, week after week. This time though, they were literally caught flat-footed. There was no chance for defensive measures, no chance for escape. Their doom was sealed. There was no way of stopping or deflecting this air-borne body. Right in the thick of it was my rabid friend.

Neilson crashed into the front row, landing squarely on a man's chest, sending him over backwards. Gregory's left arm was bent. The upper part smashed into the face of a fan, breaking his nose, I learned afterwards, sending spurts of blood everywhere. Pandemonium reigned. Blood always has a way of bringing out the beast in people. It doesn't seem to matter who the blood belongs to.

Neilson pulled himself to his feet and staggered to the ring.

230

Now I knew why he'd missed the tackle. It was my friend in the front row he'd been after. Standing back with the referee, we both watched the unfortunate man getting carried out by the officials. I felt a bit sorry for him. I mean he was in this predicament because he liked me. He did look in a bad way. I gazed into the cold blue eyes that were looking straight at me. Gregory never looked behind to see what damage he'd done. He already knew. Did I detect a flicker of amusement? His lips didn't seem to move, but I heard quite clearly what he said. "How do you think your friend will like his broken nose?" He murmured.

No need to tell me what he meant. How could I break the news to him? I decided I must, whatever the consequences. Gregory had made one error that was to cost him his revenge.

He had calculated the direction of the blow to perfection. One could admire the precision of an artist, unless you were the recipient of course. The only thing was that in changing his position by grabbing the rope, Gregory had become disoriented for a second. The fan he was after was on the right of the man he had landed on, thus misdirecting the fatal blow entirely.

"You got the wrong one." I said. "Take a look."

Neilson stared at me for a couple of long seconds, then slowly turned around. Sure enough, his enemy was sitting there large as life, but looking very pale. He may have had a few drinks on him, but he wasn't too drunk to understand how narrow an escape he'd just had. Neilson stood looking at him for a few seconds more, then turned at the referee's command to continue wrestling. As he turned, he missed my most loyal fan of the night get up from his seat, with a great show of bravado, and slowly walk away, never to return, at least not that night. He'd gotten the message, loud and clear.

23

THE LAST ROUND UP

Simon Greenberg was one of the most improbable looking wrestlers in a business of improbable looking people. I'd learned a long time before that you could not judge a person by his appearance. Mass murderers almost invariably are described by people who knew them, as quiet, humble inoffensive folk. Deranged rapists nearly always turn out to be good family men, and so forth. Strength sometimes is not always obvious. It can lurk beneath the fat body that looks all blubber, or beneath the skinny body that looks as if a strong wind would blow it over.

Greenberg was one of those very deceptive looking men that the pro wrestling business is full of. He stood about five-feet, nine-inches tall, was Jewish, and looked it. His face was like the caricatures you see of Jews the world over, big fleshy nose, round face, and thinning black hair. He sported thick glasses, and was legally blind without them. I often wondered how he could even see his opponent with such bad eyesight. His body was nothing to write home about. It was stocky and didn't look the best, and was smoother than most people expect an athlete's body to be. I'm sure he had difficulty persuading strangers that he wrestled for a living, so different was he from the normal conception people had. The only part of him that fitted the wrestling mold were his cauliflower ears. He looked like a cross between E.T. and a teddy bear.

To top it off, he would wear a leopard skin in the ring. This was not your fancy sleek skin. No. This skin looked like it had been chewed on by a pack of baboons, stomped on by an elephant or two, then left to get moldy in someone's basement for a few years. It was also a couple of sizes too big for him, which certainly didn't enhance his image of the strong man, for which he wrestled as.

All of this took place in the Tennessee area. When I first saw him I wanted to laugh, and laughing at a partner isn't the key to a successful combination. Why the promoter, in his infinite wisdom, decided to make us a tag team, I'll never know. The difference in our temperaments was extreme. His was placid, mine was not. Physically, although I didn't have a body beautiful, I enjoyed keeping myself fit and looking my best. Simon didn't seem to care about either. He was definitely an ox in sheep's clothing. He was exceedingly strong in the hands and wrists, bending nails and iron, all manner of things with apparent ease. He also did an act before he wrestled. I was his assistant. He would have an anvil, I can't remember how much it weighed, but it was extremely heavy, brought into the ring. It took four men to carry it with great difficulty. A flat piece of wood was next supplied, out of which protruded hundreds of nails. Then I would call the fans' attention to the tremendous weight of the anvil, the sharpness of the nails, and the extraordinary strength of Simon.

One day Simon and I were driving through some pleasant countryside where cattle were in abundance. Simon asked if I was a country boy. I answered no. Greenberg then explained how he'd spent his younger days on a farm where he learned to call cattle for his father. He further maintained that he'd never had to go out and collect or round them up. He could call anything bovine within hearing distance of his voice. They'd all come, pronto.

Like most wrestlers, he enjoyed tall stories, especially his own, so I took it all with a grain of salt and indulged his fantasy. Actually, I'd heard wilder ones from other wrestlers and this one seemed harmless enough. He must've seen by my face that I was an unbeliever, because he asked me to pull over a couple of miles down the road. I thought he needed to go to the bathroom and couldn't understand why he picked a spot with no shelter. We were stopped by a huge field which stretched off into the distance. I could see it was dotted with scores of cows, not steers mind you, but cows... good healthy, milking cows with their bags full of fine, rich milk. They really looked a prime bunch, the ones that were close enough to see. Greenberg seemed very excited and I couldn't understand why.

"I'll bet you twenty dollars that I can make those cows start running this way." He wheezed. He had recurring bouts of asthma which usually manifested itself when he was excited. Well, twenty dollars seemed a bit much to me, even on a sure thing. At the time I was scratching for a living, so I made him drop it to ten.

The rules were simple. He had unlimited time to get the cows coming toward us — there must've been at least five hundred — and a portion of them had to come to the fence where we were standing. So sure was I of the impossibility of the task that I started to feel a bit guilty about taking his money. Enough said, Greenberg took up his position. With legs fully spread, facing the cows, he cupped his hands around his mouth and started making a noise like a cow, steer, bull, or whatever it was.

Nothing happened. Undaunted, he called again with a long mournful "Mooooo," starting with a deep note, ending up with a sound fading slowly away. Altogether each call lasted from three to five seconds. Again nothing happened. I was starting to fidget. It was embarrassing to watch his efforts fail so miserably. We must have been there five or six minutes with his face slowly turning purple. Tugging at his sleeve I said, "Let's go Simon. Maybe southern cows are not as easily fooled as northern ones." My attempt at levity only brought renewed cow-calling, with increased vigor. Just as I was about to suggest again that we leave, as we'd be late for the show, one of the beasts close by lifted her head and started gazing in our direction, in the absent-minded way that cows do. Then a look of interest crept across the bovine face, or maybe I was imagining it. What I wasn't imagining were the few hesitant steps she was taking. "Damn!" I thought, "I hope this isn't the start of something big."

My problem wasn't the ten dollars, though money was always important to me. I hate more than anything to lose, especially to lose a bet. If this cow should start a trend then a sure-fire bet was down the tubes. Well, to my chagrin, that's just what happened.

Slowly at first, then one or two, half a dozen, now a dozen, then as far as the eye could see cows were heading our way. I couldn't believe it. Simon, in the meantime, was redoubling his efforts. Looking at his smooth face and neck, which was now livid from his efforts, I thought he was about to have a heart attack. The bright side to that was I probably wouldn't have to pay off the bet. It was then that I discovered a quality behind those inch-thick lenses that I didn't know was there. He liked to win, convincingly!

The barbed wire was over-spilling with love-lorn, wild-eyed cows, whilst across the field, down gullies, at the gallop, with full udders crashing from side to side, came what seemed thousands more! It was like the charge of the heavy brigade. When we stopped I thought there were only fifty or so cows. Boy, was I wrong. There must have been five or six hundred, and they were all headed our way at top speed!

By now I was laughing so hard I'd forgotten about losing the bet. The show was almost worth it. It was then that I felt a tap on my shoulder. Turning around I came face to face with a real hillbilly type. I had no idea how long he'd been there watching. I never heard the pick-up truck arrive. The noise of the cows was deafening.

EVERYBODY DOWN HERE HATES ME

He wore patched dungarees and a tall hat that all but hid his eyes. His weather-beaten face did not look happy. He looked like something out of "The Grapes of Wrath".

"What's goin' on heer?" He shouted, trying to make himself heard above the din. Did I detect a note of hostility? No, that couldn't be. This was too funny.

"What's going on," I shouted back. "Why, my friend is calling those cows... making like he's a bull, I guess, and those dumb cows are busting a gut to get to him. Look at those tits swing! It'll be all butter by tonight, not milk! Isn't it the funniest thing you've ever seen, eh?" I turned my back on him to watch Simon, who by now was mooing like his life depended on it. It nearly did. Hundreds of cows were pressing against the fence, starting to make it groan under all the pressure. I started to get a little worried. What if it busted? Would the cows stampede over us? My thoughts were suddenly interrupted in a way I had not expected.

Something cold and hard pressed just behind my ear. I thought I knew what it was, but no, it couldn't be. I turned slowly. The laughter died in my throat. I was looking down the barrel of a shotgun that was larger than life. Right then it looked more like a cannon.

"You stupid sons-a-bitches!" Snarled the funny-looking hillbilly, who didn't look funny any more. "Those are my cows and I don't see nothin' funny. Y'all tell 'ya friend that if'in he don't quit whatever he's a' doin', right now, I'm a goin' ta blow off some heeads!"

I almost shit right there. I couldn't even talk. This nut looked mean and mad enough to do just what he said. I realized how close I was to this crazy hick. I'd be the first to go. Keeping one eye in his direction, I tried to focus my other one on Simon, a bit like a chameleon. Grabbing Greenberg by the shoulder, I shouted, "Simon!" My voice sounded like a bullfrog calling its mate. "Simon, this man here wants to talk to you."

I know it sounded stupid, but when you're peering down the

business end of a cannon, you have a hard time thinking of the right things to say. Greenberg didn't even look around. He stopped calling long enough to wave me away with his hand, then continued with his fun. He was going to give me my money's worth, plus he was getting a little sadistic pleasure rubbing my nose in losing our bet.

I got a jab, a very hard one, in the back of the ear. By now there must've been hundreds of cows pressed against the barbed wire fence, which looked on very shaky ground, as I did right then. I was expecting the strands to break at any moment. The thought entered my head, would he shoot me as I went under the avalanche of cattle, or would the stranger just let the stupid beasts take care of things for him?

Desperation engulfed me. Taking my eyes off the hillbilly, I grabbed Greenberg by the shoulders, spinning him around to face the cannon. The "moooo" died right on his lips. His sallow complexion was a bright red from his efforts. His eyes even looked bloodshot.

"What's wrong?" Simon asked nervously, looking from me to the cannon to the hillbilly. "Have you ever seen anything so funny?"

"Funny?" Came the reply. "Funny! Y'all stupid sons-of-a-bitches! I don't think it's funny, 'ya assholes!"

I couldn't talk. The main reason was the stranger kept moving his gun back and forth, first pointing it at me, then at my partner. What really scared the hell out of me was his hands were shaking. I kept wondering if the gun was a one shot or not. I wished I knew more about shotguns, but then at that distance one shot would suffice for both of us. I'm sure I could see his trigger finger whiten, just like I'd read in books.

I've got to give Greenberg his due. He could still talk, even if he was a little hoarse, in fact very hoarse. Never-the-less he said a few words. "Why don't you think it's funny?" Simon managed to croak out. Already I knew, but couldn't explain, my throat had dried up. The stranger became even more enraged under his tall hat. I thought he was going to have a heart attack.

I kept thinking strange things like, would rigor mortis set in fast enough to pull the trigger if he died? Would his trigger finger straighten, not firing the gun, or would it bend more in the throes of death? You can read all kinds of books on self-defense, how to kick him in the balls whilst deflecting his arm upwards. Whoever wrote that bullshit never looked down the wrong end of a shotgun held by a mad Tennessee hillbilly farmer!

"Them's my cows y'alls fuckin' with." The words were like ice picks right into my heart.

This was when you could tell we were a tag team. Our reaction was simultaneous and instantaneous. We advanced to the rear, as they say in Ireland, in unison, dividing only when we reached the car.

I scrambled behind the steering wheel, started the engine, put the car in gear, and took off, faster than I had ever done in my life. How was I to know Simon wasn't in the car? I'd never taken my eyes off the shotgun which had followed our every movement. Mercifully, the farmer was now looking at his cattle as I stepped on the gas. The car took off almost smashing into the fence. I'd put it in reverse. This gave Simon time to leap aboard while I was changing gears. Then we roared down the road straight to the show.

We were very subdued when we arrived in town. Both of us knew how close a shave we'd had. Farmers in Tennessee are not known to be the softest people in the world, especially with those who are screwing around with their livestock. They've blown people away for a lot less. So our silly bet came unstuck. Simon was so shook up, he forgot to ask for his ten dollars. I forgot to give it to him at the time. When you've just saved your own lives, what's ten dollars?

It was time for our match. We were on last which meant after the intermission, an interval long enough to give the concessions time to make some money. In small towns especially, concessions were run by the local promoter. I believe they were a gold mine.

People who go to wrestling eat and drink out of proportion to their numbers.

The anvil was already in the ring, along with the bed of nails, plus a large sledge hammer. Greenberg would lay on his back in the center of the ring. The bed of nails would be placed carefully on his chest and belly, with the nails pointing down into his skin. This part always gave me goose pimples, heightening my admiration for my partner. I would never do anything like this, or even try. There were too many things that could go wrong. . . like the anvil falling off the board on your face.

The fans would line up and come into the ring, one by one. Each would have the opportunity to swing the sledge hammer and hit the anvil on top of Simon, then return to their seats happy at having participated in the show. It was amazing how popular the whole production was. Many people came to the matches just to swing the hammer. I got quite a kick out of watching the variety of people who would climb in the ring, young and old, men and women. My part was vetting the audience. I was to let into the ring only the people whom I thought could lift the hammer and swing it, which was no mean feat for the average punter. This whole business made us very popular with the fans, so God help our opponents when and if they broke the rules. We were involved in many riots in the halls when our fans felt we were being taken advantage of. The police would have to escort the other wrestlers out of the ring, sometimes out of the town!

This particular night we'd had the usual collection of fans come up to hit the anvil, then leave giggling and happy. The line was getting shorter. I had just given the okay for a fan to duck through the ropes to take his turn. He looked like he'd be strong enough to swing the hammer, so I gave him his instructions.

"Spread your legs about shoulder width. Grasp the handle firmly. Take your time. Feel the weight of the sledge. Hold on to the handle with the other hand holding it almost at the head."

EVERYBODY DOWN HERE HATES ME

Before the fan could grasp the hammer, he was pushed aside violently by a tall, lean man who jumped through the ropes. Grabbing the big sledge hammer handle in both hands, the man seemed to go berserk. Wild-eyed, he jumped back and hoisted the hammer over his head. I was paralyzed. There was nothing I could do to stop him. He seemed demented. His large work-worn hands came together at the end of the handle.

It was like slow motion, I can still see the arc of the hammerhead as it headed up to the full length of his long arms, and slowly started to come down. If I had jumped in to stop him, God-knows-where the hammer head would've landed! Greenberg was laying there without his glasses, almost asleep, blissfully unaware of what was happening. His trust in me was implicit. We had done this many times. The sledge came down, gathering momentum all the way. This idiot was swinging with all of his might. It missed the anvil completely. I held my breath. Vividly I could visualize brains splattered all over the mat. Fortunately, it missed Simon's head by a couple of inches, burying itself in the ring, smashing the boards like matchwood. There was complete and utter silence. Greenberg knew something was wrong. He'd heard the crash, felt the ring floor shake, but he couldn't figure out what had happened. His head swiveled frantically around. His eyes were squinting. Bewildered, he tried to see what the hell was going on. Eventually his gaze fell on the handle that was sticking out of the ring. He squinted even more. He brought his arm up and felt it. Disbelief flooded his face. Suddenly he was galvanized into action. Putting both his hands on the sides of the board where there were no nails, he pushed with superhuman strength, and did the impossible...
he lifted the board, nails, anvil, and everything off his body, hurling it to one side. I couldn't believe his awesome strength. Fans had to leap out of the way. The pile came crashing down, narrowly missing legs. I'd never seen him move so fast before. His eyes were bulging from both the effort of lifting the anvil and, I suspect, the fright he'd gotten on feeling the handle so

near to his head. That blow, if it had struck his head, would've crushed his skull like an eggshell. Simon must have realized this instantly. He may have been legally blind, but he wasn't stupid!

"Are you okay, Simon?" I asked him, my voice sounding strained. He looked around desperately trying to see where I was amongst the fans. I guess he focused on the bare skin in the sea of clothed bodies, for he rushed straight over and grabbed my arm.

"What stupid prick did this?! Where is he? I'll murder him! He tried to kill me! He could have! He almost did!" Simon was babbling on while painfully squeezing my arm. I really felt sorry for him. It just wasn't his day. For that matter, to a lesser degree, it wasn't mine either. I looked around for the long, lean bastard who had swung the hammer. Rage started to take over from fright. If I could get my hands on him I'd teach him a lesson he wouldn't forget. I blamed myself for not preventing the wild swing. Rampaging around the ring, I searched for the lunatic. But the swine was wisely taking his leave.

I could see his tall figure heading for the door. Grabbing the top rope, I shouted after him, "Stop that bastard, somebody!" I knew I couldn't catch him through the press of people. I don't know whether he heard my voice, but he looked over his shoulder for an instant. It was then that I got the shock of my life. In that split second I saw the face of the farmer who had pointed the shotgun at us earlier that afternoon.

To this day I wonder if he'd recognized us from TV, and came to the matches to get his revenge. The thing that really bothers me is did he really mean to kill Simon, or was his miss an accident?

Things were never quite the same after that incident. The promoter split us up shortly thereafter. I believe he blamed me for screwing up a good gimmick. There's no room for fuck-ups in the wrestling world. Not being a stupid person, I left the green hills of Tennessee.

24

WRESTLING WITH THE LAW

Based out of Omaha, Nebraska, I wrestled in the surrounding Midwestern Corn Belt states. Traveling one night, at my usual hundred miles an hour, with three sleeping wrestlers in my car, I suddenly saw lights appear in my rear-view mirror. Obviously some local cop had been hiding down a side lane, I thought, waiting for the unwary traveler like myself to speed past. Now he was on my trail, trying to get a fix on my speed. It had to be a cop, I could tell by the shape of the head lights that it was a new car, and in that part of the country there were not too many of them. Plus the good law-abiding citizens were all in bed at this hour of the night. Barrett's Law is when in doubt, slow down. Well, I was a traveler, but not your usual run-of-the-mill kind. Perhaps this sounds like conceit, but I prided myself on not being caught by police very often. When working I never went under ninety on the highway, if I could help it. This was not luck, but a format I'd worked out. One rule was at night, if lights came on or appeared, slow down immediately until you discover who's on your tail. The police, I'm told, are supposed to follow for a certain distance to establish your speed before writing a citation, or making an arrest. I always watched my rear-view mirror carefully for the first sign of lights or a strange car. Radar was something else. I depended on my Fuzz

Buster to alert me to that. In this case, I slowed down before the lights came on to the main highway. The Fuzz Buster had remained silent, so radar was not involved. By that time I was driving quite nicely, doing the limit and no more.

The car behind came up very fast. When it was right behind me, on came the dreaded blue lights. Pulling over immediately was part of my plan to appease the police, showing no resistance. When you are a fairly large man this is important, and I never like to make anyone nervous who carries a gun. Easing out into the headlights, letting him see both hands were empty, I asked, "What's wrong, officer? Is there a problem?"

"Yes." He said. "You were speeding... over ninety miles an hour. Lemme see your license."

By now my passengers were somewhat awake. I could hear them grumbling about my driving, how they'd always told me to keep it down, what a heavy foot I had. It was 2:30 a.m. These were the same men who, a couple of hours before, had said how delighted they were to be riding with me as I always got them home at a reasonable hour, especially on these long trips. Some of the wrestlers just crawled along, and even pulled over to have a nap. I figured if I could hear them grousing, so could the cop. I tried to move a little farther away from the car, but he blocked my way. His hands were on his belt, one suspiciously near to the butt of his gun.

"What made you imagine I was speeding?" Was my next question. Perhaps he had radar... Yes, that was it. The crafty so-and-so had radar. But why hadn't my radar detector warned me? Did he have a new type of radar that my detector couldn't pick up? I tried to look past him into the car. But because he had switched on his spotlight, plus his high beams, I was nearly blinded. All I could see was little more than his silhouette. I was beginning to feel like I was Wyatt Earp, with the sun in his eyes at the OK Corral, except that I was unarmed.

"Followed you." Was his laconic reply. "Timed you over a mile."

243

EVERYBODY DOWN HERE HATES ME

This was a down-right lie. I was overcome with indignation that this country cop — we were definitely out in the boondocks, about a hundred and twenty miles from Lincoln — was lying.

"That's impossible!" I snapped, an edge coming to my voice. "I saw you pull out of that side road just back there. I'm not dumb enough to be speeding." My mind was racing. No radar. He certainly didn't follow me for a mile, especially at ninety mph, so there should be no problem. I went into phase two.

"Look, Officer, I definitely wasn't going too fast. Why I have to drive so much in the wrestling business, I have to watch my speed or else I'd be working for the state, instead of myself, paying off the tickets with the amount of driving I do!"

He was peering at my license while I was talking, shining his flashlight on it to get a better look. I'd given him an out-of-state license, one of about four I always used to carry. Every state I wrestled in I took a test, telling them I had no license, having just arrived in the country a short while before. This way I never had too many tickets on any one license. Most of the time, we were out-of-state and the police tended to let you go, as there was a lot of paperwork and bother in booking you, especially late at night. At the mention of the word "wrestling", his head jerked up. I got the full glare of the light in my face.

"Knew I recognized you from somewhere!" He chortled. "Watch you on TV all the time! Who've you got in the car?" All of this gushed out in one breath. The flashlight shifted toward the back window where a couple of sleepy, disgruntled faces were peering out.

I'm sure I heard a voice mumble from inside the car, "Turn that fucking light off!"

He moved to a side window, shining his light inside. "Mad Dog Vachone!" He shouted with glee, shifting the light again, shining it straight into another face. "Reggie Parks!" His voice got higher with excitement.

This was a real wrestling fan. No problem here I thought, no ticket from such an obvious fanatic. The third wrestler he didn't

244

recognize. He was new to the area, so hadn't had the exposure on TV. Then the cop was back to me.

"God I love that skirt you wear into the ring! What do you call it?" He may have noticed my pained expression at the mention of the word "Skirt". Sometimes I wore a kilt into the ring. If the people liked me, they cheered at the sight of it. Women of all ages would whistle and stomp when I took it off, as if I was doing a male strip-tease act, and might have nothing on underneath. Now if it was somewhere I wasn't liked, then I was called choice names like "Fucking Queer Fag" among other things. Luckily in this area I was liked, so this should be a breeze.

It's funny, but cops who are paid to escort wrestlers to the ring, especially unloved wrestlers, would viciously fight the hordes to defend their charges against being brutalized. When I was in a town where I was hated, the cops tended to shy away and would keep their distance if I wore the kilt. I noticed this especially in the Midwest and South. I think they suspected me somewhat of practices that should remain nameless, else why would I wear a "skirt"? I often felt like kissing them on the cheek, just to see what they would do, but I was afraid they might not have a sense of humor.

I explained the history of the kilt briefly, wishing to wind this scene up. It was obvious we weren't going to get booked, being from out-of-state and all. But more important, we were big-time wrestlers. This country cop was so happy to meet us, he was a real fan judging by his enthusiasm, he wouldn't pull us in. It was really late. He wouldn't want all that paperwork at this hour of the early morning.

"Listen," I said. "When we're wrestling around here next, any one of us," My arm swung wide to embrace the car and its occupants, "bring the family along. We'll make sure you get seats. Free. Be our guests. Right, guys?" I shouted to my passengers. There were grunts of affirmation. Turning back to the cop, I gave him my most ingratiating smile.

245

"That's great." He said. "I'll do that, but we've never had wrestling near our town." This was getting to be a bore.

"What's the name of where you live? Where are we anyway?" I queried. He mentioned some obscure place I'd never heard of before, not only that, but I couldn't remember it five seconds later.

"Look, give me your name and address," I said. "I personally will send you tickets to the wrestling. How many in your family?... Five, eh... Okay. Five tickets ringside to the wrestling in the nearest town to yours I wrestle in. How's that suit you?" As I talked I reached for my license he was holding, but he made no attempt to give it to me. In fact, his grip on it remained firm.

"Great. Great!" He said. "The wife and kids would love that. Could my boy meet the wrestlers? Like Mad Dog? He's a great fan of his. Would he shake his hand? He'd love that!"

"Sure... Sure... " came the sleepy reply from the car. "Anything... now let's get the fuck out of here. It's been a long day." This was Vachone trying to be nice. I could tell it was a real effort.

"Go? Go where?" The cop sounded genuinely puzzled.

"Go home." I gently reminded him that we had another hundred-odd miles to drive. "It's very late."

"But what about your speeding?" He said ignoring our pleas. "At least you've got to come with me to meet the judge. Why he'd never forgive me if I didn't bring you all along to meet him! He's your greatest fan. Always watches you guys on the tube every chance he can. He watches more than me!" This was almost an apology.

Was I dreaming? Was this some kind of nightmare from which I'd soon wake up? The voices from inside the car were no longer sleepy.

"Judge? What judge? When? Surely you can't mean now! You mean when we wrestle near here... You want tickets for the judge... No problem." It was a confused babble from all four of us. He couldn't mean we were to meet a judge now, out here, at 3 a.m. in the middle of nowhere. But that, unfortunately, was exactly what he meant.

"I'll hold on to this," He said, waving my license. "Just follow me. It's only five minutes down the road to court." The language in the car had deteriorated dramatically. There were words like "fucking judge", "shit", and "screw the court". The things said in French were a lot worse, I'm sure, Mad Dog being a French Canadian. He was a real tough nut who'd come up from the streets, and fought his way to the top in amateur wrestling. From there, he became one of the biggest names in the world as a pro. Voices that had spent years shouting above crowds of angry people carried far on a quiet Midwestern night. The cop must've heard them, but he gave no indication. He just got in his car, started the engine, then waved me to follow. I'd been standing there stunned. The man must be mad. Everything was falling apart. My little routine was crumbling. This couldn't be happening, not with this hayseed!

We had no choice in the matter. Everybody was wide awake. The general consensus was we'd fallen foul of a lunatic dressed up as a cop. There was nothing to do now but to follow his instructions.

It was a typical one-horse town that dots rural America. Actually places like these make up the backbone of this great country. Not a light was on. Everyone was snug in their beds, secure that life would go on uninterrupted for the next fifty years, just like it had for the last fifty. The cop stopped at a gas station. The building behind the pumps was two-story, from what I could see of it. It looked like the working part of the station was downstairs, and the living quarters were upstairs. He climbed out of his car, walked leisurely to a doorway, and rang the doorbell. I couldn't see very well from where I was but I saw him poke his finger toward the door jamb. Soon after a light came on upstairs, a window was pushed up, and out protruded a head. It was a typical Midwestern woman's head, large and beefy, plus this one had a headful of decorations on it in the shape of hair curlers. The eyes were small and puffy, but I could tell from where I sat that they were neither surprised at the scene below nor at the time of night.

"Is that you, Sheriff? Do you want to see the judge?"

"Sure do." The unhurried drawl was so opposite to the rantings and ravings that were coming from my car, it was obvious he'd never get high blood pressure. Turning his smiling face without a hint of animosity toward us, he gave a wide wave as big as the great outdoors, beckoning the whole car full of nasty, grumbling, farting wrestlers inside. We'd all dined on beer and salami a few hours before, which we'd picked up at an all-night grocery, but we managed to control ourselves enough to squeeze through the door which he opened.

Up the stairs we were ushered, into a front room which was modestly, but comfortably, furnished with a big sofa against one wall, an easy chair and a couple of dining chairs around a small table. The walls were covered with hunting and fishing pictures, and photos of children of all sizes — small, medium, and large. A whole life history in that one room. Our friend Joe, the cop, told us to make ourselves comfortable, which we did. The sofa groaned under the combined weight of three wrestlers. It was sturdy, but not that sturdy.

There was silence for a few moments. Joe leaned against the door jamb with his hat in his hands, clearly a man without a care in the world. Abruptly a door opened. A man who looked in his late sixties bustled in.

"Well." He said. "What have we here, Joe?" His face lined from hard work and time, turned to the lawman. The cop's face lit up like a Christmas tree.

"Bill, you won't believe who I've got for you here!" He pointed in our direction. Why did I feel like a landed fish, gasping for life on the shore, when he did that? Bill looked us over warily at first, then I saw recognition coming slowly to his eyes.

"It can't be! It just can't!" He exclaimed. "Why that's Mad

Dog Vachone! His eyes flicked to me then widened. "It's the Irishman! You're... " He struggled with my name. I hadn't made as big an impression as Mad Dog I guess, but then not many people had. He reeled off the other names with a little help from all of us. We definitely had a first-class fan. Everyone was very relaxed now. Mad Dog was trying to smile, but that would be expecting too much from him, even in the presence of a judge.

Bill's questions came tumbling out, but first he hadn't forgotten his Midwestern hospitality. He told his wife to bring us coffee and sandwiches, which she did with great charm and speed. Even wearing the curlers, she had a quiet dignity serving the refreshments. She behaved as if it were the most natural thing in the world to be offering four wrestlers, from different parts of the world, coffee at 4 a.m.

The conversation went on for a couple of hours, everyone calling each other by their first names, the air heavy with smoke and farts. At one point Bill, the judge, had Mad Dog on the carpet in a face lock, receiving the muffled encouragement of "Goddamit Bill, tighten it up! That's as weak as a baby's ass!" All this with a distinct French accent.

I glanced at my watch. My God! It was 6 a.m.! Time to get going. It had been a long day of driving and wrestling. The others had had a good sleep, but by now I'd been up twenty-three hours. It was time to get this show on the road. I was definitely starting to flag, and still had a hundred miles to go.

"Sorry to break things up." I said. I really was sorry as everyone seemed to be having such a good time. Even the judge's wife had tried her hand at putting holds on me. She was surprisingly strong and quick to learn. She said it came from raising four sons. I believed her.

"Right!" Bill said, "It is getting late, or early, eh?" With a chuckle. "Let's see... What are we to do?"

The four of us stopped dead in our tracks which were heading for the door.

EVERYBODY DOWN HERE HATES ME

"What do you mean, Bill?" I asked innocently. Surely after all this camaraderie I thought there'd be no talk of speeding, not from good old Bill and Joe. Suddenly Bill's whole demeanor was taking on a transformation. This Dr. Jekyll was becoming Mr. Hyde right before my eyes. Then he was all business. He straightened his tall, lean body, brushed back his thinning hair with a large boney hand, then pulled his dressing gown into order. It was like Peter Cushing becoming Count Dracula, I could see his teeth getting longer. His wife disappeared like a well-trained hound into the other part of the house, taking all the coffee cups and plates, and what seemed like all signs of friendship with her.

The room temperature seemingly dropped several degrees.

"Sit down, gentlemen." Bill commanded, taking a seat at the table. "What are the charges, Sheriff?" He demanded all in one breath.

It'd difficult to catch men who gamble with their lives all by surprise, but Bill, or maybe I should say "Judge", did just that. I looked at the shocked faces around me. What happened to Joe and Bill, the good old boys? They were replaced by two strangers named Sheriff and Judge, cold, impersonal men that would give no quarter.

"Speeding, Judge." Joe said. "They were speeding . . . doin' about a hundred, but I'm dropping that down. The charge will be ninety."

The hawk face turned to us. "Who was driving the car? Why were you going such a speed? How do you plead?"

My wits returned. "Not guilty, Your Honor." I realized they were having their fun. Play this little charade out, then all would have a big laugh. We'd all go home and everyone would be happy. "Judge," I said. "I was not speeding. In fact I never go over seventy." This I explained with a straight face. After all, how could he disbelieve one of his heroes?

"That so! What do you say, Sheriff? Did you follow him?"

"Yes, Judge. He drove over a hundred, near enough, for over a mile."

Now I know police sometimes lie. Hell, I trained, got drunk, and chased girls with some of them all over the world. Joe, the sheriff, struck me as such a straight, stand-up type guy. It was impossible to believe that such a sweet man would lie through his teeth. I'd watched this man pull out in my rear-view mirror. No way did he follow me at a hundred miles per hour!

"Judge," I pleaded, "That's impossible!" I proceeded to explain why. He politely listened then gave his verdict.

"Pat." He spoke almost kindly. "I've known the sheriff here," He paused. "How long have I known you, Sheriff?" He asked. The formality of everything now, after all the frivolity, was not lost on me.

"Fifty-odd years... must be at least that," replied Joe, looking like he was searching his memory. "Closer to sixty." I looked hard at Joe. He certainly didn't look over fifty-five. The judge studied his hands as he dropped the hammer.

"Pat." He repeated. "I've known the sheriff here almost all my life, and he's never lied to me in all that time. Have you, Sheriff?"

"Never," came the prompt response.

"Now how long have I known you? Two, maybe three hours?" Then he gave a little laugh. "Anyway, you can see why I've got to believe the sheriff. He's never lied to me before. Why would he start now?"

How could I answer? He had me by the balls. We both knew it. Everybody in the room knew it. I've had them squeezed before by experts, but this man was one of the best.

"The bail will be one-hundred-eighty dollars, cash." Came the decision.

"You're joking!" I heard my own voice say, as if from a thousand miles away. Growls erupted from beside me. We became a mad angry mob. Even though I was seeing red, my mind was clear. Was it an accident, or did I imagine it? Joe's hand was resting on his gun, and the holster clip was off.

"No, Pat. It's no joke."

EVERYBODY DOWN HERE HATES ME

"I can't pay that! I know I don't carry that much cash!" I snapped, not bothering with the niceties any more. "What happens then?"

"No problem at all." Bill reassured me. His eyes twinkled. "No problem. We have a nice comfortable cell out back. Very comfortable. My wife would love to cook for you fellas. She'd never get tired of talking wrestling. You'd be well looked after and could stay as long as you like... 'till the money arrives, that is. But then your boss, I'm sure, won't leave you with us too long. You're too valuable for that." He made it sound like a rest home for retired wrestlers, except we all knew exactly what he meant.

Being a winner means knowing when you can't win a situation, when to regroup, and when to retreat. This was one of those times. We all dug deep and came up with the money, and left as fast as we could. I'm sure they had some chuckles in that small town about the "Big Time Wrasslers." Looking back on it all, I can smile to myself, but that drive home in my car that day was blue with bad language and sour dispositions.

25

WATERING HOLES

New York has always held a special place in my heart. I've wrestled in Madison Square Garden many times, both the old one and the new. The atmosphere in the old hall was electric. It was always a marvelous feeling to stand in the ring and let the waves of human emotion flow over and around me. It was a fitting hall to grace such a marvelous city. So I was very sad when I heard it was being torn down. In the past I've seen old venues pulled down and new ones go up, unfortunately something is nearly always missing in the new ones. Oh, the dressing rooms are better, more comfortable. Now there is hot water, where before there was only cold. The new showers give the right mix of hot and cold, no more finding yourself freezing your ass off one minute, then scalding yourself the next. The doors on the toilets are always a much-appreciated improvement. Not many people, even wrestlers, object to a little privacy when nature calls.

The new Madison Square Garden was glittering. The dressing rooms were a pleasure to be in. On my first match in the new place I just sat for awhile, drinking in the sights, sounds, and smells that surrounded me. The hall was packed to capacity. One could feel the mass of humanity, even in the dressing rooms, through concrete walls. I thought what a strange business I was in. Just a few days before, in Massachusetts, I wrestled in a small dingy place. To call it a hall would be flattering. All of us on the card that night were crowded into one room, sweating and cursing. There was no shower, just a sink. Wrestling that night in that small town, were some of the top talents in the business, names seen on TV and avidly watched by literally millions. The matches were just as exciting as those seen in Madison Square, yet the small town hall was only a quarter full. These people would be your hard-core wrestling fans. It was difficult to understand why it wasn't full, spilling over with enthusiastic onlookers. In one week you could hit the height of the business, like the Garden, then hit rock bottom, like the little dump in Massachusetts. The reason for running small towns was a mystery to me. I was told it kept small promoters in business, and in turn, nurtured the beginners and upcoming stars of the mat world. A star has to start its journey somewhere. Myself, I think the promoters like to keep their men hungry and humble, and this is as good a way as any.

The new Garden's atmosphere was everything the old one was, and more. It had all the old Garden's excitement with the addition of modern day comforts and glamour.

After everything was over that night, Kevin Sullivan and I went to have a couple of drinks. Well, one drink led to another, with fans toasting our victory, and everyone in the place having a great time. We stayed until closing, with all that conviviality, time had no meaning.

Kevin and I were driving back to Connecticut that night, definitely the worse for wear, when he decided he needed to take a piss. Now I thought, that wasn't a bad idea, after the quantity of beer I had put away I was ready. I started to look for a place to pull over and stop, preferably grassy. Don't ask me why it would have to be grassy. I just believe most men would sooner relieve themselves on grass than on concrete, obeying some primitive urge. I also had my ninety-two pound Pit Bull Terrier in the car with me. I know he definitely preferred grassy places. It was time to let him out too, even though he hadn't been drinking. He was partial to an odd pint of beer, but that particular night he was on the wagon. Then I spotted it. A huge lawn materialized out of the foggy night. It was perfect. We were still in New York City so this was a godsend. I stopped the car. Kevin seemed to have a little difficulty getting out of the seat of my car, for that matter so did I. It would've appeared to have shrunk. We both made it after a brief struggle. The dog had no problem jumping straight out and going about the business that all dogs go about.

There we were, blissfully watering the lawn, all three of us, when the whole world seemed to light up. I'd been blinded by the sun that had sprung up out of nowhere. God but the night was awfully short! Maybe I was dazed by too much drink. My thoughts were completely disoriented. I heard a tough New York-accented voice shouting at me. Slowly the words sunk into my brain. "What the fuck do you think you're doing here?"

With great dignity I drew myself up, still pissing and squinting hard, I could just make out the outline of the patrol car. Two cops were standing beside it, their hands on their gunbelts. I answered them with a question, surely they couldn't be that dumb. "What does it look like we're doing?" I demanded, a little truculently. Then I answered myself. "Taking a piss. Can't you see?"

The voice boomed out again, "What's he doing there?" Slowly I turned around. What could the dumb cop be talking about? Standing, oblivious to everything, Kevin was still pissing at full force. It couldn't be Sullivan the cop was talking about. Then I saw my dog, Rocky.

Rocky traveled with me all over the country, loving every minute of it, riding on the floor where the front-seat passenger put his feet. He'd ridden with me since he was a pup, in that very same place. He'd made it his own. If a wrestler was sitting in the front, he could put his feet on Rocky, without the dog so much as blinking an eye. Just as long as he could stay up there, all was well. He hated to be put in the back, and seemed to hold the person who was in the front with me responsible. A reign of terror would begin, starting with grumbles and building from there. If this didn't work the dog would get very quiet, then suddenly rise like the Phoenix, attacking the real or imagined enemy. The thing that frightened everyone was the enemy always seemed to manifest itself outside the car, just behind the unfortunate passenger's head. Rocky was a nasty looking individual, absolutely fearless, caring for none in the world but me. He could be as evil as he looked, when he wanted to be. He was as tough as all hell, saving my skin many times when I was surrounded by screaming kicking fans. With him on a short leash, snarling and lunging, we would cut through the mob like a hot knife through butter.

This dog was a traveler from the word go. Like any good traveler, he took his food, sleep, and bowel movements when the right opportunity presented itself. Now, on this convenient lawn, was the right time in his mind for the works. He might not get another chance for quite some time. Where else would a dog find such a good place to take a nice healthy crap in New York City?

Turning to the policeman, with great patience, I explained what the dog was doing. I've often heard that the NYPD are a very harassed bunch, but these two showed great restraint.

"I know exactly what you are all doing." The uniformed man in blue said. "It's *where* you are doing it that I object to."

"What's wrong with here?" I asked querulously. "Seems as good a place as any!"

"I'll tell you what's wrong." Snarled the policeman. I felt he was starting to lose his patience. "This is the front lawn of the United Nations building!"

I couldn't remember any building being there, let alone the United Nations building, when I stopped my car. Sure enough, there it was, larger than life, rearing up behind us in all its magnificence.

"Now do something for me," A voice cut through my

befuddled brain. "Get your asses out of here before I put all three of you in jail!" At the sound of that horrible word "jail" I suddenly felt as if I'd had a cold shower. Without hesitation Kevin, who seemed to also get cold sober at the thought, climbed into the car with me. This time the car was back to the correct size. Rocky, reading the situation as calling for a speedy finish to his business, cut it short, and bounded into his favorite position on the floor. Then with a final reproachful look, and a big sigh, closed his eyes and went to sleep. There were times when I wished my life was as simple as his.

26

ONE MORE TIME

I was trying to see through the suffocating smoke. My eyes were beginning to water again, my breath was catching in my throat. How could these extras, some of whom looked so old and frail as if one foot was in the grave and the other on a banana skin, keep up the screaming and shouting? They were being exhorted to do this by the director time and again, forever it seemed to me. Finally I made my escape outside into the sunlight, away from this madhouse that was the set of a wrestling movie I was in.

All of this had come about after a phone call one evening from Red Bastien. "Pat, my boy. How would you like to be a movie star?" He had asked with a chuckle in his voice.

"Again?" I quipped back. "Why not!"

It was good to hear his voice on the phone. We went back many years, enjoying many good times together. Red was very articulate with a great sense of humor. The only dark cloud over our relationship was when he was promoting in Modesto, California. Several times he paid me peanuts, and once he conveniently forgot to send my check altogether. Even so I found it impossible to dislike the man. The thing I found interesting was that his memory in other directions was crystal clear. The loss of the small payoff was discounted by the many times we

258

enjoyed drinking together, the best beer in the world for me . . . good old Irish Guinness.

The first time I heard about him I had only been in the states a short while. The promoter I was working for was raving to me about how much I reminded him of a wrestler by the name of Red Bastien. At that time, Bastien was one of the hottest properties on the American wrestling scene. After being told this many times over a period of a couple of months, my curiosity was at a peak.

He was not a big man as U.S. wrestlers go, weighing a mere two-hundred, thirty pounds or so. But as a performer, his style was the forerunner of one seen today by the W.W.F. (World Wrestling Federation). Aerial maneuvers were his forte. Combinations of spectacular airborne assaults on his opponents would drive fans into a frenzy. I didn't know this was his style before I met him. All I knew was he had red hair, somewhat like mine, and was fair-skinned and smaller than most heavyweights, as I was.

I was wrestling in St. Louis one night and Red was on the card. Watching his match in awe, I saw him do some suicidal moves. That's what it looked like to my horrified eyes. How could anybody describe my style of wrestling as being similar to this aerialist? I prided myself on moving faster than just about any heavyweight in the wrestling business. But those high-flying high jinx were not for me.

When I arrived back in the dressing room, the booker greeted me with a smile and a handshake. Then he said the fatal words, "Pat, I believe you're another Red Bastien."

Looking him straight in the eye, I said, "Forget that! I'm no high-flyer, so I hope you don't expect it! I like terra firma, the more firmer, the less terror."

He gave me a puzzled look and a nervous laugh. It was obvious my caustic humor had gone over everyone's head, even if I hadn't.

Later on, when wrestling in Hawaii, Bastien surfaced again.

I learned a valuable lesson about the business from him, though he didn't mean to teach me one.

When I first arrived there, the booker, Lord Blears, an English wrestler of considerable charm, had asked if I would stay in Hawaii for a year or so, as he believed my style would go over well with the people. I had already been on the island for a few weeks and found it very constricting. This may seem strange, after all, Ireland is also a small island. But by this time, I was spoiled by the vastness of America and hated the physical limitations of the islands. So my answer had to be "No". I would be staying only about four months. The promoter had intended teaming me with Jim Hady, who was the Hawaiian champion at the time, and immensely popular. This would've meant top billing for me, and also top money.

Bastien arrived on the scene shortly after and fitted into the spot, giving them assurances that he would be staying for a very long period, and therefore would guarantee a good return on the promotion's investment.

As it turned out, he left before I did, making a lot more money and having a lot more prestige to further his career. I learned a very valuable lesson right there. Honesty, in the pro wrestling world, is not always the best policy.

First, before he left, he visited my apartment one evening, saying he was feeling a little down in the dumps. I was going to a movie with a girlfriend and invited him along, which he declined. Feeling a little sorry for him, I told him to help himself to some of my special imported German beer that I had gone to a lot of trouble and expense to procure. Telling him to lock up after he left, we departed to the cinema.

When we arrived back, he had gone, so had twenty-three bottles of beer out of my case of twenty-four! The empties were placed neatly in rows on my table. Rage engulfed me. I wanted to kill him. I'd been looking forward to a nice session of drinking when I got back. To make matters worse, he had left for the mainland the next morning, so I couldn't do anything about getting him to buy me a case to replace it. Then I heard through the grapevine, the biggest insult of all. The day he left Hawaii he went on the wagon; for eight months, not a drop of liquor passed his lips. I kept asking myself why the hell hadn't he started a day earlier, and left my booze alone?!

All this came back to me as we talked on the phone. I hadn't heard from him in some time, since he became trouble shooter for the W.W.F. on the West Coast. Red had been retired from active wrestling for awhile. He'd had both his hips replaced and was in pretty good shape, all things considered. We got to talking about retirement and its effects. Red said the hardest thing was nobody called him anymore. The phone just didn't ring. This is something that many wrestlers have to face when they quit, the loneliness of no one wanting them anymore. Their whole lives were bound up in their business. Now that they are no longer a part of it, there appears a giant void that they aren't prepared for. It was heart-breaking to see old-timers coming into the dressing rooms at Madison Square Garden, talking to the young turks who did not listen. I remember Antonio Rocca, one of the all-time greats, doing exercises in the dressing room that most athletes today couldn't do. He wanted to show how flexible he still was. No one paid any attention to him. He was just another anachronism of the business to most there. The saying "You're only as good as your last match" holds true.

The movie, Red explained, was about wrestling, a fictional story, very far-fetched, but exciting. He'd read the script and gave it his approval. Anyway, the deal was that I would be paid for a day's shooting, plus meals and two night's hotel bills. That sounded all right to me because I wanted to visit Los Angeles for business purposes, and could kill two birds with one stone.

The boredom on the set was getting to me. I'd arrived there at 8:40 a.m. and still I waited for my call. At first the shooting was interesting to watch, but after about fifty takes it became boring, so I went back to reading a book I had brought along. By now it was 6 p.m., I hadn't been used to and disliked all this inactivity.

The director was a fanatic for detail and was driving everyone mad with all his retakes of scenes. Finally he wanted a close-up of a kick from the star, Steve Strong. When Steve told him to stick his head between the ropes to get the shot, the director balked.

"You'll kick me!" He said.

"No, no." Steve reassured. "I promise I won't. You're quite safe. I know what I'm doing."

The director, who should've known better, stuck his head and shoulders through the ropes, with the camera glued to one eye. The action started. Steve started kicking. Suddenly there was a lot of screaming from both the people around the ring and the director. The screaming was totally unrehearsed, and sounded very natural to my experienced ears. It was quite different from what had gone on before, when they were filming the wrestling crowd scenes. So different was it that it penetrated my thoughts, which were miles away at the time. Looking over at the milling crowd, I noticed the director was clutching his eye. I knew instantly what had happened. Steve had misplaced a kick which had driven the camera's viewfinder into the moviemaker's face. Looking up at the ring with his good eye, the director's face suffused with both rage and fear, he shouted up at Steve, "You kicked me! You kicked me! You promised you wouldn't! Why did you do it?"

Steve's face couldn't be seen because it was behind a grotesque mask, but his words showed he wouldn't be losing any sleep over what had happened. Leaning over the ropes he nonchalantly said, "Welcome to the wrestling world!"

There was a stunned silence from the cast, then a few nervous titters. The wrestlers in the cast weren't the only ones who saw the humor in it. But they were the only ones who made it obvious. It took three stitches to sew the director's eye up, so it was not too bad.

That evening, at about 8:30 p.m., my call came. The scene

was to be a violent one, with Steve Strong going wild and simultaneously wiping out three wrestlers. We were discussing how best to do the choreography for the fight scenes. The choreographer, a wrestler himself, suggested I be thrown bodily over the top ropes, into the waiting arms of extras. He said this without cracking a smile. I could tell he was serious. I was very disappointed in him, he knew me quite well and my reputation was not one for taking those kind of stupid chances. When I started in the business I might've done it. But I'd learned to be wary, especially of my competition, and every wrestler is a competitor. I had visions of myself flying through the air with the greatest of ease, and no one there to catch me. I was not as trusting as the director, plus it was my body that was on the line. So I told them there was no way I'd do it. It would have to be changed. After much argument, we agreed to a different finish to the scene.

Finally it came time to shoot. Action was called for. The first wrestler was slammed, none too gently by Steve, on to the mat, then kicked out of the ring. The second wrestler and I attacked, a few seconds later. We were smashed into each other, which eliminated the second fellow. Then I swung a punch that would've taken Steve's head off, if it had connected. Steve ducked, grabbed me in a headlock, and pummeled my head before hurling me into the ropes. When I bounced off, his huge arms wrapped around me in a Sleeper hold. This was all arranged and it was supposed to be gently done.

The massive arm slammed around my neck then started squeezing. I realized that he was wound up and was forgetting to take it easy. There was nothing I could do, but hang in there till the scene ended. It was close. I could feel my senses start to slip away.

Dimly I heard the call, "Cut!", which terminated my agony. Steve Strong flopped back on the canvas exhausted, for him it was the culmination of many scenes, takes, and retakes that day. He was really earning his money, for most of the scenes were physical. The cast, as well as he, bore the marks of combat.

The director said it was wonderful, perfect, but in the next breath said he'd like to shoot it again. We got back into the standing position with a sigh. The signal was given and away we went. Everything went as before, except this time I slipped my hand and wrist between the big bicep and my neck, just in case the director was a little late in giving the "Cut" call.

Then it was over. Steve again rolled over on his back. He was really beat. Everybody who was anybody seemed happy again with the scene, except — that is — the director. He would've made a perfect guard for a Nazi concentration camp. Looking up into the ring he said, "That was perfect, but do you think you could do it one more time... if it's not too painful?" It was not a request, it was an order. I could see that, even though I hadn't made that many movies.

Leaning over the ropes, I whispered to the director, "My friend, I will do it one more time, but if you ask again, then I will show you what the Sleeper hold really feels like. That's a promise." He looked up into my eyes, then shrugged and walked away. We went through it again, from start to finish. So violent was the scene, the punch in the gut the first wrestler got even made me wince. Again the big arm came around my neck, tucking my chin in to my chest to minimize the squeezing I hung in there until it was all over. There was silence for a couple of seconds, then the director shouted, "That's it! That was great! We can all go home!" There was tumultuous applause. It was now 9:15 p.m. Most people, including myself, had been there since 8:30 a.m. It was a long day. I don't know whether my little talk had any effect on the director's decision, but I like to think that it had.

When the noise had died down, a voice through the smokey air shouted, "Let's take it one more time!" My heart stopped for a second, then I recognized the voice. Though I couldn't see its owner, I knew it was Bastien.

"Fuck you, Bastien!" I shouted. "You want it again, YOU

do it!'' This brought laughter all around, and I could hear his deep belly laugh amongst the others. I spotted him sitting in the bleachers with a baseball cap on, drinking a beer, with a big silly grin on his face. For a second he had us all going.

After I got cleaned up, I went to supper with the other wrestlers, the producer, and the financial backer. This was laid on by the movie people. It was really fabulous. Polish sausage, all we could eat, sliced boneless chicken that I never knew existed, a feast for a king! The meat was so tender and there were so many dishes, I couldn't taste them all, though I gave it a good try. The thing that touched me most was the producer and the backer, both of Irish descent, got me some Guinness beer to go with it. We sat at big picnic tables until after midnight, telling stories about ourselves and each other.

I looked around at the other wrestlers eating, drinking, telling stories, laughing and slapping each other on the back with gusto. It was hard to imagine looking at this friendly brotherhood, that all these men were fierce competitors who would cut each other's throat to get to the top.

It will be moments like these that I will miss when I retire. There is a joke in the wrestling business that is more truth than we realize. . . that old wrestlers have been known to get in their cars, late at night, when everyone else is in bed, and drive around the block several times, drinking a six-pack of beer. Old habits die hard!

ABOUT THE AUTHOR

When Pat Barrett is looking for sympathy or trying to distract the opposition in an argument over international politics, he lays on his thick Irish brogue and refers to himself as "a poor Irish immigrant."

Malarkey, this immigrant has been around the capitalistic block a time or two, and in this book proves he can weave a yarn with the written word. The professional wrestler has brought together a collection of spellbinding stories based on his career and life, both in the ring and out. Who could be better qualified than a seasoned international wrestler who's held, among his many titles, the W.W.F. World Heavyweight Tag Team Championship, World's Undisputed Junior Heavyweight Title, and numbers among his peers such greats as Andre the Giant, Hulk Hogan, Randy "Macho Man" Savage, Cowboy Bill Watts, Ted DiBiase and Bruno Sammartino just to mention a few?

Barrett continues his wrestling career from his Pensacola Beach home where he combines speaking engagements with his writing. Born in Dublin and formally educated at the city's Wesley College where his areas of concentration were economics and world history. Barrett has appeared in English and American movies, done television commercials and has stage and theater experience.

His specialty skills include dialects, poetry and narrative reading; body building and physical conditioning; his business experience ranges from imports and real estate; and he teaches obedience training to guard dogs.

Barrett created a copyrighted "VCR Library Log" to complement video recording systems, and is the author of lyrics and music to "All My Life."

He and his wife Peggy enjoy beach life with their three dogs: Sammy, Champ and Rip, and a cat named Sinbad.